D1254012

SOUTHERN LITERARY STUDIES

SOUTHERN LITERARY STUDIES

Louis D. Rubin, Jr.
Editor

A Season of Dreams: The Fiction of Eudora Welty
ALFRED APPEL, JR.

The Hero with the Private Parts
ANDREW LYTLE

Hunting in the Old South: Original Narratives of the Hunters
EDITED BY
CLARENCE GOHDES

Joel Chandler Harris: A Biography
PAUL M. COUSINS

John Crowe Ransom: Critical Essays and a Bibliography
EDITED BY
THOMAS DANIEL YOUNG

A Bibliographical Guide to the Study of Southern Literature
EDITED BY
LOUIS D. RUBIN, JR.

Poe: Journalist and Critic
ROBERT D. JACOBS

Love, Boy: The Letters of Mac Hyman
EDITED BY
WILLIAM BLACKBURN

The Complete Works of Kate Chopin
EDITED BY
Per Seyersted

Kate Chopin: A Critical Biography
Per Seyersted

Without Shelter: The Early Career of Ellen Glasgow
J. R. RAPER

Southern Excursions: Essays on Mark Twain and Others
LEWIS LEARY

The Poetry of Randall Jarrell
SUZANNE FERGUSON

Death by Melancholy: Essays on Modern Southern Fiction
WALTER SULLIVAN

The Sovereign Wayfarer: Walker Percy's Diagnosis of the Malaise
MARTIN LUSCHEI

THE
SOVEREIGN
WAYFARER

THE
SOVEREIGN
WAYFARER

Walker Percy's Diagnosis of the Malaise

MARTIN LUSCHEI

LOUISIANA STATE UNIVERSITY PRESS/BATON ROUGE

To Glenna
and
To the memory of my father
Erich G. Luschei
1898–1936

ISBN 0–8071–0239–3
Library of Congress Catalog Card Number 72–79333
Copyright © 1972 by Louisiana State University Press
All rights reserved
Manufactured in the United States of America
Printed by
LithoComp, Inc., Smyrna, Georgia
Designed by A. R. Crochet

Preface

To judge from the reviews of his recent novel, a rather surprised conviction seems to be emerging that Walker Percy is one of our most gifted writers. This book is addressed to those who find themselves concurring or skeptical without really knowing why—specifically to those who have read one or more of his novels and want to know more about him.

Many of Percy's readers know that he began as a physician, but few are aware that he has published a dozen philosophical articles in professional journals. He is a living writer in mid-career, and a study of his novels would not be justified at this point if he were not an extraordinarily demanding writer.

What has made critical assessment of his work so difficult is that Percy is a multifaceted writer and no one to date has assembled all his writings to give anything like a measure of the man. This book undertakes to do that. Its burden is primarily explication. Percy deserves and will surely get better treatment of his artistry than is offered here, but we need to understand what he is attempting before we can appraise the attempt. As Sartre said of Faulkner, it is necessary to define a writer's metaphysics before evaluating his fictional technique.

My approach is dictated by Percy's development. He did not arrive where he is by the customary routes. He is esteemed as a Southern and a Catholic writer, but to me—and I am neither a Southerner nor a Catholic—he has always been a contemporary American voice. To approach his novels by the light of conventional notions—Southern, Catholic, or American—is to see only dimly and in part. Accordingly this book begins with a brief intellectual biography and then goes into the philosophical backgrounds of his novels before offering a detailed reading of each in turn.

Those sources turn out to be mostly European and existentialist. A close reading of the novels persuades me that our favored ways of seeing cannot pierce the surrounding dimness. The lenses we customarily reach for, manufactured with precision by the scientific method, are apt to intensify the obscurity. We cannot hope to penetrate the malaise by such devices. We have to develop alternative ways of seeing, as Percy has done—not simply more tools of analysis by which to determine what A and B have in common with X, Y, and Z, but new eyes adapted to the darknesses of an individual human life. Our vision needs existential and not merely logical correction.

That conviction, born of my reading of Walker Percy, animates this study of his novels. I thank my wife and children, who have paid a price for this book; the American Studies Program at the University of New Mexico, which sheltered it; and my committee there—Paul B. Davis, Patricia Sanborn Glassheim, and George Arms—who could value the rude beginnings from which it grew.

M. L.

San Luis Obispo, California
March 1972

Contents

	Preface	ix
1	The Making of a Novelist	3
2	Some Light from the Existentialists	19
3	A Moviegoer Living in New Orleans	64
4	Ground Zero to Santa Fe	111
5	The Ruins of Consensus	169
6	Toward a Rediscovery of Being	233
	Bibliography	245
	Index	251

THE
SOVEREIGN
WAYFARER

I myself sometimes thought of [*The Notebooks of Malte Laurids Brigge*] as a hollow form, a negative mold, all the grooves and indentations of which are agony, disconsolations and most painful insights, but the casting from which, were it possible to make one (as with a bronze the positive figure one would get out of it), would perhaps be happiness, assent—most perfect and most certain bliss. Who knows, I ask myself, whether we do not always approach the gods so to speak from behind, separated from their sublimely radiant face through nothing but themselves, quite near to the expression we yearn for, only just standing behind it—but what does that mean save that our countenance and the divine face are looking out in the same direction, are at one; and this being so, how are we to approach the god from the space that lies in front of him?

Rainer Maria Rilke

1

The Making of a Novelist

During those years I stood outside the universe and sought to understand it. . . . The greatest success of this enterprise, which I call my vertical search, came one night when I sat in a hotel room in Birmingham and read a book called *The Chemistry of Life*. When I finished it, it seemed to me that the main goals of my search were reached or were in principle reachable, whereupon I went out and saw a movie called *It Happened One Night* which was itself very good. A memorable night. The only difficulty was that though the universe had been disposed of, I myself was left over. There I lay in my hotel room with my search over yet still obliged to draw one breath and then the next.[1]

In his middle twenties Walker Percy, like Dante midway in life's journey, found himself in a dark wood. He had come into it a medical student, bound for a career in psychiatry; he went out from it a novelist. What he encountered there seems to have been a realization like the one Binx Bolling arrives at in *The Moviegoer:* that though the universe had been disposed of, he himself was left over. If the birth of Walker Percy the novelist can be dated, it is from the moment of that recognition,[2] for what drove him forth was the aware-

1. Walker Percy, *The Moviegoer* (New York, 1967), 69–70. Page references here are to the Noonday edition. The original hardcover edition was published by Alfred A. Knopf in 1961.
2. Percy was born in Birmingham, Alabama, on May 28, 1916. The biographical facts in this chapter have been authenticated by Percy himself. The interpretations, unless otherwise indicated, are mine.

3

ness that he was still obliged to draw one breath and then the next and had best be charting his course. And though more than ten years were to pass before the first documents saw light—and almost two decades before *The Moviegoer* would appear as a preliminary outline of his pilgrimage—the starting point for a study of his novels is this pivotal epoch in which he turned from medicine to the writing of fiction.

The decisive stroke was pulmonary tuberculosis, which cut short his medical career and sent him to the Adirondacks for two years of enforced invalidism while his two younger brothers went off to war. What is less well known is that this personal catastrophe coincided with personal and philosophical crises in a powerful conjunction of circumstances. One circumstance was the death of "Uncle Will," his father's cousin William Alexander Percy, who had done his best to raise Walker and his brothers after the death of their parents more than a decade earlier. At the time his uncle died, Walker as a medical student had spent three years in Freudian analysis. No doubt the trauma of his father's suicide when Walker was eleven contributed to his personal difficulties,[3] as did his mother's death in an automobile accident two years later. For Will Percy, a lifelong bachelor, raising the three boys of his favorite cousin could never have been easy. He suddenly found himself charged with the responsibility of "directing young lives," he wrote in his autobiography, "in a world that was changing and seemed to [him] on the threshold of chaos." Those "youngsters" of the boys' generation "crave community of aspiration and purpose, they fear to be alone and outcast," he remarked, going on to speak of the "beautiful dead language" of Christianity as something that could not save them.[4] As the world moved

---

3. Ellen Douglas, a novelist from Greenville and a friend of the family, speaks of a "thread of suicide" in the family going back to the first Percy to settle in Mississippi in the eighteenth century. Her pamphlet *"The Last Gentleman": Introduction and Commentary* (New York, 1969) gives some valuable background on the family as well as the novel.

4. William Alexander Percy, *Lanterns on the Levee* (New York, 1941), 310, 315. The chapter entitled "For the Younger Generation" demonstrates the kind of one-

into the chaos of the Second World War, Will Percy died,
leaving Walker the eldest of three brothers, about to be strick-
en with tuberculosis.

Compounding the personal difficulties was a philosophical
crisis that bears directly on Percy's view of the novel. His
education had been scientific. In his premedical school years
at the University of North Carolina he had majored in chemistry. Whether or not he was ever really enthusiastic about
a medical career is uncertain,[5] but he admired the elegance
and simplicity of science and was particularly drawn to the
notion of "the mechanism of disease" of which his professors
spoke.[6] "Under the microscope, in the test tube, in the col-
orimeter, one could actually see the beautiful theater of disease and even measure the effect of treatment on the disease
process." Percy still admires the rigor of the scientific method
but even then was beginning to feel a discomfort with the
concept of mechanism which so attracted him. Following his
graduation as an M.D. from Columbia's College of Physicians
and Surgeons in 1941, he went to work as a pathologist at
Bellevue Hospital in New York, where with eleven other
interns he conducted autopsies, often on tuberculous patients.[7] Then came the cataclysm. He was struck down by
"the same scarlet tubercle bacillus [he] used to see lying
crisscrossed like Chinese characters" in the sputum and

---

way sermonizing that Walker and his brothers must have encountered, which, as
Jim Van Cleave has pointed out, finds its way into *The Moviegoer.* See Van Cleave's
"Versions of Percy," *Southern Review,* n.s. VI (1970), 990–1010.

5. Percy told me recently he went to medical school mostly to please Uncle
Will, he now thinks, though he is not sure that Will Percy actually wanted him
to. He felt that it was expected of him somehow but cannot recall ever putting
the question directly to his uncle.

6. "It struck me then, as now," he says, "as an idea of the most revolutionary
simplicity and beauty; namely, that even the *dis*-order of *dis*-ease, which one generally
takes to be the very disruption of order, could be approached and understood
and treated according to scientific principles governing the response of the patient
to the causative agents of disease. This response *was* the disease as the physician
sees it!" See Walker Percy, "From Facts to Fiction," *Writer,* LXXX (1967), 27. This
is the best account Percy has given of his transformation from physician to novelist,
and I have drawn on it extensively in this chapter.

7. Evidently they were careless, conducting autopsies without masks or gloves.
Of the twelve, four contracted tuberculosis.

lymphoid tissue of the patients. "Now," he says, "I was one of them."[8]

The catastrophe brought a radical shift of perspective. It was during his ordeal as a patient, when he was forced into physical inactivity, that he became aware of a limitation of the scientific method. With time on his hands Percy began to read extensively—Dostoevski, Camus, Sartre, Marcel, Heidegger, and especially Kierkegaard. It was Kierkegaard who brought home to him a limitation of the scientific method, "the quite spectacular limitation that science cannot utter a single word about an individual as individual but only insofar as he resembles other individuals."[9] This recognition carried the force of an illumination. After twelve years of scientific education, Percy says, he felt rather like Kierkegaard when he finished reading Hegel: "Hegel, said Kierkegaard, explained everything under the sun, except one small detail: what it means to be a man living in the world who must die." Something was missing. "Did my eyes deceive me or was there not a huge gap in the scientific view of the world (scientific in the root sense of the word, knowing)? If so, it was an oversight which everyone pretended not to notice or maybe didn't want to notice."[10] A man whose view of the world is constructed entirely by the scientific method, Percy said recently, "sees the world ordered in scientific constructions with himself as a great lacuna, a great vacuum."[11] Percy found himself rather in that predicament.

So Walker Percy, in this dark wood of his life, found himself receptive to the tremendous illumination he received from Kierkegaard, which began slowly to transform his world. The European writers he had begun to read almost took over his life for a time. Dostoevski's novels were instrumental, especially *Notes from Underground,* as was Sartre's *Nausea.* The

8. Percy, "From Facts to Fiction," 28.
9. Walker Percy to Martin Luschei, April 19, 1970.
10. Percy, "From Facts to Fiction," 28.
11. John Carr (ed.), "Rotation and Repetition," in *Kite-Flying and Other Irrational Acts: Conversations with Twelve Southern Writers* (Baton Rouge, 1972), 39.

place these novels helped to fill is suggested in a passage from an article Percy once cited by the psychiatrist Leslie H. Farber. Speaking of the difficulty of arriving at an adequate definition of the "fully human," Farber offers a number of excerpts from writings on psychopathology and goes on to comment:

> Without examining these normative statements in detail, the reader can see why psychiatry is so often charged with being reductive. For while the creatures described above may bear some resemblance to animals, or to steam engines or robots or electronic brains, they do not sound like people. They are in fact constructs of theory, more humanoid than human; and whether they are based on the libido theory or on one of the new interpersonal theories of relationships, *it is just those qualities most distinctively human which seem to have been omitted* [emphasis added]. It is a matter of some irony, if one turns from psychology to one of Dostoevski's novels, to find that no matter how wretched, how puerile, or how dilapidated his characters may be, they all possess more humanity than the ideal man who lives in the pages of psychiatry.[12]

The "huge gap" in the scientific new of man of which Percy spoke is made up, as Farber says, of "just those qualities most distinctively human." In the reductive process by which science undertakes to generalize about the similarities between one person and another, the individual is lost. "You stop short at the very point where it matters to [the individual] man," Percy says, which is "what he is in himself."[13]

All this is not to suggest that Percy abandoned his respect for the scientific method. He began to see instead that art—and specifically the novel—had equal value, at least potentially, as an instrument of truth, an instrument that might complement the scientific method in exploring those lost areas of experience that were inaccessible to science. That was what Sartre seemed to be attempting with his phenomenological explorations in *Nausea*. Percy became interested in anthropology "in the European sense of the

12. Leslie H. Farber, "Martin Buber and Psychiatry," *Psychiatry: A Journal for the Study of Interpersonal Processes,* XIX (1956), 110. One of the excerpts quoted is from Jung: "A person is a psychic system which, when it affects another person, enters into reciprocal reaction with another psychic system."
13. Carr (ed.), "Rotation and Repetition," 39.

word, in a view of man as such, man as man,"[14] a concern
that probably impelled him toward the Catholic view he subsequently came to, and these philosophical European writers
were of enormous value to him—not only Sartre and Kierkegaard but Heidegger, Jaspers, and Gabriel Marcel, along with
Dostoevski and Camus. They suited his temperament and
his condition. Modern European thought focuses on
"concrete life-situations rather than abstractions," he once
explained, and is mainly interested in "the *predicament* of
modern man, afflicted as he is with feelings of uprootedness,
estrangement, anxiety and the like. It is quite natural, therefore, for philosophers like Sartre and Marcel to write plays
and novels."[15]

It is in this sense of seeing man in a predicament that
Percy can be called an existentialist, and it began to seem
natural to him that he too should write novels. For much
of the time that he was confined as a patient these writers
were his constant and intimate companions. It was they, not
the poet Virgil or any beatific Dantesque vision, who led
him forth from the lonely wood he had entered. There is
an analogue in his philosophical outlook for that exodus,
as we shall presently see, but the important thing to note
here is that in Percy's writings there are two streams. One
is his fiction, the other his writings on the philosophy of
language, which are little known to date. Percy attaches at
least equal importance to these writings on language.[16] The
two streams are of course related and the language essays
have a bearing on his fiction that I want to explore in the
concluding chapter, but the primary interest of this study
lies in the novels.

A conjunction of most painful circumstances, then, turned

14. *Ibid.*, 38.
15. Percy quoted by Judith Serebnick in "First Novelists—Spring, 1961," *Library Journal*, LXXXVI (1961), 597.
16. This dual interest may help to explain one of Percy's most engaging personal qualities: a genuine modesty with no visible literary pretensions. Though he does not much like the distraction of interviews, I found him very cooperative, seemingly a little puzzled as to what all the fuss was about.

Percy from medicine to philosophical investigations and writing. There was one auspicious condition that enabled him to pursue his new interests seriously: he had enough money to give him independence. Will Percy's greatest contribution to the literary values he esteemed may prove to have been the economic freedom he was able to grant his cousin's oldest son. So in a sense Walker Percy is right in saying that tuberculosis liberated him. "Let's just say I was the happiest doctor who ever got tuberculosis and was able to quit it," he told an interviewer.[17] His need was accompanied by the great boon of time and opportunity, and the failed physician he felt himself to be was able to advance in the direction that beckoned.

The foregoing account should make it clear just how Percy "got out from under William Faulkner," to borrow the phrase Louis D. Rubin, Jr., uses in describing a major problem for Southern writers today.[18] He was simply never under Faulkner's influence, though Faulkner often played tennis with his Uncle Will. He leapfrogged Faulkner and other writers Southern and American, with the sole exception of Mark Twain,[19] and went to Europe. By the time he came home he could see and speak for himself.

The literary impulse had been with him since an early age. The long line of lawyers from whom he was descended had often shared in a Southern tradition of writing on the side, especially Will Percy, to whom Walker is most indebted. But even before he moved to Greenville, Mississippi, to live with Uncle Will, he had tried his hand at writing. As a boy of ten or twelve he submitted a short short story to the old magazine *Liberty* that was never dignified by a rejection slip. "I probably didn't even get the address right," he says. "But it seemed like a good way to live, to sit down and write some-

17. Carlton Cremeens, "Walker Percy, the Man and the Novelist: An Interview," *Southern Review*, n.s. IV (1968), 290.
18. Louis D. Rubin, Jr., *The Curious Death of the Novel* (Baton Rouge, 1967), 282–93.
19. Percy told me he thought Hemingway was close to the truth in saying that all modern American literature comes from a book called *Huckleberry Finn*.

thing and send it off to a magazine."[20] A few years later
he wrote a gossip column for the Greenville High School
Pica.

Will Percy's house in Greenville was the center of a sort
of literary society. The town was a very enlightened place,
Percy says, and besides Faulkner, Carl Sandburg and Langston Hughes would drop in to see Uncle Will.[21] Walker knew
David Cohn, who lived in Greenville, and he went to school
with Shelby Foote in Greenville and later in Chapel Hill.
In high school Walker became proficient in writing sonnets
for sale at fifty cents to fellow students who needed them
for English classes. The greatest single literary influence on
him was surely Will Percy himself, who had the gift of a
good teacher for "making you see a poem or a painting the
way he sees it." Will Percy read Shakespeare and Keats to
Walker and introduced him to classical music, played on a
"huge monstrous" Capehart. David Cohn came to the house
for a weekend and, having just retired from business, stayed
a year. Cohn announced he was going to write and did.[22]
For ten years and more that was the kind of house Walker
Percy called home.

Entering the University of North Carolina as a chemistry
major, fresh from a reading of *The Sound and the Fury,* Percy
wrote one long unpunctuated Faulknerian paragraph for
his English qualifying exam and was placed in a "retarded
English Class."[23] While at Chapel Hill he wrote two pieces
for the *Carolina Magazine,* the campus literary magazine. One
was called "The Willard Huntington Wright Murder Case,"
an article on S. S. Van Dine which argued that Wright, a
promising scholar, had committed a murder of sorts in

20. Cremeens, "Percy, the Man and the Novelist," 287. Faulkner said something
very similar about the literary trade as he claimed to have observed it in Sherwood
Anderson.

21. Ashley Brown, "An Interview with Walker Percy," *Shenandoah,* XVIII (1967),
4–5.

22. Carr (ed.), "Rotation and Repetition," 36. Percy remarks jokingly that in
providing Shelby Foote with an example by writing poetry he launched Foote on
his literary career.

23. Brown, "An Interview," 3–4.

becoming "S. S. Van Dine," the author of best-selling whodunits in the twenties and thirties. The other has a familiar ring: "The Movie Magazine: A Low 'Slick.' "[24] The titles alone suggest how far from antebellum nostalgia his interests roamed even then. Percy is impatient with the notion that he was prompted to write by the oral tradition of Southern storytelling: "Whatever impulse I had towards writing owes nothing to sitting on a porch listening to anybody tell stories about the South, believe me."[25]

When he left for New York to begin medical training, clearly, Percy took along a literary valise or two among his luggage. Though he had not selected a literary vocation, he had developed the sensibility along with his bent for science. In a rather ominous literary sense, he was ready.

Then came his ordeal by tuberculosis. Following his recovery he taught pathology at Columbia Medical School until he suffered a mild relapse. This time he went to Gaylord Farms Sanatorium in Connecticut, where Eugene O'Neill had spent a year in 1912 and had written his first plays.[26] Disheartened by the relapse, Percy abandoned the medical career altogether and took to writing. In his subsequent development as a writer to this date, it is possible to discern three phases, each a consolidation growing out of the previous: his marriage and move to Covington, Louisiana; his breakthrough with *The Moviegoer;* and his further literary achievement culminating in his third novel, *Love in the Ruins.* The first two phases demand some attention.

Late in 1946, two years or so after he had first left the confinement of the sanatorium, he married a Mississippi girl, Mary Townsend, who had been a medical technician in the

24. Percy told me someone had tracked these down and written something about them, but as yet I have been unable to locate any such item.

25. Carr (ed.), "An Interview," 54.

26. In fact, Percy says, he occupied the same bed, which rather eerily recalls Hawthorne occupying the Old Manse in Concord where Emerson had written *Nature.* Percy doubts that he was affected by the coincidence. The really interesting thing is the parallel, since O'Neill, during his year of enforced leisure, developed an intense interest in drama, read the Greeks, Elizabethans, and moderns, and began writing plays.

Greenville clinic where he had worked the summer following his graduation as an M.D. They moved to Covington, the small town across the lake from New Orleans where they still live, and were converted to Catholicism. Alfred Kazin suggests in a recent profile that Percy's ordeal brought out in him one of those personalities William James called the "twice-born." Kazin comments, "In becoming a writer, as in his professing Catholicism, he declared himself born again, born to a new understanding."[27] It appears to me that in embracing what amounts to a way of life after the troubled probings of three years of psychoanalysis and an anguished existentialist quest, Percy was not only being born again in the sense Kazin describes but also consolidating his life, making a major synthetic move to reassemble the elements. Percy remarked not long ago that the Freudian view of man would be a difficult position from which to write novels,[28] and the move from psychoanalysis to Catholicism suggests a change tending to reinforce the conversion from medicine to literature.

He began to write. In this early phase his writings were predominantly philosophical, though the range of his essays is impressive. His first published work, if we except the pieces he wrote for the literary magazine at Chapel Hill, was an essay called "Symbol as Need," which came out in 1954 as a response to Suzanne Langer's *Feeling and Form*. Langer's new book sent Percy back in excitement to her earlier *Philosophy in a New Key*. In a sophisticated argument that shows professional competence in philosophy, he praises her for clarifying "once and for all, we hope . . . the generic difference between sign and symbol" and for recognizing the symbol as "a *basically human need.*" Then he faults her for dropping the epistemological implications of her discovery and goes on to urge an existentialist and Thomist position.[29]

27. Alfred Kazin, "The Pilgrimage of Walker Percy," *Harper's,* CCXLIII (1971), 85. Kazin spent a weekend in the Percy household and his sketch of Percy has some interesting sidelights. A valuable source.
28. Carr (ed.), "An Interview," 46.
29. Walker Percy, "Symbol as Need," *Thought,* XXIX (1954), 381–90. Percy quotes

In 1956 Percy published an arresting essay called "The Man on the Train" that defines some of the existential tools by which he was seeking deliverance. The essay is prophetic.[30] "There is no such thing, strictly speaking, as a literature of alienation," he announced at the outset, and went on to differentiate between the reading and nonreading commuter on the train: "The nonreading commuter exists in true alienation which is unspeakable; the reading commuter rejoices in the speakability of his alienation and in the new triple alliance of himself, the alienated character, and the author. His mood is affirmatory and glad: Yes! that is how it is!—which is an aesthetic reversal of alienation."[31] Shortly thereafter he wrote of a coming crisis in psychiatry, and in 1958 published one of his most provocative essays, "The Loss of the Creature," which discusses the packaging of experience by experts for the consumer.[32] In *Lanterns on the Levee* there is a passage suggesting a parallel in the way Will Percy sought to deal with the spiritual questioning of his nephews that would lead one to doubt the efficacy of packaged religion.[33] And obviously Walker Percy's quest was not satisfied by such expedients. In a parable-essay the following year called "The

Marcel here on naming or symbolization as "the foundation of what Marcel calls the metaphysics of *we are* instead of *I think.*" Note that Percy was writing five years before Noam Chomsky wrote his devastating review of B. F. Skinner's book *Verbal Behavior* (*Language: Journal of the Linguistic Society of America*, XXXV [1959], 26–58). Percy considers Chomsky's subsequent work to be largely consistent with his own views on language. In December of 1971 he was reading proofs on a new article advancing a triadic theory of meaning. This aspect of Percy's writings is beyond the scope of my book but constitutes a worthy field of investigation.

30. Walker Percy, "The Man on the Train: Three Existential Modes," *Partisan Review*, XXIII (1956), 478–94. It was the discovery of this essay in an otherwise tedious bibliographical search that led me to a study of Percy.

31. *Ibid.*, 478. For a discussion of the implications of this idea in Percy's fiction, see my final chapter.

32. Walker Percy, "The Loss of the Creature," University of Houston *Forum*, II (1958), 6–14. This essay is important and my title for this book is taken from it.

33. "Yet, knowing how purblind a guide I was, I sent them to the churches. It seemed to matter little what sect they sought for guidance: they and their young friends returned confused, resentful, and distressed" (William Alexander Percy, *Lanterns on the Levee*, 313). Walker Percy has some important things to say on the aesthetic problem of approaching the too-familiar. The problem is taken up in my concluding chapter.

Message in the Bottle," he portrayed man as a castaway longing for news from beyond the seas.[34]

Through most of the early 1950's his apprenticeship as
a novelist was continuing. The novel seemed a promising
instrument for exploring those dark interstices of experience
unillumined by science. Marcel had voiced a similar aim in
saying that writing plays "appeared to me as a way out of
the labyrinth into which I had been led by my abstract thinking; through it I hoped to emerge into the light of an
organized human landscape of which it was my aim to understand the structure."[35] Percy too was looking for an exit,
though his early efforts were fumbling and ineffectual.[36]

The first novel he attempted was the standard apprentice
novel, a long rambling thing in an eclectic style owing more
to Thomas Wolfe than to anyone else. The novel was called
The Charterhouse and had a country club for its setting. Percy's
idea was that the country club with its golf course had displaced the medieval cathedral as the center of communal
activity around which people lived.[37] He submitted the novel
for publication and got it back with rejection slips or with
"pained notes which began, 'Despite some occasional splendid
passages, I am sorry to have to inform you—' etc." He sent
it to Caroline Gordon, the only writer he knew, who returned
it with thirty pages, single-spaced, of comment and criticism,
an effort for which he still expresses astonishment and
gratitude. Allen Tate, who was then married to her, wrote
Percy two or three sentences: "This is dreadful—you've simply got to put some action in it!"[38] Percy wrote a second
novel, this one about a pathologist doing autopsies on tuberculous patients in Saranac Lake, a sort of American *Magic*

34. Walker Percy, "The Message in the Bottle," *Thought,* XXXIV (1959), 405–33.
35. Gabriel Marcel, *The Philosophy of Existentialism,* trans. Manya Harari (New
York, 1961), 108.
36. So he says. No one else has seen them. Percy is glad they are not in print.
37. A charterhouse was a monastery of the very strict order of Carthusians,
which was founded in France in the eleventh century. Stendhal called one of his
masterpieces *The Charterhouse of Parma.*
38. This is the way Percy recalled it (Brown, "An Interview," 4). It is possible
Tate was more tactful.

Mountain whose only virtue, he says, was that it was short. It never reached a publisher.

When he sat down to write *The Moviegoer,* something happened. He broke through suddenly, following great discouragement, in a "paradoxical moment of collapse-and-renewal in which one somehow breaks with the past and starts afresh." The terms in which Percy describes the process of trying to create something new are illuminating: "not the picture of a man setting out to entertain or instruct or edify a reader but [the] picture rather of a scientist who has come to the dead end of a traditional hypothesis which no longer accounts for the data at hand." He likens the serious novelist today to the physicist at the turn of the century coping with the overthrow of Newtonian physics. Now it is "man himself who is called into question and who must be defended"; it is the "very nature of man which must be rediscovered." So after repeated failures, his traditional hypothesis unable to account for the data now at hand, Percy began *The Moviegoer* with "a *man* who finds himself in a *world,* a very concrete man who is located in a very concrete place and time," who might be represented as *"coming to himself* in somewhat the same sense as Robinson Crusoe came to himself on his island after his shipwreck, with the same wonder and curiosity."[39]

It happened with the first sentence he wrote. By the time he had finished the opening paragraph, which stands as he then wrote it, he had found his voice. The voice in *The Moviegoer* owes a good deal to Albert Camus, as Percy has acknowledged, but it is impossible to miss the distinctive Percyan tone.[40] What he stumbled onto, by his own account,

39. Percy, "From Facts to Fiction," 46.
40. Compare Percy's opening paragraph with that of Albert Camus in *The Stranger,* taken from the Vintage edition (New York, 1946), trans. Stuart Gilbert. First Percy, then Camus:

This morning I got a note from my aunt asking me to come for lunch. I know what this means. Since I go there every Sunday for dinner and today is Wednesday, it can mean only one thing: she wants to have one of her serious talks. It will be extremely grave, either a piece of bad news about her stepdaughter Kate or else a serious talk about me, about the future and what I ought

was a closer relation between style and content—more specifically a laconic tone which allowed him to treat his recurring themes without Faulknerian or Wolfean excesses. Stanley Kaufmann, his editor at Knopf, was of tremendous help to him. Percy wrote *The Moviegoer* in a little over a year. He says that writing it was better therapy than three years of psychoanalysis.[41]

The rest is publishing history. Percy's breakthrough with *The Moviegoer* following his long apprenticeship recalls a sentence from Emerson's famous letter to Whitman upon the publication of *Leaves of Grass:* "I greet you at the beginning of a great career, which yet must have had a long foreground somewhere, for such a start." Winning the National Book Award for 1962 with his first published novel was a literary coup, but such a start can only be understood in light of the long foreground I have tried to sketch here. Percy was forty-five. Some reviewers were dismayed to see the prize go to *The Moviegoer.* Alfred Kazin summarizes the trade gossip in his profile of Percy.[42] The sudden critical success of *The Moviegoer* made Percy feel the pressure to demonstrate in his second novel that the first was not a fluke. He was gratified that *The Last Gentleman* was a runner-up for the same award in 1967. *Love in the Ruins* drew highly respectful reviews, for the most part, when it came out in May of 1971. Some reviewers—wisely, I think—showed an instinct to hedge, as if in recognition that Percy was onto something best treated with respect whether or not one could really follow it. Walker Percy the novelist had arrived.

There is no trace of literary vanity in Percy's manner. He lives a modest and outwardly conventional life in an attractive

---

to do. It is enough to scare the wits out of anyone, yet I confess I do not find the prospect altogether unpleasant.

Mother died today. Or, maybe, yesterday; I can't be sure. The telegram from the Home says: YOUR MOTHER PASSED AWAY. FUNERAL TOMORROW. DEEP SYMPATHY. Which leaves the matter doubtful; it could have been yesterday.

41. This he told me in conversation.
42. Kazin, "The Pilgrimage of Walker Percy," 81.

brick house of French provincial style overlooking the Bogue
Falaya River, which in Choctaw means river of mists. A
lifelong inhabitant of Covington and New Orleans to whom
I spoke had never heard of him. A private person who rather
guards his privacy yet converses easily, he is devoted to his
family. His wife considers him a doting grandfather: no discipline at all. One has only to be with him for a few minutes
to recognize the cant-free solidity of the man whose pilgrimage is charted in his novels. He does not see himself particularly in a literary role; writing novels is one of the things
he does. Directly confronted on the question, he identifies
himself as a failed physician. Pressed for positive definition,
he adds that he is a person who takes an interest in something
and sees it through.

There is something fateful in the way Percy was put to
trial at the outset of the war that marks such a turning point
in American life. The postwar mood has been an almost
steadily rising malaise, a malaise finally unaccounted for that
threatens the psychic annihilation of us all. "The mood of
crisis has come as an unwanted but permanent guest," Ernst
Breisach says, bringing with it a "fervent, often frenzied"
search for causes. The technicians, "convinced that a quick
repair is all that is needed," urge one solution or another
to "one particular, simple-to-grasp problem [such as] the
dwindling of the topsoil [or] 'bringing ethics into line' with
our advanced technology, etc., etc." The traditionalists blame
Western man's "straying away from time-honored and well-
proven ways," others the "stifling routine of modern life."[43]
But the causes are deeper and more complicated and must
be sought by various means—even nonscientific means. It
remains for some to explore the gaps left in our knowledge
by the scientific method we so revere. In such times it is
good to hear from a physician-philosopher-novelist who
encountered the malaise early, in a highly personal form,
and has been thinking it over.

43. Ernst Breisach, *Modern Existentialism* (New York, 1962), 3.

Walker Percy today is not the same doctor who peered through the microscope with such fascination at the scarlet tubercles. Fate removed his detachment. Now he deals with mysteries as well as problems. "A problem," Marcel said, "is something which I meet, which I find complete before me, but which I can therefore lay siege to and reduce. But a mystery is something in which I myself am involved."[44] The doctor is very much involved. And because it is impossible to understand his novels fully without some knowledge of their sources in philosophical existentialism, it is time we turned to those sources for some illumination.

---

44. Gabriel Marcel, *The Mystery of Being*, trans. G. S. Fraser (2 vols.; Chicago, 1960), I, 260.

2

Some Light from the Existentialists

A problem arises when we try to probe this new malaise: the condition is aggravated by our attempt to diagnose it. The malaise is partly the *result* of our effort to understand it! Consider the predicament of Binx Bolling cited earlier. By his vertical search he has disposed neatly of the universe, only to find himself left over. In that discovery he could hardly be more American, for surely never in history has there been a society so dedicated to the scientific outlook. And the scientific method, which has yielded such dividends in providing for our material wants and to which we reach almost instinctively in the attempt to save ourselves, produces the opposite effect: the *method* becomes an agent of alienation. We intensify the malaise by our effort to see it.[1]

That is why Walker Percy, who discovered the shortcomings of the method for himself when he read Kierkegaard, had to learn to see with new eyes. And that is why American readers who want to understand Percy's new vision of things, and to see it without distortion, need a working acquaintance with the existentialists. Such an acquaintance does not come

1. As Percy himself put it ("The Man on the Train," 480): "The estrangement of the existing self is not capable of being grasped by the objective-empirical method simply because the former is specified by the latter as its reverse. . . . it is just when the Method tries to grasp and categorize the existential trait that it is itself reversed and becomes a powerful agent, not of progress, but of alienation."

easily;[2] it seems to go against the grain. There is truth—or
used to be—in the widespread assumption that existentialism
is foreign to the pragmatic temper of most Americans.
Perhaps we have to come to the "dead end of a traditional
hypothesis," as Percy himself did, before we can be open
to a new understanding. The traditional hypothesis in this
case would be an exclusive faith in the scientific method.
The new understanding has to come by way of the existentialists, for that is the way Percy took. In order to penetrate
the malaise he developed existentialist modes of perception,
or ways of seeing, that we need if we are to see what he
sees—and perhaps to see the malaise for what it is.

A reviewer discussing *Love in the Ruins* refers to Walker
Percy, in the realm of fiction, as "the chief diagnostician of
our American anomie."[3] The description is exact, as the subtitle of this study indicates, provided we understand that
the doctor here is not standing off from the patient, as from
a medical problem that can be reduced, but involved along
with him in the mysterious surrounding element. For it is
in the nature of the malaise that the diagnostician is a partici-
pant.

There is an analogue for his philosophical views in the
personal exodus charted in his writings, his departure from
the dark wood in which he found himself as a young man—
that tangle of difficulties through which he had to find a
way. His exodus was essentially a movement from confinement to openness. I want to follow the general course of
that movement here, pausing long enough en route to define,
insofar as is possible, the modes of perception by which he

2. There have been moments in which it seemed to me that Percy had taken
for his own the attitude Søren Kierkegaard assumed mockingly on the part of
Johannes Climacus, one of his pseudonyms, who muses to himself: "You must
do something, but inasmuch as with your limited capacities it will be impossible to
make anything easier than it has become, you must, with the same humanitarian
enthusiasm as the others, undertake to make something harder" (*A Kierkegaard
Anthology*, ed. Robert Bretall [New York, 1946], 194, from *Concluding Unscientific
Postscript*). However, I have found in every case that the difficulty was inherent
in the subject, the question only the extent to which I could understand it.

3. Peter S. Prescott, "The Big Breakdown," *Newsweek*, LXXVII (1971), 106.

sought to find his way. Following the clues in his own writings, I have searched the writings of the existentialists for light to bring to his novels. Obviously I cannot presume to speak for Percy, only to consider the evidence carefully and in good faith. In presenting the focal concepts I have been able to identify I am not enshrining them; they are only critical tools. Nor am I trying to reduce the novels to philosophical abstractions. What I hope to do here is simply to discover conceptual light for the often obscure landscape of Percy's pilgrimage before proceeding to the novels. The aim is illumination.

The first thing Percy does philosophically, in his confinement, is to survey his surroundings. One thing he discerns is a phenomenon he calls *everydayness,* which is almost omnipresent in *The Moviegoer.* Binx Bolling speaks of the impression growing on him that everyone is dead:

> It happens when I speak to people. In the middle of a sentence it will come over me: yes, beyond a doubt this is death. There is little to do but groan and make an excuse and slip away as quickly as one can. At such times it seems that the conversation is spoken by automatons who have no choice in what they say. I hear myself or someone else saying things like: "In my opinion the Russian people are a great people, but—" or "Yes, what you say about the hypocrisy of the North is unquestionably true. However—" and I think to myself: this is death. Lately it is all I can do to carry on such everyday conversations, because my cheek has developed a tendency to twitch of its own accord. Wednesday as I stood speaking to Eddie Lovell, I felt my eye closing in a wink.

The condition described is everydayness, a term Percy borrowed from Heidegger— *Alltäglichkeit.* "Everydayness," Binx tells us, "is the enemy."[4]

This condition can be defined as a generalized loss of awareness that walls a person off from his surroundings and diminishes his vitality. It is connected with routine and the anonymity of people in the mass, and it results in numbness and anxiety. Kierkegaard and Heidegger have written of

4. Percy, *Moviegoer,* 99–100; 145.

it most explicitly, though Marcel too speaks of a "twilight state" of non-vision which is not, however, a state of quite complete non-awareness."[5] Kierkegaard described the phenomenon in terms of dispersion and anonymity. Defining his own age as "essentially one of understanding lacking in passion," he wrote: "By comparison with a passionate age, an age without passion gains in *scope what it loses in intensity.*"[6] The result is a kind of human leakage, a devitalized existence that loses itself in trivia. In one of his most pithy remarks Kierkegaard summed up the consequence: "The majority of men are curtailed 'I's'; what was planned by nature as a possibility capable of being sharpened into an I is soon dulled into a third person."[7]

Kierkegaard's extended lament over the condition of mid–nineteenth–century Denmark has much in common with Percy's portrayal of contemporary America. The kind of death described by Binx Bolling corresponds remarkably with a passage from Kierkegaard:

> Nowadays one can talk with any one, and it must be admitted that people's opinions are exceedingly sensible, yet the conversation leaves one with the impression of having talked to an anonymity. . . . People's remarks are so objective, so all-inclusive, that it is a matter of complete indifference who expresses them. . . . There is no longer any one who knows how to talk, and instead, objective thought produces an atmosphere, an abstract sound, which makes human speech superfluous, just as machinery makes man superfluous.[8]

What is striking here is Percy's demonstration that a phenomenon isolated in Europe by Kierkegaard in 1846, while Emerson was preaching self-reliant individualism in the New World, has permeated American life so deeply that we can all find ourselves at times talking about hypocrisy or the Russians like interchangeable parts of a big machine.

5. Gabriel Marcel, *The Mystery of Being,* trans. G. S. Fraser (2 vols.; Chicago, 1960), I, 79.

6. Søren Kierkegaard, *The Present Age,* trans. Alexander Dru (New York, 1962), 68.

7. Søren Kierkegaard, *The Journals of Kierkegaard,* trans. Alexander Dru (New York, 1959), 248.

8. Kierkegaard, *Present Age,* 76–77.

Heidegger describes everydayness more in terms of loss or forgotten-ness. Man finds himself—or in Heidegger's terms, *Dasein* finds itself[9]—thrown into this world without having been consulted. In such a condition he has like any living animal a basic connection with Being; but as man he is heir to a second dimension, the possibility of *inquiring into* his connection with Being, of transcending other beings. But that is just the problem, for this second dimension, as Ernst Breisach points out, is only a possibility: "Man can ignore this question and just not ask it. He can float and coast along. He can exist like other beings not knowing and not caring about his connection with Being." Coasting along in this fashion, he becomes lost in everydayness, "thrown down among beings and immersed in them," to quote another interpreter of Heidegger, his "unique prerogative . . . lost in forgotten-ness. This is [his] every-day condition."[10]

A special feature of everydayness is loss of visibility. As Marcel said, "all of us tend to secrete and exude a sort of protective covering within which our life goes on."[11] Sometimes our symbolizing tendency contributes to the loss of visibility. A commonplace thing like a sparrow, Percy has written, tends to become invisible in ordinary life because it vanishes into its symbol. When the sparrow is first named, as it is by a child, it has the freshness of discovery; we can see it. "But when names no longer discover being but conceal it under the hardened symbol, when the world comes to be conceived as Alice's museum of name-things: shoes and ships and sealing wax—then I am bored."[12] One is lost in the boredom of everydayness, which is a serious predicament,

9. I am following Ernst Breisach here, who interprets *Dasein* to mean man as seen by Heidegger (*Modern Existentialism* [New York, 1962], 83). Particularly with Heidegger I am relying on authoritative interpreters of his work.
10. *Ibid.*; William J. Richardson, S.J., *Heidegger: Through Phenomenology to Thought* (The Hague, 1963), 48. Richardson translates *Dasein* as There-being and speaks of it in the neuter. I have taken the liberty of adapting his language to my discussion.
11. Marcel, *Mystery of Being*, I, 79.
12. Walker Percy, "Naming and Being," *Personalist*, XLI (1960), 153–54.

for boredom can be just what Kierkegaard called it, the root of all evil.[13]

A second hazard Percy identifies in his surroundings is *inauthenticity*. We find a good example of inauthenticity in *The Moviegoer*. When Binx Bolling first moved to the middle-class New Orleans suburb of Gentilly, he tells us, he bought a two-door Dodge sedan, a conservative and economical car, "just the thing, it seemed to me, for a young Gentilly business-man." But then a curious thing happened:

> When I first slid under the wheel to drive it, it seemed that everything was in order—here was I, a healthy young man, a veteran with all his papers in order, a U.S. citizen driving a very good car. All these things were true enough, yet on my first trip to the Gulf Coast with Marcia, I discovered to my dismay that my fine new Dodge was a regular incubator of malaise. Though it was comfortable enough, though it ran like a clock, though we were spinning along in perfect comfort and with a perfect view of the scenery like the American couple in the Dodge ad, the malaise quickly became suffocating. We sat frozen in a gelid amiability. Our cheeks ached from smiling. Either would have died for the other. In despair I put my hand under her dress, but even such a homely little gesture as that was received with the same fearful politeness, I longed to stop the car and bang my head against the curb. We were free, moreover, to do that or anything else, but instead on we rushed, a little vortex of despair moving through the world like the still eye of a hurricane.[14]

What Binx recounts here is an inauthentic experience. The reference to the American couple in the Dodge ad is a clue: Binx finds himself playing a role alien to him. He is comfort-able and smiling, all his papers are in order, and he sits next to a beautiful girl. A recipe for happiness, by all the guidelines set up by the advertising industry. But the two of them have fallen into inauthenticity and the malaise moves in on them.

Inauthentic existence in the broadest sense is the antithesis of a meaningful life for all the existentialists. In this study

13. Søren Kierkegaard, *Either/Or*. See Bretall (ed.), *A Kierkegaard Anthology*, 22. Because of the convenience of this anthology I will generally make page references to it where possible, rather than to the individual books themselves.
14. Percy, *Moviegoer*, 121.

I am using the term in a more limited sense, in the way I see it functioning in Percy's novels. Inauthenticity in the novels involves a surrender of personal sovereignty. We can distinguish several ways of yielding sovereignty. The first lies in general conformity to the crowd or to the prevailing myths—not the minimal adaptation necessary to live in society, but what Ernst Breisach calls "conformity as a fetish."[15]

Kierkegaard voiced an early and heartfelt protest against the crowd and thus raised the battle cry of the existentialists on behalf of the individual. "A crowd in its very concept is the untruth," he proclaimed. "What a falsehood! The falsehood first of all is the notion that the crowd does what in fact only the *individual* in the crowd does, though it can be every *individual*. For 'crowd' is an abstraction and has no hands: but each individual has ordinarily two hands, and so when an individual lays his two hands upon Caius Marius they are the two hands of the individual, certainly not those of his neighbour; and still less those of the ... crowd which has no hands." The crowd, moreover, is cowardly and not brave: "For every individual who flees for refuge into the crowd, and so flees in cowardice from being an individual (who had not the courage to lay his hands upon Caius Marius, nor even to admit that he had it not), such a man contributes his share of cowardliness to the cowardliness which we know as the 'crowd.' " Truth resides in the individual, and "no witness for the truth dare become engaged with the crowd."[16]

This cowardice of the individual in the crowd constitutes a grave threat to the authentic life in modern democratic society, with its weapons of propaganda and advertising and its tyranny of the majority. Percy has mounted increasing attacks on conformity in his novels, especially in *Love in the Ruins*, which is an all-out satire, among other things.[17] His treatment of conformity often deals with the phenomenon

15. Breisach, *Modern Existentialism*, 190.
16. See Søren Kierkegaard, *The Point of View for My Work as an Author: A Report to History and Related Writings*, ed. Benjamin Nelson, trans. Walter Lowrie (New York, 1962), 109–20, from which this discussion is taken.
17. He has also expressed a scornful view of what is called the liberal intellectual

of role-playing—what we might call living the cliché. *The Moviegoer* is built upon a highly sophisticated awareness of role-playing. As he spins along in his new Dodge, his "little vortex of despair," Binx Bolling encounters this form of inauthenticity and the trip becomes a charade.

To be aware of playing a false role and go on deceiving oneself about it is to be guilty of what Sartre calls bad faith, a concept derived from Heidegger's view of the inauthentic. Bad faith is a deadly component of the malaise in contemporary society. In the simplest terms it means "the art of retaining together an idea and its negation."[18] Sartre's phrase *mauvaise foi* has also been translated as self-deception.[19] Suppose that Binx realizes he is unhappy as he coasts along in his Dodge but proclaims to himself that he is enjoying a splendid experience. He is then guilty of bad faith, which is commonly received by others as hypocrisy.

Bad faith has ominous implications when we consider the ultimate reality that each of us confronts in his own life, the fact of finitude or personal death; for as Heidegger has stressed, a man's recognition of the fact of his own death is what leads him to the threshold of authentic existence.[20] And almost everything in modern society conspires to mask death and nourish inauthenticity, to curtail man's possibility of becoming an I, in Kierkegaard's terms. Death is commonly spoken of, Heidegger says, as an occurrence that comes to man but "belongs to nobody in particular. . . . Dying, which is essentially mine in such a way that no one can be my

---

establishment, referring in one of his interviews to "this intellectual herd in the North who profess to be free creative spirits." For the context of his remark see Cremeens, "Percy, the Man and the Novelist," 279.

18. Wilfrid Desan, *The Tragic Finale: An Essay on the Philosophy of Jean-Paul Sartre* (New York, 1960), 24.

19. Walter Kaufmann, *Existentialism from Dostoevsky to Sartre* (New York, 1956), 241–70. Kaufmann altered the translation of Hazel E. Barnes, who has given a more extended definition of bad faith in her book *Humanistic Existentialism: The Literature of Possibility* (Lincoln, Nebr., 1959), 50–55. Jean-Paul Sartre's treatment of *mauvaise foi* can be found in his *Being and Nothingness: An Essay on Phenomenological Ontology,* trans. Hazel E. Barnes (New York, 1966), 86–116.

20. Breisach, *Modern Existentialism,* 89.

representative, is perverted into an event of public occurrence which the 'they' encounters." It is considered "a cowardly fear" to reflect upon death. *"The 'they' does not permit us the courage for anxiety in the face of death."*[21] Bad faith is a central factor in all this, since no man can escape an occasional intimation that he must one day die. But undertakers have long since been converted into morticians and then into funeral directors, and only the stark reality of death itself is any longer buried. Under such conditions it is a simple matter to drift along in bad faith believing one will never die and remain the "curtailed I" of which Kierkegaard spoke.

Another way of yielding sovereignty is by abdicating, or deferring to the experts. Percy himself has written a good deal on this question. The best statement of his concept of sovereignty is in his essay "The Loss of the Creature," in which he analyzes some of the ways men are disinherited in modern techological society. The predicament of a man in such circumstances is that he becomes a consumer in a society divided between "expert and layman, planner and consumer, in which experts and planners take special measures to teach and edify the consumer.... The expert and the planner *know* and *plan,* but the consumer *needs* and *experiences.*"[22] The student has no right to one of Shakespeare's sonnets; Miss Hawkins will present it to him in an experience-package, with appropriate instructions. Nor has the boy in the biology class at Scarsdale High much hope of seeing the dogfish on the desk in front of him. Both are consumers receiving packaged experiences; the living creature is lost to them.

No one has really *seen* the Grand Canyon since its discovery. The sightseer's view is blocked by the National Park Service presentation and compromised by the frame of expectancy

---

21. Martin Heidegger, *Being and Time,* trans. John Macquarrie and Edward Robinson (New York, 1962), 297–98.

22. This essay contains highly original elements, though Percy is clearly indebted to Marcel. See for example Gabriel Marcel, *Man Against Mass Society,* trans. G. S. Fraser (Chicago, 1952). Percy, "Loss of the Creature," 11.

through which he unconsciously gazes on it. Most likely it will not measure up. Only the experts are qualified to see: "In the New Mexico desert natives occasionally come across strange-looking artifacts which have fallen from the skies and which are stencilled: *Return to U.S. Experimental Project, Alamogordo. Reward.* The finder returns the object and is rewarded. He knows nothing of the nature of the object he has found and does not care to know. The sole role of the native, the highest role he can play, is that of finder and returner of the mysterious equipment."[23] In modern society we all tend to become "natives," denied authentic experience. That is why we have to learn, all over again, to see.

Dispossession of the layman has deadly consequences in psychiatry. The patient, Percy writes in the medical journal *Psychiatry,* is all too prone to fall into what Whitehead called the fallacy of misplaced concreteness: that is, bestowing upon theory, "or what [the patient] imagines to be theory, a superior reality at the expense of the very world he lives in." The patient's problem is not, like the scientist's, one of interpreting the data before him but of living in a world which he, like Binx Bolling, has "disposed of theoretically." He fails to realize that science cannot tell him how to live; he "does not conceive a higher existence for himself than to be 'what one should be' according to psychiatry." Viewing himself objectively, he applies for relief to the scientist, who is the source of his world view, but his "seduction by theory" has placed him almost out of reach of the therapist. "Paradoxically," Percy notes, "it is his veneration of psychiatry which all but disqualifies him as a candidate for psychiatric treatment."[24] He has abdicated.

Still another way of surrendering personal sovereignty is by forfeiting one's right to participation in the intersubjective communion—the I-Thou community of the truly human.

23. *Ibid.,* 11.
24. Walker Percy, "The Symbolic Structure of Interpersonal Process," *Psychiatry: A Journal for the Study of Interpersonal Processes,* XXIV (1961), 39–52.

"Lying cuts you off," says Tom More, the narrator of *Love in the Ruins*,[25] and there are manifold forms of lying. A person forfeits his participation in the intersubjective communion principally by viewing others as objects and treating them accordingly.[26] Kierkegaard's "Diary of the Seducer" contains an admirable demonstration of the process. Johannes the seducer has just sighted the beautiful young Cordelia and ascertained that she has no ring on her fourth finger: "Ought I to give her up? Ought I to leave her undisturbed in her happiness?—She is about to pay, but she has lost her purse.—She probably mentions her address, I will not listen to it, for I do not wish to deprive myself of surprise. . . . No impatience, no greediness, everything should be enjoyed in leisurely draughts; she is pointed, she shall be run down."[27] Johannes lives entirely on Kierkegaard's aesthetic plane, which will be discussed later. His imagery is coolly direct: the girl is a quail to be run down. She will pay.

The cost to the seducer is less obvious. Essentially he forfeits his own place in the community of being; in taking her for an object he makes an object of himself. Percy has written nothing explicit on the ethical question here, but in an essay that is probably the best introduction to his overall philosophical position he suggests what is implicitly the case. I plan to deal more fully with this question presently; for the moment it is sufficient to say that he takes issue with Sartre on the question of the other. Symbolization is an intersubjectivity in its very essence, involving a "mutuality between the I and the Thou and the object which is in itself prime and irreducible." Consequently the "two term subject-object division of the world, as the situation in which [according to Sartre] one finds oneself, is not the original predicament of consciousness but rather a decadent 'inauthentic' state,

25. Walker Percy, *Love in the Ruins* (New York, 1971), 77.
26. To do so is a form of abstraction as well. It should be apparent by now that these are existential and not logical categories. They overlap and are neither precise nor mutually exclusive, nor does the sum of them exhaust all possibilities. They do however shed light on what it is to live an individual human life.
27. Bretall (ed.), *A Kierkegaard Anthology*, 39.

a falling away from an earlier communion."[28] Authenticity involves a sharing.

Percy's view of sovereignty is not an egoistic concept, but the assertion of one's claim within the community of others, which entails an acceptance of the claims of others on oneself. It is a sovereignty-within-intersubjectivity, for want of a more palatable term. And to forfeit one's sovereignty here, or in any of these areas, is to fall into inauthenticity and be prey to the malaise.

There is no more lethal component in the malaise than something Percy has identified as *abstraction,* which is prominent in all his novels and central in his most recent. One of his victims of abstraction is Jamie Vaught, the brilliant adolescent of scientific gifts in *The Last Gentleman* who is slowly dying of leukemia. The narrator, Will Barrett, reflects on the contrast between himself and Jamie:

> If Jamie could live, it was easy to imagine him for the next forty years engrossed and therefore dispensed and so at the end of the forty years still quick and puddingish and childish. They were the lucky ones. Yet in one sense it didn't make much difference, even to Jamie, whether he lived or died—if one left out of it what he might "do" in the forty years, that is, add to "science." The difference between him and me, [Barrett] reflected, is that I could not permit myself to be so diverted (but diverted from what?). How can one take seriously the Theory of Large Numbers, living in this queer not-new not-old place haunted by the goddess Juno and the spirit of the great Bobby Jones?[29]

Jamie's view of himself, as Will defines it, involves the kind of abstraction in which a person takes a purely functional view of himself, seeing his own life not as his personal opportunity to experience life but as an activity that yields a certain return on the world's investment.

28. Walker Percy, "Symbol as Hermeneutic in Existentialism: A Possible Bridge from Empiricism," *Philosophy and Phenomenological Research,* XVI (1956), 522–30. Percy attempts to form a bridge from empiricism to existentialism on the basis of symbolization, pointing to the need for "an experiential and heterodox empiricism which . . .would include the method of Gabriel Marcel."
29. Walker Percy, *The Last Gentleman* (New York, 1966), 231.

Abstraction in this sense means the absorption of the concrete human personality into its theoretical shadow, which can happen by the objectification of self, where one's person becomes irrelevant to oneself, or by the objectification of others, where human beings vanish into mere symbols or masses. The two modes reinforce each other, either sliding imperceptibly into the other. Marcel has illustrated the juncture at which they meet in discussing the feeling one has in filling out what we call identity papers: "I have not a consciousness of *being* the person who is entered under the various headings thus: *son of, born at, occupation,* and so on. Yet everything I enter under these headings is strictly true."[30] The I here encounters the image an institution has of it, but still hears the small voice within protesting that *that* is not what it *is.* The personality is not yet extinguished.

Self-objectification is an occupational hazard of the scientist, who as scientist, Marcel notes, is concerned with "an order of truths which he must consider as wholly outside of, and completely distinct from, his own self." That is the "strange greatness of his task... that he really is lifted out of himself in this way.... the self has, in so far as it possibly can, vanished away."[31] He can easily become "dispensed," as Barrett imagines Jamie to be in the quotation above, whether he be doctor or patient. And one of the most pernicious forms of self-objectification, as we have seen, is the pride of the psychiatric patient who has learned to view himself in the abstract.

Modern technical society threatens the individual with self-objectification by valuing his function rather than his person and giving primary importance to efficiency. Marcel has written extensively on this process. He cites the instance of a country which in confronting the cruel predicament of displaced persons wanted only those who could make shoes, and points out that in contemporary society it is the man

30. Marcel, *Mystery of Being,* I, 104.
31. *Ibid.,* 265.

whose output can be objectively calculated, the man functioning most like a machine, who is taken as the archetype.[32]
It is a constant struggle for the individual not to be absorbed
into his function, which is far more important to the gross
national product or the five-year plan than is his person.[33]

The second mode, objectification of others, has taken
shapes in our day that Kierkegaard, who launched the existentialist revolt against abstraction, could scarcely have
imagined. But Kierkegaard saw the potentiality of what he
called the "hopeless forest fire of abstraction."[34] He felt it
with his entire being, especially in the all-enveloping form
of Hegelian idealism: "Being an individual man is a thing
that has been abolished, and every speculative philosopher
confuses himself with humanity at large, whereby he becomes
something infinitely great—and at the same time nothing
at all." Modern philosophy, he said, was open to the criticism
"not that it has a mistaken presupposition, but that it has
a comical presupposition, occasioned by its having forgotten,
in a sort of world-historical absent-mindedness, what it means
to be a human being."[35]

If the philosopher is capable of omitting his own existence
in a "world-historical" oversight, what then of the state or
the massive forces of history? Even with a friend we know
well, Marcel has observed, we sometimes fall prey to abstraction. Someone asks us for an opinion of our friend and we
offer a "summary, inexact judgment" which begins to form
a simulacrum of him in our own mind that obstructs our
concrete knowledge of him. It may even effect a change
in our attitude toward him.[36] If abstraction can operate with

32. Gabriel Marcel, *The Decline of Wisdom* (New York, 1955), 17; Marcel, *Man Against Mass Society*, 179.

33. The humanities divisions of our universities often do their hiring in what are forthrightly called slave markets, where the objects bought and sold are labeled medievalists or eighteenth-century men unless the sorting process reveals them to be fit only for composition or survey functions.

34. Kierkegaard, *Present Age*, 81.

35. Bretall (ed.), *A Kierkegaard Anthology*, 206, 202–203. The first quotation is from *Concluding Unscientific Postscript*.

36. Marcel, *Mystery of Being*, I, 66–67.

such force in the presence of personal knowledge and affection, its destructive power is immensely magnified in their absence. And when Kierkegaard's nemesis the crowd is involved, poisoned by what he recognized in 1847 as *ressentiment*[37] and undergirded by philosophies of the state that deny value to the individual, abstraction truly becomes a conflagration consuming everything in its path. It may be difficult for us in the English-speaking world, with our empirical temper, to feel the tremendous force of collective abstractions—*le peuple, el pueblo, das Volk*—unless abstraction takes on the more familiar demonic shapes of "communism" or "fascism."

Marcel speaks of the "spirit of abstraction," a concept that is very important to Percy. In an autobiographical essay Marcel relates his experience with the Red Cross Information Service during the First World War, where in most cases the information he reported to anxious relatives was the news of death: "In the end every index card was to me a heart-rending personal appeal. Nothing, I think, could have immunised me better against the power of effacement possessed by the abstract terms which fill the reports of journalists and historians of the war."[38] The spirit of abstraction involves a "contempt for the concrete conditions of abstract thinking." Abstraction itself is a necessary process of clearing the ground for action; the evil enters when we forget the methodical omissions made for the sake of the process.[39] The result is an "effacement," a kind of reduction related to Whitehead's fallacy of misplaced concreteness, to which Percy makes frequent reference. Contrary to appearances, this operation is not essentially intellectual: "We should have at this point [if we wish to understand what happens] to make a direct attack on general formulations of the type, '*This* is only *that*

37. Kierkegaard, *Present Age,* 49–52.
38. Gabriel Marcel, *The Philosophy of Existentialism,* trans. Manya Harari (New York, 1961), 121. A contemporary parallel is obvious: there is a vital difference between the weekly casualty figures from Indochina and the printing by *Life* of the photographs of all the Americans who died in a particular week.
39. Marcel, *Man Against Mass Society,* 155.

... *This* is nothing other than that ...', and so on: every depreciatory reduction of this sort has its basis in resentment ... and at bottom it corresponds to a violent attack directed against a sort of integrity of the real, an integrity to which only a resolutely concrete mode of thinking can hope to do justice."[40]

The spirit of abstraction, then, represents a malignant form of the objectification of the individual, which from day to day manifests itself most often in the relatively benign form of indifference. Either way its consequence is the eradication of personality. The victim of objectification is likely in the end to see himself as he is seen, and to look upon others in the same way. He is a good candidate for Kierkegaard's crowd. Whether by self-objectification or objectification by others, the individual is annihilated, and the effective agent is abstraction.

The concepts we have been considering up to now are modes of alienation in modern industrial society. As components of the malaise pervading contemporary life, they plague men with peculiar intensity. But underlying the predicament of contemporary man is the necessary condition of man as man. In that sense, in his anthropology, Percy dissents vigorously from most of the current notions and sees *man as wayfarer.*

This concept of man holds increasing importance in Percy's novels and is central to his latest, in which the narrator, Dr. Thomas More, remarks toward the end, "Some day a man will walk into my office as ghost or beast or ghost-beast and walk out as a man, which is to say sovereign wanderer, lordly exile, worker and waiter and watcher."[41] The sovereign wanderer and lordly exile Dr. More envisions is man as wayfarer, *homo viator,* a conception of man that goes back through Marcel to Thomas Aquinas. The best way to approach it may

---

40. *Ibid.,* 155–56. The "resolutely concrete mode of thinking" Marcel describes would serve as a thumbnail definition of existentialist thought.
41. Percy, *Love in the Ruins,* 383.

be through Binx Bolling, that contemporary of ours who narrates *The Moviegoer.*

"My belief was invincible from the beginning," Binx reflects, lying on his cot in the dark. "I could never make head or tail of God. The proofs of God's existence may have been true for all I know, but it didn't make the slightest difference. . . . I have only to hear the word God and a curtain comes down in my head." He tosses restlessly, "locked in a death grip with everydayness," until its hold loosens and he can scribble the following entry in his notebook:

REMEMBER TOMORROW

Starting point for search:

It no longer avails to start with creatures and prove God.

Yet it is impossible to rule God out.

The only possible starting point: the strange fact of one's own invincible apathy—that if the proofs were proved and God presented himself, nothing would be changed. Here is the strangest fact of all.

Abraham saw signs of God and believed. Now the only sign is that all the signs in the world make no difference. Is this God's ironic revenge? But I am onto him.[42]

Binx refers to his search frequently throughout the novel; his quest is clearly important to the book. But what of "one's own invincible apathy"? Why should the appearance of God change nothing? These questions, clearly portentous in their implications, baffle the mind; and until we can suggest answers to them we can never fathom the invisible substratum of Percy's novels or understand man's placement in the world as he sees it. We need to consult Marcel, to whom he is closest in his view of man, and his own writings, which furnish important clues.

Culturally speaking, he once wrote, "our posture is something like the cat in the cartoon who ran off the cliff and found himself standing in the air. May be he can get back to earth by backing up; on the other hand he might be in for a radical change of perspective." The cliff in this cartoon

42. Percy, *Moviegoer*, 145–46.

is the erstwhile security of Western culture in the Christian faith. The ethical secularist has been living on its "accumulated capital" and can afford to ask himself, as Binx does: "how is it that even if these things were all true, could be proved, it would make no difference to me?" One starting point—the only possible starting point, Binx remarks—for a consideration of this question is just this "strange fact" of one's invincible apathy. It is possible, Percy says, that the dislocation of the times might be related to "this very incapacity to attach significance to the sacramental and historical-incarnational nature of Christianity." For the imminent change in perspective is radical in the root sense: "the relation of Christianity to Western culture and one's own culture is much too radical to be settled by one's fancied aversion to this particular dogma or that particular churchgoer." Percy's position here is constructively negative. He cautions against an unthinking haste in dismissing the entire Christian tradition, but he is not proselytizing nor is he recommending religious conversion. "For 'religion' is itself apt to be conceived in terms specified by the very worldview for which it is prescribed as a cure."[43]

If we want to overcome this incapacity, Percy says, we must somehow disengage our world view from the slough of scientific humanism. From his unique perspective Percy has offered compelling criticisms of scientific humanism. "The suspicion is beginning to arise," he wrote in 1957, "that American psychiatry with its predominantly functional orientation—its root-concepts of drives and counter-drives, field forces, cultural criteria—is silent [on the great themes raised by existentialist critics like Kierkegaard and Marcel] because, given its basic concept of man, it is *unable* to take account of the predicament of modern man." Most American social scientists "have no criterion for evaluating illness except as a deviation from a biological norm." By definition the normal person *cannot* be ill. But what of the alienated commuters,

43. Walker Percy, "The Culture Critics," *Commonweal*, LXX (1959), 250, 249.

those "normal" residents of Park Forest or the suburbs of Cleveland whose "needs" are fully met, who can be certified by experts to be mentally healthy, yet who "experience themselves as things, as commodities, or as nothing"?[44] What if their ills are not biological but metaphysical?

Percy has a special antipathy for behaviorism, which, as Arthur Koestler says, has "a kind of flat-earth view of the mind": "Or, to change the metaphor," Koestler continues, "it has replaced the anthropomorphic fallacy—ascribing to animals human faculties and sentiments—with the opposite fallacy: denying man faculties not found in lower animals; it has substituted for the erstwhile anthropomorphic view of the rat, a ratomorphic view of man."[45] Such a view of man, in "denying man faculties not found in lower animals," is practicing a form of reductionism akin to the spirit of abstraction, if not consciously animated by it. But man is not simply a physical organism functioning in space and time, Percy says, and if we want to understand the malaise pervading our lives we must go beyond this "ratomorphism," with its sociology of motivations, in search of a larger view of man that "takes account of what man is capable of and what he can fall prey to."[46] To get a more encompassing view we must undergo a fundamental shift of perspective and see man as a wayfarer.

The term *wayfarer* comes from Marcel. It is impossible to give an adequate account of Marcel's thought here or to offer more than a few hints as to the reorientation necessary to understand his nonsystematic way of viewing things. A wayfarer by definition is a man who is not at home but on the road. Marcel has called him "the man *on his road to*," or simply "man," for a man "no longer on a road to anywhere

44. Walker Percy, "The Coming Crisis in Psychiatry: I," *America,* XCVI (1957), 392.
45. Arthur Koestler, *The Ghost in the Machine* (New York, 1967), 17. Percy has read Koestler's book, as becomes quite evident in *Love in the Ruins.*
46. Percy, "The Culture Critics," 248. Percy adds: "There is not really such a thing as a consumer or a public or a mass man except only as they exist as constructs in the minds of sociologists, ad men, and opinion pollsters."

would be a man no more." The wayfarer is an exile, "a being who is not at one with his actual surroundings"; he has a glimpse of a distant prospect. We should not be misled by the spatial analogy, for this distance presents itself as an "inner distance, as a land of which we should have to say that it is the land we are homesick for."[47]

One interpreter of Marcel, in discussing his concept of disquiet, describes the wayfarer's condition in the following terms:

> Disquiet is experienced in the same way that a secret is, like the feeling of a promise still unrealized, or the childhood phantasy of mysterious and inaccessible places. Or again, the sense of disquiet is similar to the expectation of a channel opening out to the sea. Most important, it resembles the nostalgia of an exile, yearning for a home. All [of Marcel's metaphors for disquiet] include a present state, a distant state and an intense desire to bridge the gap between the former and the latter.[48]

This desire to bridge the gap is man's need for transcendence, not a transcending of experience, for there is nothing beyond experience, but an inner transformation suggested by the kind that sometimes takes place within a personal relationship. If we can imagine experience to be a kind of solution receptive to varying degrees of saturation, this inner need for transcendence might coincide with "an aspiration toward a purer and purer mode of experience." Salvation for the wayfarer is better conceived as a road than as a state. He is a pilgrim on a journey toward the light.[49]

Transcendence, says Percy, is one feature that all existentialists recognize to be an inveterate trait of human existence. "Some[,] like Gabriel Marcel, may regard it as the true motion of man toward God; others, like Jean Paul Sartre, may regard it as an absurd striving, the 'useless passion.' But, atheistic or theistic, they would all agree that transcendence is the one distinguishing mark of human existence. In Friedrich

47. Marcel, *Mystery of Being*, II, 142, I, 237.

48. Patricia Sanborn, "Gabriel Marcel's Conception of the Realized Self: A Critical Exploration," *Journal of Existentialism*, VII (Winter, 1967–1968), 146.

49. Marcel, *Mystery of Being*, I, 59, 68, II, 204–205, 210.

Nietzsche's words, man is he who must surpass himself."[50] Marcel says, "My life infinitely transcends my possible conscious grasp of my life at any given moment; fundamentally and essentially it refuses to tally with itself."[51] Man is not at home in the world; he has a passion, useless or not, to transcend his condition. In the words of Loren Eiseley, "Man is not man. He is elsewhere."[52]

In his essay "The Message in the Bottle" Percy describes man's condition as that of a castaway, an exile marooned on an island where he has lived all his life and yet is not at home. Deep within himself he knows that "life on the island, being 'at home' on the island, is a miserable charade." He suffers the fate of Karl Jaspers' "shipwrecked man," the condition Heidegger called *Geworfenheit*, or "thrown-ness," which Percy interprets to be that of a castaway.[53] The castaway hungers for *news*. What he wants is not news of the island, which relates to his immediate needs: news of food or water, let us say. Nor is it knowledge, the knowledge *sub specie aeternitatis* which is available to anyone anywhere, at any time—the kind, say, that is experimentally verifiable by science. The castaway cannot put on the objectivity of the scientist, nor is his sickness to be cured by tidbits of island news. He is a man in a predicament. What he longs for is news from beyond the seas.

The news he awaits entails three canons of acceptance. It must be relevant to his predicament. It must be borne by a newsbearer whose credentials are good, preferably a brother or friend who knows his predicament and approaches him soberly and in good faith; news is often unheeded

---

50. Percy, "The Coming Crisis in Psychiatry: II," 417.

51. Marcel, *Mystery of Being*, I, 206.

52. Loren Eiseley, "The Uncompleted Man," *Harper's*, CCXXVIII (1964), 54. "There is within us," he continues, "only that dark, divine animal engaged in a strange journey—that creature who, at midnight, knows its own ghostliness and senses its far road." Eiseley, an anthropologist, goes on to say, "The terror that confronts our age is our own conception of ourselves," and concludes that the "deadliest message man will ever encounter in all literature" is the one carried to Macbeth by the witches: "that what we wish will come."

53. Percy, "The Message in the Bottle," 427, 430.

because it is shrieked at one emotionally, which can be done on any island and at any time and has no particular relevance to the castaway's predicament. And it must not be an obvious impossibility or something inappropriate, such as the suggestion that molten sulfur will appease his thirst. The Christian message is the kind of news the castaway is waiting for: not a piece of knowledge *sub specie aeternitatis,* "not a teaching but a teacher . . . not a member in good standing of the World's Great Religions but a unique Person-Event-Thing in time." The peculiar character of the Christian claim is "its staking everything on a people, a person, an event, a thing existing here and now in time." But this good news will not be recognized by a castaway "who believes himself to be at home in the world, for he does not recognize his own predicament. It is only news to a castaway who knows himself to be a castaway."[54]

Man is a castaway, then, whether he recognizes it or not. But the image of man as wayfarer more accurately reflects Percy's overall view. The shortcomings of spatial analogies as images of man's condition have been repeatedly stressed by Marcel, and what he says about the central theme of his own *Metaphysical Journal*—"precisely the impossibility of thinking of being as an object"—applies equally well to Percy: "Being can not be indicated, it cannot be *shown;* it can only be alluded to."[55] In the terms of the epigraph from Rilke that heads this study, we cannot approach the god from the space that lies in front of him.

Man's condition is that of wayfarer. Modern industrial society exposes him to the further hazards of everydayness, inauthenticity, and abstraction. To be afflicted in all these ways is essentially to be closed in, to be closed off from one's being: an exile longing for news from across the seas; a consumer-cipher walled in by everydayness, dispossessed of his sovereignty, and lost in abstraction: the anonymous "one"

54. *Ibid.,* 418–22, 425–26, 432.
55. Gabriel Marcel, *Metaphysical Journal,* trans. Bernard Wall (Chicago, 1952), viii.

of "one says," a "curtailed I." And yet that is not the worst.
To know the worst we should look to something Percy says
about despair:

> It is not for me to say here that [the castaway] should believe such
> and such. But one thing is certain. He should be what he is and
> not pretend to be somebody else. He should be a castaway and not
> pretend to be at home on the island. To be a castaway is to be in
> a grave predicament and this is not a happy state of affairs. But
> it is very much happier than being a castaway and pretending one
> is not. This is despair. The worst of all despairs is to imagine one
> is at home when one is really homeless.[56]

Man the wayfarer is closed in. His hope lies in the search
for a way out, and his journey must begin in the recognition
of his exile.

Having recognized his predicament and identified some
of the shapes assumed by the malaise that surrounds him,
Percy begins looking for egress. The ways he finds open
are mostly through existentialist terrain. One avenue familiar
to any reader of his novels is *ordeal*. Will Barrett, the protagonist of *The Last Gentleman*, has the impression that people
feel better in hurricanes and other natural disasters. The
one hurricane he has experienced left an imprint:

> A window broke. They helped the counterman board it up with Coca-
> Cola crates. Midge and the counterman, [Will] noticed, were very
> happy. The hurricane blew away the sad, noxious particles which
> befoul the sorrowful old Eastern sky and Midge no longer felt obliged
> to keep her face stiff. They were able to talk. It was best of all when
> the hurricane's eye came with its so-called ominous stillness. It was
> not ominous. Everything was yellow and still and charged up with
> value. The table was worth $200. The unexpected euphoria went
> to the counterman's head and he bored them with long stories about
> his experiences as a bus boy in a camp for adults (the Southerner
> had never heard of such a thing) somewhere in the Catskills.[57]

We can readily identify two kinds of alienation obliterated
by the storm. Everydayness has been shattered and the yellow
light of euphoria now vivifies everything, and with the nox-

---

56. Percy, "The Message in the Bottle," 428.
57. Percy, *Last Gentleman*, 24.

ious particles dissipated, Midge has been emboldened to drop her inauthentic "Eastern" pose and be herself.

Such dispensations are all too rare and should be received with gratitude. But ordeal has deeper significance in Percy's novels, and we can distinguish two forms of it. The first is shock, an unexpected rending of the everydayness that veils reality. At times shock turns out to be no ordeal at all, but a kind of surprise bonus, like the famous blackout in Manhattan. Sometimes the shock of ordeal helps us recover vision, Percy says, as in the case of the sparrow that vanishes into the everydayness of its symbol: "Only under the condition of ordeal may I recover the sparrow. If I am lying wounded or in exile or in prison and a sparrow builds his nest at my window, then I may see the sparrow."[58]

Figuratively speaking, the value of ordeal is this rediscovery of vision. We may proceed uneventfully from day to day, Marcel points out, until the people around us become "almost part of the furniture," but let a serious illness come along: "the break in habit that an illness brings with it enables us to grasp the precariousness of that everyday atmosphere of our lives which we thought of as something quite settled."[59] Suddenly we are aware of contingency, "that shock," as Ernst Breisach calls it, "which enables man to become aware of his special position among beings."[60] And in this confrontation with contingency in the form of shock, perhaps in the illness or death of another, I may encounter the second and ultimate form of ordeal: nothingness and finitude, my own personal death. Let one being be annihilated, Heidegger would say, and the world which has seemed so commonplace suddenly becomes mysterious.[61] The veil is drawn aside and I confront a reality I can ignore only at the greatest peril to myself. I can ill afford to conduct myself, Percy suggests,

58. Percy, "Naming and Being," 154.
59. Marcel, *Mystery of Being*, I, 257.
60. Breisach, *Modern Existentialism*, 193.
61. *Ibid.*, 86.

like the man Pascal described three hundred years ago, "who comes into this world, knowing not whence he came nor whither he will go when he dies but only that he will for certain die, and who spends his time as though he were not the center of the supreme mystery but rather diverting himself."[62]

The second form of ordeal, then, is my recognition that death is not a general phenomenon, but comes to *me*. For the existentialist the anxiety attending such a discovery is not simply a negative condition. Though in the view of Freud or Harry Stack Sullivan anxiety is the symptom of a disorder to be gotten rid of, Percy says, Kierkegaard saw it as the "discovery of the possibility of becoming a self."[63] To Heidegger anxiety is "that basic disposition which grips the whole person, makes him aware of his estrangement from Being, makes him feel completely threatened, and in doing so sets free liberating forces."[64]

The person who in bad faith deludes himself about death is truly lost in despair. He is dead to news from across the seas because he does not know himself to be a castaway. Since at least the time of Kierkegaard it has been all too easy to drift along. Kierkegaard's young man in *Repetition* admired Job because Job would not let the "passion of freedom within him [become] stifled or tranquilized by a false expression."[65] Our society today is grossly overstocked with inauthentic tranquilizers by which "anguish is denied or converted into manageable theories," as one interpreter of existentialism has put it. But to achieve authentic existence man must confront his anguish directly.[66]

---

62. Percy, "The Coming Crisis in Psychiatry: II," 415.

63. Percy, "Naming and Being," 154, and for the remark on Sullivan, "The Coming Crisis in Psychiatry: II," 416.

64. Breisach, *Modern Existentialism*, 88.

65. Soren Kierkegaard, *Repetition: An Essay in Experimental Psychology*, trans. Walter Lowrie (New York, 1964), 112. Kierkegaard's "trial of probation" has a connection here that I will explore later.

66. Patricia Sanborn, *Existentialism* (New York, 1968), 104.

The horror which all the existentialists have of these tranquilizers is summed up in a passage from Rilke's *The Notebooks of Malte Laurids Brigge:*

> Who, today, would still give anything for a well-executed death? No one. Even the rich, who could after all afford to die elaborately, are beginning to become negligent and indifferent; the wish to have a death of one's own is becoming rarer and rarer. A little while yet, and it will be as rare as a life of one's own. God, it's all there. One comes along, one finds a life, ready-made, one only has to put it on. One wants to go or is forced to go: well, no trouble at all: *voilà votre mort, monsieur*. One dies at random; one dies whatever death belongs to the disease one happens to have: for since one knows all the diseases, one also knows that the different lethal conclusions belong to the diseases and not to the human beings; and the sick person, as it were, doesn't have anything to do.[67]

Not a "lethal conclusion" but a "death of one's own," and along with it a life of one's own: that is the claim the existentialist makes on human existence.

Ordeal takes various shapes in the different existentialists, and issues in widely varying "solutions." Marcel, for example, has said that one's own death is easier to accept than one imagines; true ordeal is more likely to come with the death of a being one loves.[68] Marcel's interpretation of death of course is at the opposite pole from Sartre's. In Percy's novels we can define ordeal as man's first encounter on the road to being, whether in the form of shock, as a preliminary piercing of the curtain of everydayness, or as that paradoxically final recognition by which man in his freedom guides his life into authentic existence.

Another possible escape from the malaise is through *rotation*. Percy's most able practitioner of rotation is Binx Bolling, who passes his spare time in the company of his secretaries:

> Naturally I would like to say that I had made conquests of these splendid girls, my secretaries, casting them off one after the other

---

67. Quoted from Kaufmann, *Existentialism from Dostoevsky to Sartre*, 114.
68. Marcel, *Mystery of Being*, II, 169.

like old gloves, but it would not be strictly true. They could be called love affairs, I suppose. They started off as love affairs anyway, fine careless raptures in which Marcia or Linda (but not yet Sharon) and I would go spinning along the Gulf Coast, lie embracing in a deserted cove of Ship Island, and hardly believe our good fortune, hardly believe that the world could contain such happiness. Yet in the case of Marcia and Linda the affair ended just when I thought our relationship was coming into its best phase. The air in the office would begin to grow thick with silent reproaches. It would become impossible to exchange a single word or glance that was not freighted with a thousand hidden meanings.... No, they were not conquests. For in the end my Lindas and I were so sick of each other that we were delighted to say good-by.[69]

The ancient ritual that Binx is honoring here Kierkegaard would have called rotation. Its essence is novelty or possibility. Percy borrowed the term from Kierkegaard, who regarded it narrowly as a lower stage to be surmounted on the road to higher things. Rotation has been dismissed by one critic of Percy as a mere "bromide,"[70] but Percy values it more highly than such a judgment suggests. In the depths of the malaise rotation can be a strategy for defeating everydayness and breaking momentarily into authentic existence.

Even Kierkegaard seems to have savored outlining his formula for the rotation method. His spokesman is A the aestheticist, who could have offered Binx some expertise in managing his love affairs: "When two beings fall in love with one another and begin to suspect that they were made for each other, it is time to have the courage to break it off; for by going on they have everything to lose and nothing to gain." Loss or gain of course is interpreted solely in terms of pleasure. A disdains the vulgar and inartistic rotation that has to be supported by illusion: "One tires of living in the country, and moves to the city; one tires of one's native land, and travels abroad; one is *europamüde,* and goes to America, and so on." This is the extensive method, which is self-defeating. A recommends the intensive approach. Instead

69. Percy, *Moviegoer,* 8–9.
70. Anselm Atkins, "Walker Percy and Post-Christian Search," *Centennial Review,* XII (1968), 82.

of changing the field, you change the method of cultivation, enlisting the principle of limitation, which stimulates invention. You avoid business and friendship and shun marriage at all costs, for when you are one of several your freedom is gone. You cultivate acquaintances, letting them lie fallow at times, and harness the powers of the arbitrary: "One does not enjoy the immediate, but rather something which he can arbitrarily control. You go to see the middle of a play, you read the third part of a book. By this means you insure yourself a very different kind of enjoyment from that which the author has been so kind as to plan for you."[71]

The tone of all this is blasé and *europamüde,* and it is self-evident that rotation as customarily practiced by those of jaded appetite becomes a trap, a self-enclosed circle in which one never leaves the sphere in which he moves. But in his essay "The Loss of the Creature" Percy urges a similar tactic with an air both sly and serious. The malaise is far more perfidious than old-style European lassitude; to circumvent its myriad forms of inauthenticity we need all the stratagems we can devise. We need to distinguish between two modes: the extensive, which is often accidental, and the intensive, which is deliberate. Both involve zone-crossing and novelty. The extensive mode—which is the sense in which Percy himself speaks of rotation, as "the quest for the new as the new, the reposing of all hope in what may lie around the bend"[72] —is a device of restricted value, often a mere bromide. But the deliberate mode, or cultivation, which we can extrapolate from Percy's writings, is a part of the strategy of the search, a valued tool for the recovery of being.

In extensive rotation the zone-crossing tends to be accidental. We may go to a movie with the deliberate expectation of leaving the zone of everydayness, but whether we achieve a successful vicarious escape or are plunged back into deeper alienation is a matter of chance—for example, whether we can identify with the hero, or whether the whole affair has

71. Bretall (ed.), *A Kierkegaard Anthology,* 25–32, excerpted from *Either / Or,* I.
72. Percy, "The Man on the Train," 481.

the stench of falsehood. When it is good it is what Binx calls it: "the experiencing of the new beyond the expectation of the experiencing of the new."[73] This kind of rotation is perfectly suited to transmission in art, where it serves as a "mode of deliverance from alienation."[74] But when it is bad it leads to anxiety and despair, the fruit of bad art. Percy suggests that the television Western, a descendant of Owen Wister's novel *The Virginian,* has come to be "the native expression of that very anonymity of which the Virginian was conceived as the antithesis." The hero is a deracinated abstraction with no human kin who must always move on. He is presented to us as the most secure and easy-going of men, but like his story he is "sodden with anxiety: Everything, absolutely everything depends on a perfection of gesture. . . . It would not be so bad to be killed. But suppose one's gesture didn't come off?"[75] The viewer pays a terrible price in anxiety for this inauthentic art.

An extensive rotation, directly experienced, may or may not lead to authenticity. Suppose I am on my way to Guanajuato. I lose my way and stumble upon a remote Indian village engaged in a religious festival. A perfect rotation, it would seem: I have left the zone of the ordinary and happened onto something unexpected. But can I experience it? Only if I claim it for my own; not if I feel the need for an expert ethnologist to certify it for me as a genuine experience.[76]

The intensive mode, on the other hand, is a deliberate circumvention of the expected, an outwitting or evasion of it by perverse individuality. Instead of giving ground you hold your own, enjoying "something you can arbitrarily control," as Kierkegaard's A put it. You refuse the prepackaged Grand Canyon and sneak up on the original by a back road.

73. Percy, *Moviegoer,* 144.
74. Percy, "The Man on the Train," 487.
75. Walker Percy, "Decline of the Western," *Commonweal,* LXVIII (1958), 182. Percy discusses the subject more thoroughly in "The Man on the Train."
76. See Percy, "Loss of the Creature," 9–10.

Or if you cannot avoid the National Park version, you stand off, movie-maker fashion, and watch the tourists watching the canyon. You smuggle Boccaccio into Miss Hawkins' class while she presents the approved Shakespearean sonnet, or steal a glimpse at the sonnet in your biology class while the class labors over phase three of the dogfish dissection. The rotatory approach to Beethoven is to hide in the bushes outside while you listen, like the girl in *The Heart is a Lonely Hunter*. "What is the best way to hear Beethoven: sitting in a proper silence around the Capehart or eavesdropping from an azalea bush?" By such stealth I may succeed in recovering the lost creature. I cease to be the "consumer of a prepared experience" and claim my rights as a man: "I am a sovereign wayfarer, a wanderer in the neighborhood of being who stumbles into the garden."[77]

The essential thing is that as wayfarer I am *sovereign*. Whether I stumble into the garden quite by chance or as a result of my own strategy of approach, I must *assert* my claim. Rotation can lead the unwary into desperate forms of inauthenticity, and the common variety practiced by Binx with his secretaries soon exhausts its possibilities. But rotation has different levels. The higher planes are those of knowing —recovering the creature[78]—and of sharing a rotatory moment with another person, which can lead to intersubjectivity. In the grip of the malaise we cannot afford to neglect either form.

Still another way that Percy finds open is through *repetition*. One of the clearest accounts of it occurs toward the end of *The Moviegoer* when Binx makes a business trip to Chicago in the company of his cousin Kate:

> No sooner do we open the heavy door of Sieur Iberville and enter the steel corridor with its gelid hush and the stray voices from open compartments and the dark smell of going high in the nostrils—than

77. *Ibid.,* 13.
78. I suspect that this kind of knowing is allied to the sense of mystery that lies at the root of pure science.

the last ten years of my life take on the shadowy aspect of a sojourn between train rides. It was ten years ago that I last rode a train, from San Francisco to New Orleans, and so ten years since I last enjoyed the peculiar gnosis of trains, stood on the eminence from which there is revealed both the sorry litter of the past and the future bright and simple as can be, and the going itself, one's privileged progress through the world.[79]

What Binx experiences here is something everyone must have felt at one time or another. Percy calls it a repetition.

Like rotation, repetition is a Kierkegaardian term, though Percy has modified it for his own purposes. To understand Kierkegaard's concept of repetition we must begin with his three stages: the aesthetic, the ethical, and the religious. In the aesthetic stage a person is deeply involved in the world of immediacy, the moment, shunning all commitment, pursuing pleasure and easily tiring of it. He practices rotation as A defines it; the example would be Don Juan. To move to the ethical phase he must abandon the role of spectator, involve himself, and commit himself unconditionally to living within a general code, as in marriage, which to Kierkegaard could never surmount the ethical stage. He submits himself to rational ethics embodying universal demands, but the submission leads ultimately to a dead end because it still attempts the self-sufficiency of man.[80]

To transcend the ethical stage and attain the religious requires the leap of faith. This is where Kierkegaardian repetition enters, one of the most important terms in Kierkegaard's vocabulary and probably his most baffling.[81] The narrator of *Repetition* notes that repetition is always a transcendence, unlike modern philosophy, which moves only within immanence;[82] but he himself, not being religious, cannot go further. The vehicle for repetition is the young man who sacrifices his beloved by pretending he has a mistress. A reli-

79. Percy, *Moviegoer*, 184.

80. Breisach, *Modern Existentialism*, 21–22. I am following Breisach's interpretation here, though he speaks of modes instead of stages.

81. So says Walter Lowrie, one of Kierkegaard's foremost translators and interpreters. See *Kierkegaard* (2 vols.; New York, 1962), II, 634.

82. Kierkegaard, *Repetition*, 90.

gious person, the young man undergoes a trial of probation, like Job, who was able to say triumphantly in faith: "The Lord gave, the Lord hath taken away, blessed be the name of the Lord."

Job was blessed because of his faith, the young man feels, and "receive[d] everything *double*. This is what is called a *repetition*." The young man himself finally receives the repetition, which seems to mean the return of himself: "Did I not get everything doubly restored? Did I not get myself again, precisely in such a way that I must doubly feel its significance? . . . And what is a repetition of earthly goods which are of no consequence to the spirit . . . in comparison with such a repetition?"[83]

Kierkegaard later wrote that repetition was "a religious movement by virtue of the absurd" and that "eternity is the true repetition."[84] The story of Abraham and Isaac has a bearing that will be taken up later. The intricacies of Kierkegaard's concept would lead us astray here; instead of pursuing them I would like to cite an interpretation by George Price that may bear directly on Percy's more limited sense of the term. When the individual has made his leap of faith in Kierkegaard's scheme, Price says, he is forgiven: that is the repetition. Man has lost his real being by his error: "The likeness which was lost or forfeited was authentic being. . . . To go forward—that is, to start again the existential process of becoming—the self must initiate a movement in which it returns to its former state of being. . . . Forgiveness therefore is restoration—is repetition. What was lost is given back."[85]

It is in the sense of a return that Percy uses the term. A circularity is always implied. Repetition is the conversion of rotation, he says: "a deliberate quest for the very thing

83. *Ibid.*, 126. Percy makes the point that trial cannot be "re-presented" in art because it transcends the objective-empirical and thus is lost in the telling. See "The Man on the Train," 480.

84. Kierkegaard, *Repetition*, 15.

85. George Price, *The Narrow Pass: A Study of Kierkegaard's Concept of Man* (New York, 1963), 199–200.

rotation set out at any cost to avoid; the rider has turned
his back upon the new and the remote and zone-crossing
and now voyages into his own past in the search for himself."
Repetition is of two kinds: aesthetic and existential. "The
aesthetic repetition captures the savor of repetition without
surrendering the self as a locus of experience and possibility";
it is in the nature of a "connoisseur sampling of a rare emotion." The existential repetition, on the other hand, is the
occasion for the "passionate quest in which the incident serves
as a thread in the labyrinth to be followed at any cost." It
seeks to find the answer to the question, who am I? This
is the Return. Existential repetition is canceled in literature,
being transmitted only as the interesting; the serious character of the search is lost. Each man carries on his own passionate
search and can only taste another's quest in literature as a
sampling.[86]

Percy's characters experience both kinds of repetition. Binx
savors the "homeliest" repetitions, even listening to the same
radio programs day after day. His definition is cumbrous:
"A repetition is the re-enactment of past experience toward
the end of isolating the time segment which has lapsed in
order that it, the lapsed time, can be savored of itself and
without the usual adulteration of events that clog time like
peanuts."[87] The definition suggests a momentary suspension
of time, the "eminence" Binx speaks of in the passage on
the train, which is part of his reenactment of a trip made
twenty-five years earlier with his now dead father and brother.
The reenactment becomes an existential repetition connected
with his passionate search. The eminence described seems
related to the distancing from self involved in Marcel's concept of recollection, the detachment that is a necessary prelude to the return to self.[88]

Repetition, then, can be a mere sampling of emotion, a

86. Percy, "The Man on the Train," 481–91.
87. Percy, *Moviegoer*, 79–80.
88. See Marcel, *Philosophy of Existentialism*, 23–24.

breaking out of everydayness, or a moment of serious insight
contributing to the search.

The most hopeful way open to us in the depths of the
malaise leads to intersubjectivity, a key if ungainly concept
borrowed from Marcel. The closing scene of *The Last Gentleman* offers an approximation of it in a conversation between
Sutter Vaught, a run-down doctor who is bent on suicide
following the death of Jamie, his younger brother, and Will
Barrett, the boy's final companion, to whom Sutter is a father
figure:

> "Dr. Vaught, don't leave me."
> "What did you say?"
> "Dr. Vaught, listen to me. I'm going to do what I told you I planned
> to do."
> "I know. You told me."
> "Dr. Vaught, I want you to come back with me."
> "Why? To make this contribution you speak of."
> "Dr. Vaught, I need you. I, Will Barrett—" and he actually pointed
> to himself lest there be a mistake,"—need you and want you to come
> back. I need you more than Jamie needed you. Jamie had Val too."
> Sutter laughed. "You kill me, Barrett."
> "Yes sir." He waited.
> "I'll think about it."[89]

With this concession from Sutter the two of them are nearing
a condition of intersubjectivity.

As the term implies, *intersubjectivity* involves nonobjective
relations. Marcel calls it the cornerstone of his concrete
ontology.[90] The best way to approach it is by a dialectic,
starting with what it is not. To begin with, intersubjectivity
is at the opposite pole from self-consciousness. The ego shows
up in a highly aggressive form in the child, Marcel says,
as a sort of "personified here-and-now that has to defend
itself actively against other personified heres-and-nows."
Insofar as I feel myself ignored or slighted by others, even
as an adult, I become at once preoccupied with myself and

89. Percy, *Last Gentleman*, 393.
90. Marcel, *Mystery of Being*, II, 191. The discussion that follows is from Volume
I, 215–24.

hypnotized by what I imagine others think of me. This paradoxical tension, says Marcel, is what the "excellent [English] word *self-consciousness*" compactly expresses. But intersubjectivity occupies the pole opposite self-consciousness.

Suppose I find myself, in this state of self-consciousness, confronted by an older man at a cocktail party. I am apt to be on the defensive, thinking of him not as *you* but as *he*, perhaps even as *it*.[91] We have no genuine encounter. But then this stranger says to me, "I am glad to meet you. I once knew your parents." Suddenly a relaxation of tension takes place and a bond is created. Instead of being merely juxtaposed to him, I am *with* him. And in a general way, Marcel says, "it is the relationship expressed by the preposition *with* that is eminently intersubjective." I am no longer simply alongside him, as a chair is alongside a table, but "lifted right out of the here and now." This unknown person I have just met accompanies me on a sort of magic voyage. We are together in "what we must call an elsewhere"; we are "linked together by a shared secret." We cannot achieve this meaningful linkage by a complicity such as our common taste for a certain Colombian coffee or our mutual eagerness to cash in on the stock market. True intersubjectivity may come about instead when a stranger recognizes the deeply individual quality of someone I love.

We can see a continuity between intersubjectivity at the higher reaches of the spirit, as in artistic or religious experience, and at the level of ordinary life, "a kind of graduated scale, with something like the mystical communion of souls in worship at the top end, and with something like an *ad hoc* association for some strictly practical and rigidly defined purpose at the bottom."[92] A single human relationship—marriage, for example—can work its way completely up and down

---

91. Self-consciousness seems to be the general condition accompanying Sartre's "stare."

92. The parallel with the American idealist Josiah Royce, with his communities of interpretation, becomes more and more strikingly evident. Marcel of course did a study of Royce: *Royce's Metaphysics*, trans. Virginia Ringer and Gordon Ringer (Chicago, 1956).

this scale. There is a hierarchy of invocations in such instances, "ranging from the call upon another which is like ringing a bell for a servant to the quite other sort of call which is really like a kind of prayer." When we ring the servant bell what we are invoking is "really a He or a She or even an It treated pragmatically as a Thou."[93] But even a casual incident in the street, such as an inquiry to find directions, can be touched with a passing feeling of brotherhood and bring us to the threshold of intersubjectivity. This seldom happens where people encounter each other *en masse,* particularly where passengers are physically together in a public vehicle.[94] In such a situation people are truly *with* each other only to the extent that they know each other "both in the uniqueness of their diverse beings and in the single colour of their common fate."

The mainspring of intersubjectivity is the shared secret. Two people who have an intimate relationship often feel a kind of unity that excludes a third person, centered on a secret shared by those two, whether merely a few allusions or jokes or some painful, incommunicable experience.[95] In the latter case the initiates feel that anyone who did not share the experience in the flesh has no right to speak. And it is just at this point that anthropology "strikes on something deeper than itself, something that constitutes us in our very selfhood."[96]

Egocentrism, Marcel says, is a barrier to intersubjectivity, a condition peculiar to "a being which has not properly mastered its own experience, which has not really assimilated it." Egocentrism causes a generalized blindness. It is precisely

93. Marcel's terminology is reminiscent of Martin Buber, though each man arrived at his position independently of the other.

94. Or in functional relations within institutions, we might add, where the I-It relationship of abstraction normally prevails.

95. One of the chief benefits a patient gets from the relationship with his therapist, Percy notes, is just this sense of the "we-community of scientists" that excludes people out on the street from the secret. See "The Symbolic Structure of Interpersonal Process," 52.

96. Marcel, *Mystery of Being,* I, 223. For an adequate treatment of this point, see Marcel's discussion in the original.

"because the egoist confines his thought to himself that he is fundamentally in the dark about himself," for we can understand ourselves only by starting from others: "Fundamentally, I have no reason to set any particular store by myself, except in so far as I know that I am loved by other beings who are loved by me."[97] Human love itself is threatened by egocentrism. If it becomes "centered on itself, if it sinks into a mutually shared narcissism, it turns into idolatry and pronounces its own death sentence." Love should be not closed, but open, to use Bergson's "fertile distinction." Even in choosing a metaphor for my soul—a "pearl to be drawn from the depths of the sea," a "statue to be released from the embrace of the raw stone," a "garden to be tilled"—I may fail to recognize the "higher claims of intersubjectivity"; I may sin against love.[98]

The very basis of consciousness is intersubjective, Percy writes: *"Symbolization is of its very essence an intersubjectivity."*[99] Marcel calls intersubjectivity "a metaphysic of *we are* as opposed to a metaphysic of *I think*" and adds that when Sartre "writes 'Hell—that's other people', he supplies evidence of his impossible position."[100] Percy quotes Marcel's statement on the metaphysic of *we are,* and the passage following it, in one of his essays: "Without doubt the intersubjective nexus cannot in any way be asserted; it can only be acknowledged ... the affirmation should possess a special character, that of being the root of every expressible affirmation. *I should readily agree that it is the mysterious root of language"* (Percy's emphasis). Intersubjectivity, Percy has·written, is just "that meeting of minds by which two selves take each other's meaning with reference to the same object beheld in common."[101]

97. Marcel, *Mystery of Being,* II, 8–9. This general line of thought parallels that of G. H. Mead.
98. *Ibid.,* 175, 39.
99. Percy, "Symbol as Hermeneutic in Existentialism," 525. The italics are Percy's.
100. Marcel, *Mystery of Being,* II, 10. Percy makes the same general criticism of Sartre.
101. Percy, "Symbol, Consciousness, and Intersubjectivity," *Journal of Philosophy,* LV (1958), 637, 631. The passage from Marcel is found in *Mystery of Being,* II, 10–12.

The metaphysic of *we are* has great importance for art, Percy feels, for within the intersubjective nexus we share the joy of communion in the original state of consciousness, just as a child does in naming the spherical object before him a ball: "No matter whether I give a name to, or hear the name of, a strange bird; no matter whether I write or read a line of great poetry, form or understand a scientific hypothesis, I thereby exist authentically as a namer or a hearer, as an I or a Thou—and in either case as a co-celebrant of what is."[102] The modern literature of alienation is in reality a "triumphant reversal of alienation through its re-presenting . . . an aesthetic victory of comradeliness, a recognition of plight in common," and may set forth the truth of things, how it stands with you and me, as "the supreme intersubjective achievement of art."[103]

The core of my difficulty with intersubjectivity, if I proclaim sovereignty over my own life with such insistence, would seem to be the manner in which I relate my own rights and claims to those of others. Are my own irreconcilable with theirs? Marcel has something to say on my predicament. The philosopher is the man who asks the true questions, he says, those questions "which point, not to anything resembling the solution of an enigma, but rather to a line of direction along which we must move." To philosophize is to devote myself to understanding my own life as fully as possible, to understand my own experience. "If I try to do so, I shall most likely be led to a strange and wonderful discovery—that the more I raise myself to a really concrete perception of my own experience, the more, by that very act, shall I be attuned to an understanding of others, of the experience of others."[104] To be attuned to an understanding of others: that is the precondition of real intersubjectivity. That I may achieve this attunement by knowing my own experience concretely is truly a strange and wonderful discovery. The better

102. Percy, "Naming and Being," 153.
103. Percy, "The Man on the Train," 487, 491.
104. Marcel, *Mystery of Being*, I, 15–16, II, 7.

I know myself, the better attuned I am to others; the less I know myself, the more I contribute my own anonymity to the faceless crowd. Recognition of this fact does not of course resolve the mystery,[105] but perhaps it indicates the direction in which a resolution should move.

These are the focal concepts we can most clearly identify in Percy's writings, the existentialist modes of perception that seem to be most instrumental to his novelistic vision. There is one further thing to consider, a conception of Kierkegaard's that serves to place Percy's work within Kierkegaard's spheres of existence and define the terms in which the novels function. Kierkegaard called it the *infinite passion*.

An equivalent term would be Paul Tillich's "ultimate concern," which in some ways is more exact, but I want to follow Kierkegaard rather closely here, and at some length, in order to bring out a parallel with Percy. As a young man Kierkegaard, like Percy, experienced what he called a "great earthquake," which as one of his translators puts it "shattered his world and left him stranded."[106] The cataclysm hinged upon his father, who suddenly stood revealed to him as "an unhappy man who was to outlive us all, a cross on the tomb of all his hopes." Young Kierkegaard became convinced that the punishment of God was upon the entire family, whose "outstanding intellectual gifts ... were only given to us in order that we should rend each other to pieces." In his "desperate despair" he "grasped at nought but the intellectual side in man and clung fast to it," finding his one joy in ideas and his only consolation the great intellectual powers he possessed. He soon identified his commanding need: "a truth which is true *for me*, to find *the idea for which I can live and die.*"[107]

105. We cannot call it a problem, which for Marcel is something I meet, because my relations with others are something in which I am very much involved. See the concluding paragraph of Chapter One.
106. Alexander Dru, "Introduction to the Torchbook Edition," Kierkegaard, *The Journals of Kierkegaard,* 14.
107. Kierkegaard, *Journals,* 39, 40, 44. The "earthquake" briefly was the discovery

That was what he lacked and what he longed for. Kier-kegaard compared himself to "a man who has rented a house and gathered all the furniture and household things together, but has not yet found the beloved with whom to share the joys and sorrows of his life." Up to now he had studied law so that "by putting myself in another man's role I could, as it were, find a substitute for my own life, and find distraction in outward change"; he had lived as a curtailed I. It was that missing beloved, that idea for which he could live and die, that he lacked "in order to be able *to lead a complete human life* and not merely one of the understanding." That beloved idea had to be "something which grows together with the deepest roots of my life, through which I am so to speak, grafted upon the divine, hold fast to it, even though the whole world fell apart." For otherwise, Kierkegaard noted, "how near man is to madness [living merely by the understanding], in spite of all his knowledge. What is truth but to live for an idea? Ultimately everything must rest upon a postulate; but the moment it is no longer outside him, and he lives in it, then and only then does it cease to be a postulate for him."[108] Not a *postulate* outside of himself, but an ultimate *concern* in which he lives, by which he becomes "grafted upon the divine": that is his infinite passion.

Inwardness rather than objectivity is the key here, for in Kierkegaard's view the original sin of philosophy was that it divorced thought from existence.[109] He considered the merit of his first book, *Either / Or,* to lie not in "giving any result, but in transforming everything into inwardness."[110]

---

of his father's awful secret, which apparently involved seducing the girl—years later she became Kierkegaard's mother—who had come under his roof as house-keeper for his first wife, whose death he felt responsible for. Dru says the father saw a predestinarian chain of cause and effect extending from his childhood rebellion against God down through his sensuality to the successive deaths of his children.

108. *Ibid.,* 44–45.

109. Dru, "Introduction," 20.

110. Specifically, "in the first part, an imaginative inwardness which evokes the possibilities with intensified passion, with sufficient dialectical power to transform all into nothing in despair; in the second part, an ethical pathos, which with a quiet, incorruptible, and yet infinite passion of resolve embraces the modest ethical

Inwardness is necessary because abstract thought cannot grasp the meaning of individual existence. Only feeling or passion can do that—not feeling as an isolated faculty of the mind, Alexander Dru points out, but feeling "purified by reason and will and integrated by that process with the other faculties." Passion so defined culminates in action. Starting from various points of view, Dru says, Kierkegaard's thought "moves always in the same direction, toward the moment of decision, the 'choice' in *Either-Or*, the 'leap of faith' in *Fear and Trembling*," leading up to the "*moment* in which decision and action fuse thought and existence, the *moment* in which temporal and eternal meet and man can fulfill his destiny." The choice and the leap of faith are eminently "acts of the whole man which alone give him the right to speak of existence." On the plane of existence the faculties of feeling, reason, and will are united in imagination, fused in the choice—not the choice of "something external (a view of life, a particular corpus of knowledge) but of oneself, of a complete existence." The choice is that "constitutive act" prior to which man is always in despair, consciously or unconsciously. Only after the choice does the leap of faith become possible; and for Kierkegaard it is only in faith that man begins to exist.[111]

So from the static image of a house without a beloved, Kierkegaard moves to the dynamic image of the knight living in the infinite passion. In *Either / Or* he presents the alternatives: *either* live in the immediacy of the aesthetic stage, reaping its benefits, *or* move to the ethical, but do not languish in the limbo between. If one elects the first, the infinite passion

---

task, and edified thereby stands self-revealed before God and man." Quoted from *Concluding Unscientific Postscript* in translator's preface to Søren Kierkegaard, *Either / Or*, trans. David F. Swenson and Lillian Marvin Swenson (2 vols.; New York, 1959), I, xi.

111. Dru, "Introduction," 20–23. This is a helpful introduction to Kierkegaard. The parallels with Emerson are striking, especially with regard to the necessity of action for the whole man. Kierkegaard's Knight of Faith at times looks remarkably like a Danish cousin of Emerson's American Scholar, propelled into action and mounted on a steed, possibly Rosinante. Dru says that Kierkegaard's favorite metaphor was that action is the knot in the thread that makes the end fast.

is denied him, since it can enter his existence only on the ethical or a higher plane; he entraps himself in the aesthetic sphere. As a precondition of escape he must commit himself to the higher plane. The infinite passion may then enter his existence as a world-defining experience that transforms him into a knight. The knight will have the power, Kierkegaard wrote, to "concentrate the whole content of life and the whole significance of reality in one single wish," lacking which his soul will be "dispersed in the multifarious" and he will "deal shrewdly in life like the capitalists who invest their money in all sorts of securities, so as to gain on the one what they lose on the other." He will next have the power "to concentrate the whole result of the operations of thought in one act of consciousness," lacking which he will "never get time to make the movements" but will be "constantly running errands in life," always forgetting something for which he must go back and thus sinking "deeper and deeper into the mire."[112]

The movement is imperative. The knight then finds two ways open to him: he may become a knight of the infinite resignation or he may become a knight of faith.[113] Suppose a young man falls in love with a princess and finds his love impossible to realize. Bravely he lets love "creep into his most secret, his most hidden thoughts, to let it twine in innumerable coils about every ligament of his consciousness" so that he will "never be able to tear himself loose from it." But seeing its impossibility, he makes the movement to resignation. He does not "forget the whole thing," but instead remembers everything, and the remembrance is pain to him, "yet by the infinite resignation he is reconciled with existence." It is easy to recognize the knights of the infinite resignation: "their gait is gliding and assured." There is peace and rest

112. Søren Kierkegaard, *Fear and Trembling* published together with *The Sickness unto Death*, trans. Walter Lowrie (New York, 1954), 53–54.
113. The argument becomes exceedingly intricate from this point on, and I am simplifying it by necessity. The reader can pursue it in *Fear and Trembling*, which has been combined with *The Sickness unto Death* in an inexpensive Anchor edition.

in the infinite resignation. Its sphere is Religiousness A, the
domain of Johannes *de silentio,* the pseudonymous narrator
of *Fear and Trembling.* The infinite resignation is confined
to the sphere of immanence and is "the last stage prior to
faith."[114]

The knight of faith makes the leap into transcendence,
the sphere of Religiousness B, which is always paradoxical
to anyone on a lower plane. Johannes *de silentio,* dwelling
wholly within immanence, acknowledges that he cannot talk
with God because they have no language in common. The
knight of faith, if he cannot realize his love for the princess,
makes the same movement as the knight of resignation,
renouncing his claim, and is reconciled in pain. But then
he makes "still another movement more wonderful than all,
for he says, 'I believe nevertheless that I shall get her, in
virtue, that is, of the absurd, in virtue of the fact that with
God all things are possible.' " Even more wonderful would
be to get the princess and to live with her joyfully despite
the constant risk of losing her, "to live joyfully and happily
every instant by virtue of the absurd, every instant to see
the sword hanging over the head of the beloved, and yet
not to find repose in the pain of resignation, but joy by virtue
of the absurd—this is marvellous." The man who does it
is "great, the only great man."[115] Unlike the knight of infinite
resignation, the knight of faith is vulnerable, uninsured
against loss.

The true paradigm of the knight of faith is Abraham.
Fear and Trembling is an exploration of the paradox of
Abraham, which cannot be grasped by anything short of
faith. Johannes *de silentio* cannot understand Abraham, he
concedes, and those who "want to swindle God out of the
first movement of faith, the infinite resignation," in the

114. Kierkegaard, *Fear and Trembling,* 49–57. The distinction between Religiousness A and Religiousness B is spelled out in *Concluding Unscientific Postscript*
but summarized in the translator's notes to *Fear and Trembling* (265).
115. Kierkegaard, *Fear and Trembling,* 57–61. Kierkegaard acknowledged that
if he had faith he would have married Regina.

attempt to do so, are simply trying to "suck worldly wisdom out of the paradox." What did Abraham do when required by God to sacrifice his son?

> He mounted the ass, he rode slowly along the way. All that time he believed—he believed that God would not require Isaac of him, whereas he was willing nevertheless to sacrifice him if it was required. He believed by virtue of the absurd; for there could be no question of human calculation, and it was indeed the absurd that God who required it of him should the next instant recall the requirement. He climbed the mountain, even at the instant when the knife glittered he believed ... that God would not require Isaac. He was indeed astonished at the outcome, but by a double-movement he had reached his first position, and therefore he received Isaac more gladly than the first time.

As a knight of faith Abraham was able to receive Isaac back joyfully; he received the repetition. Johannes confesses that in such a position he "would have been in embarrassment." Having already resigned himself to the loss, he could not risk going further.[116]

Abraham believed not that he would some day "be blessed in the beyond, but that he would be happy in the world. God could give him a new Isaac, could recall to life who had been sacrificed. He believed by virtue of the absurd; for all human reckoning had long since ceased to function." He lived in the infinite passion; with equal faith he could lose Isaac or receive him back. We cannot explain Abraham or understand the paradoxical religiousness from a lower plane, but Kierkegaard offers a dancing image that suggests what happens in the movement. It is supposed to be the most difficult task for a dancer "to leap into a definite posture in such a way that there is not a second when he is grasping after the posture, but by the leap itself he stands fixed in that posture. Perhaps no dancer can do it—that is what this knight does."[117]

The leap into a definite posture without grasping after it: that is the decisive act by which the knight leaps into

116. *Ibid.*, 46–48. Though Abraham receives the repetition, Johannes cannot.
117. *Ibid.*, 47, 51.

faith. And only in faith does man truly begin to exist, not by a postulate outside of himself but in the infinite passion that transforms his existence and enables him to become an authentic individual.

Perhaps now we can see the landscape of Percy's fiction. The wayfarer who is contemporary man finds himself wandering in the malaise, assailed by its deadly forms of inauthenticity and abstraction, its numbing everydayness. As a dweller in the malaise I may find that ordeal will break its hold on me, or rotation give me momentary release from it, but I can never hope to escape its suffocation except by my own decisive act. Somehow I must transcend my everyday condition. The first step is to recognize that condition for what it is. Then I must assert my claim to existence by the leap into the intersubjective communion, by which I acknowledge the claims of others upon me and within which I seek the answer to the question *who am I?* If I prove to be a knight of faith, I may arrive at the incomprehensible faith of Abraham. In any event the choice is mine: I can languish in the malaise as a "curtailed I" or I can live transformed by the infinite passion. To resume the primal metaphor, I must recognize my condition as wayfarer, a man on the road to somewhere, and undertake the search by which I may become a *sovereign wayfarer,* not a lone traveler seeking the lost road to being, but a co-celebrant sharing the joys of my pilgrimage.

3

A Moviegoer Living in New Orleans

Walker Percy's first novel is his most intensive diagnosis of the malaise. Like a surgeon, he probes the malaise through a character deeply rooted in the New Orleans of the 1950's, "a *man* who finds himself in a *world*," as Percy has said, "a very concrete man who is located in a very concrete place and time."[1] His instrument is the laconic tone he hit upon when he began writing *The Moviegoer*, a tone that contributes immensely to the novel but can mislead the unwary reader. Near the end of the book, for example, Binx Bolling endures a severe dressing down from his great-aunt and falls into bitter reflection:

> Now in the thirty-first year of my dark pilgrimage on this earth and knowing less than I ever knew before, having learned only to recognize merde when I see it, having inherited no more from my father than a good nose for merde, for every species of shit that flies—my only talent—smelling merde from every quarter, living in fact in the very century of merde, the great shithouse of scientific humanism where needs are satisfied, everyone becomes an anyone, a warm and creative person, and prospers like a dung beetle, and one hundred percent of people are humanists and ninety-eight percent believe in God, and men are dead, dead, dead; and the malaise has settled like a fall-out and what people really fear is not that the bomb will fall but that the bomb will not fall—on this my thirtieth birthday, I know nothing and there is nothing to do but fall prey to desire.[2]

1. Percy, "From Facts to Fiction," 46.
2. Percy, *Moviegoer*, 228. Subsequent page numbers will be given in the text.

To the reader who has been following Binx's narrative light-heartedly, as I did when the novel first appeared, this passage comes as a shock. It blocks the way to an effortless reading. Up to this point the reader can glide over the many anticipations of despair on the strength of Percy's humor. Now suddenly he is confronted by the recognition that there is more to it than that, far more; and the passage gives notice that until every detail in it makes sense the novel has not yielded its full meaning.

The watchful reader will have noted that Binx's recognition comes on Ash Wednesday. The author does not point this out; in fact it is several pages later that Binx himself comes to realize what day it is. The reader will be aware too that virtually the entire action of the novel is sandwiched between two Wednesdays, the last week of Carnival in New Orleans. Clearly Binx is celebrating a very personal Mardi Gras, more a Lean than a Fat Tuesday, but the reader must search as hard for meanings as Binx himself does. *The Moviegoer* in fact is a highly elliptical novel, with key elements implied or omitted. Much of the framework is missing.

A close scrutiny of the novel's framework reveals a dialectical process in the life of Binx Bolling.[3] The dialectic is philosophical and finds expression in the three temporal phases with which it coincides. Percy enters the dialectic at the end of the antithesis phase, which culminates in the week's action and the recognition cited above. The dialectic begins with a phase of *thesis* antedating the book's action and involving the inheritance Binx receives from his forebears, which he has rejected as meaningless for him in the *antithesis* phase, his present exile in Gentilly, a condition that remains pleasantly noncommittal until the possibility of the search reawakens after years of dormancy and his recognition propels

---

To keep the clutter to a minimum I will limit such citations mostly to sizable passages quoted or quotations drawn from sections of the novel not then under discussion.

3. A dialectic may seem out of place in a novel showing such an existentialist affinity, but the existentialists, it is well to remember, despite the vehemence of their attacks on Hegel, were profoundly influenced by him. Kierkegaard's aesthetic, ethical, and religious phases can certainly be read as dialectical.

him into a *synthesis* phase, scarcely under way at the novel's end, in which he makes an existential leap into a future constructed on different premises. Such a framework helps to illuminate the processes at work in the novel and I want to pattern my discussion upon it.

THESIS: THE INHERITANCE

What Binx has rejected is embodied in the person of Aunt Emily, his great-aunt, who has been a major influence in his life. It was she who sent him off to prep school after his father's death and sheltered him under her roof during his college years. She is unable to grasp his objections or to condone his present behavior. The contrast comes into sharpest focus during the scene preceding his recognition, when Aunt Emily calls him to task for betraying "that poor child," her stepdaughter Kate. "I try as best I can," Binx tells us, "to appear as she would have me, as being, if not right, then wrong in a recognizable, a right form of wrongness. But I can think of nothing to say." In Aunt Emily's eyes there is a right form even for wrongness.

The forms she prizes are those of the white Southern aristocracy. "More than anything I wanted to pass on to you the one heritage of the men of our family," she tells Binx in her distress, "a certain quality of spirit, a gaiety, a sense of duty, a nobility worn lightly, a sweetness, a gentleness with women—the only good things the South ever had and the only things that really matter in this life." As the last of the older generation of Bollings, the much younger sister of three brothers now dead, she constitutes the only link with these values of the past and has tried valiantly to pass them on to Binx, the last scion of the clan. Earlier in the novel she sends him a memo to convey a second thought following one of their serious talks: "Every moment think steadily as a Roman and a man, to do what thou hast in hand with perfect and simple dignity, and a feeling of affection and freedom and justice. These words of the Emperor

Marcus Aurelius Antonius strike me as pretty good advice, for even the orneriest young scamp" (78). Her choice of Marcus Aurelius reflects Percy's view that the values she cherishes have come down to her from the Stoics.[4]

Like a Sartoris watching the rise of the Snopeses, Aunt Emily sees the fabric dissolving, "the going under of the evening land," as she calls it. But for her, Binx says, "even the dissolving makes sense. She understands the chaos to come." And she has a clear vision of his proper role: "It seems so plain when I see it through her eyes. My duty in life is simple. I go to medical school. I live a long useful life serving my fellowman. What's wrong with this? All I have to do is remember it" (54). She has imbued him with the same values most of his life. At the age of eight, when his brother Scotty died of pneumonia, Emily had taken him aside to break the news: "Scotty is dead. Now it's all up to you. It's going to be difficult for you but I know you're going to act like a soldier" (4). Binx comments: "This was true. I could easily act like a soldier. Was that all I had to do?"

Emily's virtues are admirable and we can feel the author's sympathy with them, but the final question in the boy's mind is pertinent to the whole novel. It is easy enough to follow the old forms, to act like a soldier. Is that all one needs to do? The old forms have their shortcomings; the novel undertakes to examine the overriding question of what Binx must do.

Binx is not the first Bolling to sense that something is missing from the old ways. His father had shown early symptoms of a kindred affliction. Binx finds a clue in his aunt's living room. He inspects a picture on the mantelpiece of the two surviving Bolling brothers and his father, who is

---

4. Percy cites the same quotation as an expression of the best of the South in Walker Percy, "Stoicism in the South," *Commonweal*, LXIV (1956), 343, and discusses the Southern heritage in "A Southern View," *America*, XCVII (1957), 428–29. Jim Van Cleave, in "Versions of Percy," treats the parallels between Emily and Will Percy, and Lewis A. Lawson explores Will Percy's Stoicism in depth in "Walker Percy's Southern Stoic," *Southern Literary Journal*, III (1970), 5–31. I found the Lawson article particularly valuable.

much younger, in the Black Forest during their grand tour in the early twenties. The elder Bollings are "serene in their identities. Each one coincides with himself." But not his father: "His feet are planted wide apart, arms locked around an alpenstock behind him; the katy is pushed back releasing a forelock. His eyes are alight with an expression I can't identify; it is not far from what his elders might have called smart-alecky. He is something of a dude with his round head and tricky tab collar. . . . Again I search the eyes, each eye a stipple or two in a blurred oval. Beyond a doubt they are ironical" (25).

Though the elder Bollings remain "serene in their identities," Binx's father no longer "coincides with himself": the outward forms no longer correspond to the inner reality. An important concern throughout the novel is Binx's search for clues to his father's predicament, which will be taken up in the next section. It is enough here to stress that this identity in which the elder Bollings are serene contains strong elements of romanticism. The missing brother, Alex Bolling, died in the Argonne, Binx tells us, a death that was "held to be fitting since the original Alex Bolling was killed with Roberdaux Wheat in the Hood breakthrough at Gaines Mill in 1862." Upon the outbreak of World War II, Binx's father had volunteered for the RCAF and died at Crete, in the wine-dark sea, in a grand Bolling gesture. But Binx takes another view of such gestures: "Somewhere it, the English soul, received an injection of romanticism which nearly killed it. That's what killed my father, English romanticism, that and 1930 science" (88).

Another part of the inheritance is represented by Walter Wade, Binx's old fraternity brother. The two have known each other since prep school in New Hampshire. In college Walter had been a big man on campus and an arbiter of taste, a model for freshmen. He had secured Binx's admission into the right fraternity, where they shared a "sour-senseless" style of talking and the kind of comradeship that goes with being a proper fellow. Walter at thirty-three is senior partner in a legal firm specializing in oil-lease law, but he still associates with a "damn good bunch of guys." He has never outgrown the mentality of the old Delta house and Binx is struck by "how much *older*" he seemed in college days. The relationship has become awkward: "Whenever I'm with him, I feel the stretch of the old tightrope, the necessity of living up to the friendship of friendships, of cultivating an intimacy beyond words" (40). The kind of elite represented by Walter Wade is a considerable drop from the aristocratic ideal set forth by Aunt Emily.

Still another personification of the inheritance is Uncle Jules—at any rate Jules as seen by Emily. To Emily he is the last of the heroes, a product of the "age of the Catos," though in truth, Binx remarks, Jules Cutrer is "a canny Cajun straight from Bayou Lafourche, as canny as a Marseilles merchant and a very good fellow, but no Cato." He is the only man Binx knows "whose victory in the world is total and unqualified." Why he troubles to be an exemplary Catholic is a mystery to Binx; the City of God can hold few attractions for a man so at home in the City of Man. His world is "a friendly easy-going place of old-world charm and new-world business methods where kind white folks and carefree darkies have the good sense to behave pleasantly toward each other." So long as Emily presides over his household he believes nothing can go wrong; "the worst that can happen, death itself, is nothing more than seemly."

On the surface, Jules appears to combine the best of two worlds, and there is no suggestion that Emily patronizes him. All the same it is noteworthy that she does not accept the same role for Binx, who is a Bolling. Binx manages a branch office of Jules's brokerage firm and has tentatively embraced the values that go with it. To Emily such a position is unworthy of the last Bolling, especially when accompanied by dalliance. She explains his present exile as a result of the disruption of the Korean War, which was enough to "take it out of any man." When he finishes his *Wanderjahr*, his exile in Gentilly, he will turn to his proper calling, which is "research."

Emily's imagination transforms things beyond recognition: "All the stray bits and pieces of the past, all that is feckless and gray about people, she pulls together into an unmistakable visage of the heroic or the craven, the noble or the ignoble" (49). What is noble for Jules is craven for Binx. Her expectations weigh heavily upon Binx, and through them he feels the burden of his inheritance. Its full weight must be recognized in order to grasp the meaning of his exile in Gentilly.

ANTITHESIS: EXILE

All of the present action of the novel except that of the epilogue is encompassed in the week climaxing the antithesis phase of Binx Bolling's life. Within the confines of that week Percy has offered a diagnosis of the malaise of contemporary America. It is not my purpose here to outline his diagnosis in schematic terms; the book is a novel and not a medical tract. My method here will be simply to follow Binx through his adventures, bringing to the task chiefly what should illuminate the processes of the novel. The focus throughout will be on what is there.[5]

The first chapter sounds most of Percy's themes and deserves careful attention, particularly in the opening pages where he is establishing his method and finding his voice. "This morning I got a note from my aunt asking me to come to lunch," the novel begins. Since we know what a stylistic breakthrough the first paragraph represents, the balance of it is worth quoting: "I know what this means. Since I go there every Sunday for dinner and today is Wednesday, it can mean only one thing: she wants to have one of her serious talks. It will be extremely grave, either a piece of bad news about her stepdaughter Kate or else a serious talk about

---

5. This holds true in all three chapters on the novels. When I cite what Percy has said on a given topic I am in effect admitting him as a witness to the meaning of his own work, in the terms of Monroe K. Beardsley and W. K. Wimsatt, without assuming that his intention settles the question definitively. In their terms what I hope to illuminate is the novel's actual, not its intentional meaning—really its *being*.

me, about the future and what I ought to do. It is enough to scare the wits out of anyone, yet I confess I do not find the prospect altogether unpleasant." The voice is the one we recognize as Percy's, and there is drama in the way it seems to find itself within the passage, affirming itself in the last sentence, which with its paradoxical intimation of ordeal closes the paragraph on the authoritative note of a new voice.

Following the summons from Aunt Emily the novel proceeds by what seems almost free association from one paragraph to the next. "I remember when my older brother Scott died of pneumonia," the second paragraph begins. The connection seems slight and I will return to it shortly. The paragraph recounts an incident from his childhood. His aunt "had charge" of him, he says, and took him walking behind the hospital. The scene is evoked with great economy: "On one side were the power plant and blowers and incinerator of the hospital, all humming and blowing out a hot meaty smell. On the other side was a row of Negro houses." The "hot meaty smell" is just the strong olfactory sense a boy would remember, and it heightens the mystery of his brother's illness, suggesting the physicality of death. The row of Negro houses lends a sinister element, especially since he and his aunt are being watched; this is no place for such a pair. His aunt has "all the time in the world" and is willing to talk about anything: "Something extraordinary had happened all right." She gives him a squeeze and says they have always been "good buddies."· His heart gives a "big pump" and the back of his neck "prickle[s] like a dog's": some ominous demand is about to be made on him. "Scotty is dead. Now it's all up to you." Something gigantic awaits. But no: "It's going to be difficult for you but I know you're going to act like a soldier."[6] Can that be all she wants? the boy

---

6. In *Lanterns on the Levee* (New York, 1941), William Alexander Percy published some letters he wrote from the front during the First World War. In one letter he told his mother: "One must be a soldier these days—there is no other part a man can play and be a man" (201).

wonders. "I could easily act like a soldier. Was that all I had to do?"

Percy now jumps directly to an anecdote that appears unrelated: "It reminds me of a movie I saw last month out by Lake Pontchartrain." He had taken Linda to a movie out in a new suburb, a film about a man who lost his memory in an accident and consequently "lost everything: his family, his friends, his money." Finding himself a stranger in a strange city, he was compelled to start life afresh. "It was supposed to be a tragedy, his losing all this, and he seemed to suffer a great deal," Binx notes. "On the other hand, things were not so bad after all. In no time he found a very picturesque place to live, a houseboat on the river, and a very handsome girl, the local librarian." Clearly the movie describes a rotation. But what does the incident have to do with the news of Scotty's death in the preceding paragraph, and how are both related to the summons announced in paragraph one?

Percy has accomplished several things by what seems to be random selection. Both the second and third paragraphs describe ordeal, the death of an older brother and the loss of everything by amnesia, and both suggest that ordeal is far from the worst that can happen. It may in fact be an improvement over the deadly everydayness the amnesic has been lucky enough to escape. Even the death of one's only brother, from the vantage point of eight years of age, is less fearsome than the unspeakable demand his aunt seems about to make of him. To act like a soldier is no great thing, and by the ominous residue that survives this demand Percy manages to suggest the power Emily holds over this boy she "had charge" of, the invisible force of the shadow of expectation that hangs over him. The childhood incident prefigures the adult dilemma. And that Binx finds the prospect of a grave talk with his aunt not altogether unpleasant shows that he, like the amnesic, might benefit by a rent in the veil of everydayness.

Another achievement of Percy in these two paragraphs

is the parallel suggested between the soldierly role in which Binx is cast by Aunt Emily and the counterfeit plot of the movie. Both are inauthentic. The intimation is very subtly made. But Percy moves on to Linda's discomfort following the movie as Binx stands under the marquee discussing the theater's financial troubles with the manager. While Linda fidgets we learn one of this moviegoer's eccentricities: he has a car but prefers to ride buses and streetcars. No reason is given. Linda is unhappy for the same reason he is happy, because they are "out in the sticks and without a car." Her idea of happiness is having supper in the Blue Room at a downtown hotel, and from time to time he obliges her in this fancy. At such times "she loves me because she feels exalted in this romantic place and not at a movie out in the sticks."

A picture of romantic bliss, it appears, however faded the girl's notion of happiness, until Percy does a switch: "But all this is history. Linda and I have parted company. I have a new secretary, a girl named Sharon Kincaid." This three-sentence paragraph reveals that Linda is his secretary and, in what comes like a substitution in a football game, introduces us with an appropriate swirl to the rotational pattern of Binx's life with his secretaries. The initial two-and-a-half-page section ends on an ellipsis.

Already, in paragraph two, Percy has raised the question of what Binx must do. The search for an answer will supply the unifying thread of the novel. And he has foreshadowed not only this existential search, which he will announce six pages later, but also its polar opposite, Aunt Emily's expectations of Binx. These twin perspectives, the existential and the aristocratic, are to follow parallel courses through the novel, supplying what story line it possesses and culminating in a sort of denouement. More important, in these first five paragraphs Percy has established the basic method he will use throughout the novel, a method which often seems a mere stringing together of the disconnected meanderings of Binx Bolling's mind, but which in fact constitutes a meticu-

The Sovereign Wayfarer

lous *exploratory* approach. Percy is investigating realities that
normally lie in shadow beneath the threshold of American
awareness. His method is phenomenological. He is carefully
feeling his way, articulating what he finds concretely, as we
encounter experience itself, in such a way that the reader
can explore his own awareness simultaneously and find points
of contact. To describe these realities explicitly, even where
that is possible, would be to fall into abstraction and lose
the live reality. That is why Percy has chosen the novel form.
He wants to surprise being in its lair.[7]

Before sounding the theme of existential search he proceeds in the next five pages to sketch in its context, Binx's
"Little Way," his exile in Gentilly. For the past four years,
Binx informs us, he has been living in Gentilly, a middle-class
suburb of New Orleans virtually indistinguishable from suburbs elsewhere in the country. He cannot abide the "old
world atmosphere" of the French Quarter, where he lived
for two years, or the "genteel charm of the Garden District,"
where he suffers alternately from rage and depression. Life
in Gentilly is peaceful. He lives in the basement apartment
of a raised bungalow. Binx continues in the most widely
quoted passage of the novel:

> I am a model tenant and a model citizen and take pleasure in doing
> all that is expected of me. My wallet is full of identity cards, library
> cards, credit cards. Last year I purchased a flat olive-drab strongbox,
> very smooth and heavily built with double walls for fire protection,
> in which I placed my birth certificate, college diploma, honorable
> discharge, G.I. insurance, a few stock certificates, and my inheritance:
> a deed to ten acres of a defunct duck club in St. Bernard Parish,
> the only relic of my father's many enthusiasms. It is a pleasure to
> carry out the duties of a citizen and to receive in return a receipt
> or a neat styrene card with one's name on it certifying, so to speak,
> one's right to exist. What satisfaction I take in appearing the first
> day to get my auto tag and brake sticker! I subscribe to *Consumer
> Reports* and as a consequence I own a first-class television set, an all
> but silent air conditioner and a very long lasting deodorant. My armpits

7. In his interview with John Carr, Percy defined phenomenology as "the idea
of describing accurately how a man feels in a given situation" and went on to
remark: "And that's certainly novelistic." See Carr (ed.), "Rotation and Repetition,"
43.

never stink. I pay attention to all spot announcements on the radio
about mental health, the seven signs of cancer, and safe driving—though, as I say, I usually prefer to ride the bus. Yesterday
a favorite of mine, William Holden, delivered a radio announcement
on litterbugs. "Let's face it," said Holden. "Nobody can do anything
about it—but you and me." This is true. I have been careful ever
since.

This model citizen bears a strong resemblance to the one
memorialized in Auden's poem "To an Unknown Citizen,"
with the difference that this specimen is ironically self-aware.
Binx presents himself as the ideal consumer, zestfully per-
forming the prescribed rituals. The suggestion that a man's
right to exist has to be certified institutionally, by identity
cards or receipts for money spent, announces the theme of
functionalism and dispossession in modern society that provides a surrounding medium for the novel. Binx moves on
to his moviegoing habits. Other people are said to treasure
memorable moments in their lives, "the time one climbed
the Parthenon at sunrise, the summer night one met a lonely
girl in Central Park and achieved with her a sweet and natural
relationship, as they say in books.... What I remember is
the time John Wayne killed three men with a carbine as
he was falling to the dusty street in *Stagecoach,* and the time
the kitten found Orson Welles in the doorway in *The Third
Man.*" He then supplies a passage describing his "fine careless
raptures" with "Marcia or Linda (but not yet Sharon)" and
introduces the reader to his choice of the stock and bond
business. The family, Binx concedes, was disappointed that
he did not go into law or medicine or pure science. "But
there is much to be said for giving up such grand ambitions
and living the most ordinary life imaginable, a life without
the old longings; selling stocks and bonds and mutual funds;
quitting work at five o'clock like everyone else; having a girl
and perhaps one day settling down and raising a flock of
Marcias or Sandras and Lindas of my own." This is his Little
Way.

Thus prepared, we are ready for the opening sentence
of the next paragraph: "We live, Mrs. Schexnaydre and I,

on Elysian Fields." The sentence suggests more than it says. Mrs. Schexnaydre is his landlady. Her bungalow is on Elysian Fields, the place assigned to the virtuous after death. This is the significance of the name, I think, which is not an invention of Percy's but an actual street he selected for a purpose. Binx later refers to his "secret existence among the happy shades in Elysian Fields," and one of his notions is that everyone is dead. There is something Kierkegaardian for which Percy is preparing, and I would like to go back to the basement apartment Binx occupies in Mrs. Schexnaydre's raised bungalow.

In *The Sickness unto Death*, in the section from which Percy takes his epigraph for *The Moviegoer* (" . . . the specific character of despair is precisely this: it is unaware of being despair"), Kierkegaard again likens the condition of a man's life to a house. He concludes that "unfortunately this is the sorry and ludicrous condition of the majority of men, that in their own house they prefer to live in the cellar. The soulish-bodily synthesis in every man is planned with a view to being spirit, such as the building; but the man prefers to dwell in the cellar, that is, in the determinants of sensuousness."[8] Binx is dwelling in the basement of his possibilities, in the apartment below a woman whose name could suggest the nadir of his existence.[9] Binx is Percy's Underground Man wearing the stockbroker's disguise, mocking the genteel life in Gentilly. The basement image is fundamental to Percy's oblique approach. He seldom makes such a point directly. In the terms of the Rilke epigraph that heads this study, the author cannot approach the god from the space that lies in front of him. So he has Binx occupying the basement, which leaves the rest of the house for him to expand into, if and when he chooses.

8. *A Kierkegaard Anthology*, ed. Robert Bretall (New York, 1946), 346.
9. Schexnaydre: "She's nadir." The suggestion is Brainard Cheney's in "To Restore a Fragmented Image," *Sewanee Review*, LXVIX (1961), 693. "Obviously," says Cheney, "his landlady's name is manufactured for ends of symbolism." The intent seems less obvious to me, though the interpretation fits. Cheney's perceptive review is the earliest serious consideration of the novel I have found in print.

Binx inhabits the aesthetic sphere defined by Kierkegaard. Percy has described his condition as "aesthetic damnation."[10] Somewhat in the manner of Kierkegaard, Binx dwells in a house without a beloved; his Little Way is the polar opposite of the infinite passion. But enjoying the pleasures of impersonating Don Juan, he seldom feels the despair of his exile acutely. One of Kierkegaard's interpreters notes that in his university days Kierkegaard had an absorbing interest in the legends of Faust, Don Juan, and Ahasuerus, the Wandering Jew, which to him typified doubt, sensuality, and despair.[11] In a sense Binx has passed through doubt by rejecting his inheritance outright and has immersed himself in sensuality, among other things. As the novel opens he is mired there.

Percy dramatizes his imprisonment as Binx concludes the sketch of his underground life with an account of his accustomed round on summer evenings, a shower and a stroll. He strolls to the playground of a new school next door, sits on the ocean wave, a children's ride that goes around and around, and plots a route on a city map. Then instead of taking the route he strolls around the new building in the fading light, admiring how "spick-and-span" it is with its "pretty terrazzo floors and the desks molded like wings." Over the door is a "schematic sort of bird, the Holy Ghost I suppose." He admires the "goodness of creation" that permits the brick and glass and aluminum to be extracted from common dirt. The vesper ritual of a modern pietist, it would seem; but Binx explains that the sentiment is more financial than religious since he owns stock in Alcoa. "How smooth and well-fitted and thrifty the aluminum feels!" It is not that his sentiments are somehow "wrong," but that his way of

10. Carr (ed.), "Rotation and Repetition," 51.
11. Walter Lowrie, in the notes to Søren Kierkegaard, *Fear and Trembling* and *The Sickness unto Death* (New York, 1954), 270. Lewis A. Lawson sees Binx echoing Kierkegaard's "personifications of the various aesthetic subspheres" but in a different order: "At first he is the Don Juan of simple sensuousness, then he is the bored Faust who seeks relief from 'everydayness' in the unexpected, and then he is Ahasuerus, recognizing his despair and seeing in other Jews the reflection of his own awareness." See his article on Percy and Kierkegaard, "Walker Percy's Indirect Communications," *Texas Studies in Language and Literature*, XI (1969), 874.

life represents "an existential probability which cannot win through to existence," as Kierkegaard said.[12] Thus we have Binx plotting little journeys but not taking them, continually doing his vespers, this very earthbound man with his Alcoa stock and his Marcia, his Linda, his Sharon. Around and around like the ocean wave, and going nowhere.

Now something unexpected happens. His peaceful life in Gentilly has suddenly been complicated: "This morning, for the first time in years, there occurred to me the possibility of the search." Notice how carefully Percy has prepared for this announcement. The question of what Binx must do was raised in the second paragraph of the novel, but as a major unifying theme the search cannot really emerge until we have a picture of his underground life in Gentilly, his moviegoing, and the rotational pattern of his daily round with its odd piety. Binx awoke this morning, he says, with the taste of the war in his mouth, the "queasy-quince taste of 1951 and the Orient," and remembered the first time the search occurred to him. For him everything is upside-down: "What are generally considered to be the best times are for me the worst times, and that worst of times was one of the best." Ordeal, that is, breaks everydayness. He had been wounded and was pressed hard to the ground. "Six inches from my nose a dung beetle was scratching around under the leaves. As I watched, there awoke in me an immense curiosity. I was onto something. I vowed that if I ever got out of this fix, I would pursue the search."

Naturally he forgot it as soon as he recovered; but this morning, with the taste of that time in his mouth and the curtain of everydayness momentarily drawn, it came to him again. The little pile of belongings from his pockets was visible; he actually *saw* it. "I bathed, shaved, dressed carefully, and sat at my desk and poked through the little pile in search of a clue just as the detective on television pokes through

---

12. Søren Kierkegaard, in *Concluding Unscientific Postscript,* quoted in translator's preface to *Either / Or,* trans. David F. Swenson and Lillian Marvin Swenson (2 vols.; New York, 1959), I, xi.

the dead man's possessions, using his pencil as a poker."
The idea of the search comes to him again on the bus, this
poor shade making his way down Elysian Fields. The circumstances that prompt it are instructive. He dislikes driving
a car because people on the street cannot see you; "they
only watch your rear fender until it is out of their way."
In the functional anonymity of urban society one becomes
a mere obstruction. Binx finds himself sitting opposite a
beautiful Amazon but defeated by circumstances, so off he
goes on an aesthetic rotation, movie style. "What good times
we could have! . . . What consideration and tenderness I could
show her! If it were a movie, I would only have to wait.
The bus would get lost or the city would be bombed and
she and I would tend the wounded. As it is, I may as well
stop thinking about her." The drop from this vicarious trip
to his dull ride down Elysian Fields is a jolt. "Then it is
that the idea of a search occurs to me." The value of a brief
rotation is that it breaks everydayness just enough to vivify
the fading reappearance of the search.

What is the search? "The search is what anyone would
undertake if he were not sunk in the everydayness of his
own life. This morning, for example, I felt as if I had come
to myself on a strange island. And what does such a castaway
do? Why, he pokes around the neighborhood and he doesn't
miss a trick." Here, disguised in the levity of Binx's private
idiom, is Percy's castaway. Not to be onto something, to be
unaware of the search, is to be in despair—the condition
of Binx's life for some years past. The movies are onto the
search, he notes, but they "screw it up." They show the man
coming to himself in a strange place, but inevitably he "takes
up with the local librarian," settles down, and in two weeks
is "so sunk in everydayness that he might just as well be
dead."

"What do you seek—God? you ask with a smile." Binx
turns to the reader in direct address, like Dostoevski's
Underground Man, but hesitates to answer, since the polls
show that "98% of Americans believe in God and the remain-

ing 2% are atheists and agnostics—which leaves not a single percentage point for a seeker." He is ignorant whether he is ahead or behind his fellow Americans, whether 98 percent have already found what he seeks or are so "sunk in everydayness that not even the possibility of a search has occurred to them."

In a sense it is God he seeks, but the search is more complicated than such a statement would suggest. The search, I believe, is for an answer to the question, broadly construed: "Who am I?" It involves more than personal identity and has two aspects. One is metaphysical: "How did I come to be here?" The other is more practical: "What must I do?" Remember that for Percy, man is a castaway longing for news from beyond the seas. An unhappy predicament; but the worst is to pretend that one is at home on the island. And Binx has been choking in everydayness for years. Only once in his life was its grip broken, he says, "when I lay bleeding in a ditch" (145). Only then did he feel the contingency of his existence; that is what aroused his "immense curiosity." And it is in that sense of contingency, the nascent awareness of a man suddenly coming to himself in a world he cannot account for, that Percy seeks illumination by which to give fresh scrutiny to the world Binx inhabits from day to day. He wants to subject that world to the light of the existential search. Binx's memory of the time when he lay bleeding in a ditch, experienced in the form of its taste, has now reopened the ultimate question and forced him to recognize that he has been living like Pascal's man "who comes into this world, knowing not whence he came nor whither he will go when he dies but only that he will for certain die, and who spends his time as though he were not the center of the supreme mystery but rather diverting himself."[13] He has forgotten that he is a wayfarer on this earth. Who am I? How does it happen I am here? What must I do? These are the questions to which he must address himself.

---

13. Percy's paraphrase in "The Coming Crisis in Psychiatry: II," 415.

The search reopened, Binx is vulnerable to further assaults on his defenses. A scene in the French Quarter widens the breach. Binx has gone there on the chance of seeing the actor William Holden, who is shooting some movie scenes in the Quarter. The narrative has shifted to present tense, heightening his exposed sensibilities. Holden suddenly appears out of Pirate's Alley. Binx follows him. A couple of young honeymooners from the North are following along behind Holden, unaware of him, with Binx trailing. The girl is unhappy, Binx surmises, because she knows the boy is unhappy. He is afraid their honeymoon is too conventional. "He is anxious; he is threatened from every side." They see Holden. The boy brightens, then suddenly becomes morose. "He can only contrast Holden's resplendent reality with his own shadowy and precarious existence." But Holden has stopped to ask some housewives for a match. They recognize him and fall into a blushing confusion in which no one can locate a match. Now the boy comes along, holds out a light, nods, and passes on without recognition. Holden walks along between the couple, exchanges a word, pats them on the shoulder, and moves on. "The boy has done it!" Binx exclaims. "He has won title to his own existence, as plenary an existence now as Holden's, by refusing to be stampeded like the ladies from Hattiesburg." The world opens to him again, as his girl does. "He puts his arm around her neck, noodles her head."

This little scene dramatizes what it means to be sovereign, and in the process Percy has set Binx up for another blow. As Holden moves on an "aura of heightened reality moves with him and all who fall within it feel it." That is what astounds Binx about movie stars, their "peculiar reality." When Holden has gone, everything seems diminished. "Am I mistaken," Binx wonders, "or has a fog of uneasiness, a thin gas of malaise, settled on the street?" This is the first mention of the malaise, and the scene gives us a key to Binx's moviegoing. "Ah, William Holden, we already need you again," he says. "Already the fabric is wearing thin without you" (18). The veil of everydayness has been ripped; and just as Binx felt the plunge from his fantasy with the beautiful Amazon to the reality of his bus ride down Elysian Fields, he now feels the drop from the heightened reality of Holden to the malaise.[14] Rotation is the effective agent in each case.

The fabric of deception has worn thin, and Binx is now deeply vulnerable. He very nearly feels the despair of his life in Gentilly, though as so often happens with Percy, his true vulnerability is masked by the surface levity. Before confronting Binx with Aunt Emily, Percy moves him directly from the encounter with Holden to a chat with Eddie Lovell, a lawyer married to Binx's cousin Nell. The scene with Eddie is done with such superlative realism that it almost obscures the underlying seriousness. The meeting is another little trial for Binx. The mystery of his own existence deepens as he listens to Eddie, who is "as cogent as a bird dog quartering a field. He understands everything out there and everything out there is something to be understood." Eddie is dead to troublesome mysteries, and his self-assurance undermines Binx's accommodation with life. The fabric image returns: "As I listen to Eddie speak plausibly and at length of one thing and another . . . the fabric pulls together into one bright texture of investments, family projects, lovely old houses, little theater readings and such. It comes over me: this is how one lives! My exile in Gentilly has been the worst kind of self-deception." True enough; his exile has been a self-deception, but a less total one than Eddie's. Like the men

---

14. A passage from the piece Percy wrote for the literary magazine at North Carolina, when he was eighteen, throws an interesting light on moviegoers: "The reader of *Scientific American* is in a small way an explorer in the field of science. But the steady reader of *Silver Screen* knows very little about the production of movies and cares less. *She,* for *he* is outnumbered three to one, is incapable of distinguishing a projector from an extra; yet she buys her copy or copies of Hollywood magazines and reads them till they fall apart. She is to be found only in America and is possessed with a neurotic curiosity which demands knowledge of every intimate detail of her idol's life. She does not know acting from arm-waving, yet she writes countless letters of praise and criticism to both actor and magazine. She is not satisfied with seeing a Hollywood actor perform; she must know his love life and his spinach recipe." Taken from Walker Percy, "The Movie Magazine: A Low 'Slick,' " *Carolina Magazine,* XLIV (March, 1935), 5.

whose portraits hang in the Bouville museum in *Nausea*,[15] Eddie is too secure in his refuge of bustling activity ever to face the reality of his existence. His is the despair of the novel's epigraph; he is truly lost.

Now thoroughly shaken, Binx goes on to confront his aunt. Despite detours and distractions, his search continues. He finds a clue in the picture of his father in the Black Forest with the elder Bollings. Why the ironical eyes? We feel his interest in the question and follow his search for an answer. Aunt Emily greets him as "an ingrate, a limb of Satan, the last and sorriest scion of a noble stock." Suddenly he forgets his years in Gentilly, his search. This is where he belongs after all; he has only to accept the role prepared for him. And as he is subjected to yet another assault on his fortifications, we are introduced to the inheritance he has rejected. Emily, with her "blue-white hair and keen quick face and terrible gray eyes" is "soldierly both in look and outlook," still somehow at sixty-five "the young prince." Her stepdaughter Kate has become a problem as her marriage to Walter Wade approaches. Kate is consuming barbiturates in quantity and refuses to see a doctor; Emily fears a general withdrawal. Binx is to exercise his gifts to get Kate out of the house and doing something.

The manner of introducing Kate shows her position in the family. She does not enter; she is simply present in the next scene as Percy skips directly to lunch. After two pages of table talk Binx notes, "Kate frowns at her hands in her lap." She is *there*, inconspicuous as furniture. The overtones are clear: in this house Kate is a problem, best unobserved. "Today Kate has her brown-eyed look. Sometimes her irises turn to discs." Binx recounts a "talk" he had with her fifteen years earlier, at his aunt's request, when she would sit at her desk and refuse to go out to play at recess. Now Emily

15. Jean-Paul Sartre, *Nausea*, trans. Lloyd Alexander (New York, 1964), 88–92. Percy admires this novel and freely acknowledges its influence on him. Compare Holden's effect on ordinary people, for example, with Doctor Rogé's effect on M. Achille (65–70).

begins patronizing Walter, Kate's intended. "But strangely, my aunt looks squarely at Kate and misses the storm warnings." As Emily goes on badgering Walter, Kate "utters a clicking sound in her teeth and abruptly leaves the room." Walter follows her; Emily sighs; Jules sits easy, knowing nothing can go wrong in his house. Binx alludes in the narrative to Kate's earlier "breakdown." Her position here is not pictured for us, we *feel* it: that of a troublesome presence without which everyone could share the confidence of Jules that all is well.

Now at last, in connection with some byplay with Walter, Binx reveals what prompted his withdrawal to Gentilly. For eight years he has had no friends. "I spend my entire time working, making money, going to movies and seeking the company of women." Following his return from the Orient he had taken up with a couple of fellows and struck off for Maine on the Appalachian Trail. It seemed a fine idea at the time, but he soon found himself cast in a role: "The times we did have fun, I had the feeling they were saying to me: 'How about this, Binx? This is really it, isn't it, boy?', that they were practically looking up from their girls to say this." In Marcel's terms, intersubjectivity has degenerated into self-consciousness. So Binx left behind him the inauthentic world of fraternity soulmates and hale good fellows; he still shuns the French Quarter for the same reason.[16] In Gentilly he could pursue the search. Thoreau, in order to drive life into a corner, sought the seclusion of Walden; Binx, finding the quiet desperation of the malaise even in the Appalachians, fled to the most nondescript of suburbs. Unhappily he failed to "front only the essential facts of life,"

16. "He doesn't want to be down in the French Quarter with a lot of guys who are artists and writers," Percy told John Carr. The "hip" young are "exactly the kind of people he's trying to avoid." And he goes to Gentilly in the same spirit Philip went to Gaza: "A man goes to a desert to seek something. Gentilly is a desert if ever there was one" (Carr [ed.], "Rotation and Repetition," 48). There is some confusion on the sequence of events. Binx presents his withdrawal to Gentilly as an immediate one following the Appalachian episode, though the evidence of the novel makes clear that he went to Gentilly several years later, after trying the Quarter and the Garden District.

as Thoreau aimed to do, and soon lost himself in distraction,
everydayness, and ironic half-awareness, awakening only now
to the discovery that life has driven *him* into a corner.

Emily forms a "soundless word" with her lips to signal
Binx to go downstairs and talk to Kate. He finds Kate cleaning
an iron fireplace. After the careful buildup, she speaks now
for the first time:

> "Well? Aren't you supposed to tell me something?"
> "Yes, but I forget what it was."
> "Binx Binx. You're to tell me all sorts of things."
> "That's true."
> "It will end with me telling you."
> "That would be better."
> "How do you make your way in the world?"
> "Is that what you call it? I don't really know. Last month I made
> three thousand dollars—less capital gains."
> "How did you get through a war without getting killed?"
> "It was not through any doing of yours."
> "Anh anh anh." (43)

It is clear that Kate is on a different footing with Binx than
with others. There is no self-consciousness here. Binx is with
her, not merely next to her. Kate complains that Emily looks
upon him as one of her kind, a "proper Bolling"; Jules, on
the other hand, considers him a "go-getter." But Kate is not
fooled: "You're like me, but worse. Much worse."

One reason for this camaraderie is that Kate too is in the
grip of a dialectic. Binx is concerned about her "dialectic
of hatreds" as she swings between her father and stepmother.
In the beginning she had been her father's child. Then as
a young girl she discovered her stepmother's enchantment,
and her once "formless discontents" with Jules and "his dumb
way of inner faith and outer good spirits" led her into rebellion. Emily took her in hand and freed her, but now Emily
has fallen prey to the dialectic. "It was inevitable that Kate
should catch up with and 'see into' her stepmother, just as
she caught up with her father, and that she should, in the
same swing of the dialectic, rediscover her father as the
authentic Louisiana businessman and, if not go to Mass with
him, build him a TV room." What Binx fears now is that

her dialectic will carry her not back to Emily, but into "some
kind of dead-end where she must become aware of the dialectic." So there are two dialectics at work, both of them pulling
against Emily at the moment.

Finally we have the concerned talk about Binx's future
that was forecast in the first paragraph. Emily proposes he
move back into her house and go to medical school in the
fall. Binx is hesitant. "What is it you want out of life, son?"
she asks him. "I don't know'm. But I'll move in whenever
you want me." "Don't you feel obliged to use your brain
and to make a contribution?" "No'm." That is what makes
Binx difficult to deal with: superficially he plays the role
of compliant nephew, but like Melville's Bartleby, he always
prefers not to. Emily urges him to fight the good fight, while
Binx reflects to himself: "I will say yes even though I do
not really know what she is talking about." He says aloud,
"As a matter of fact I was planning to leave Gentilly soon,
but for a different reason," and is about to mention his idea
of the search, but it seems absurd. "Of course!" Emily responds; he is doing something "every man used to do," having
his *Wanderjahr*. His heart sinks. "If I thought I'd spent the
last four years as a *Wanderjahr*, before 'settling down,' I'd
shoot myself on the spot."

There is no common ground here. Emily appeals to the
great days before he went off to war, when together they
discovered Euripides and Jean-Christophe. "You discovered
them for me," Binx remarks, suddenly becoming sleepy. That
is the key to the place she has prepared for him: *she* has
chosen it. During the conversation earlier at lunch Emily
remarks absently to Binx that he is a "depraved and dissolute
specimen," grown "fat-witted from drinking of old sack" (32).
"What I am, Hal, I owe to thee," he replies, drinking his
soup. Emily is Prince Hal to his Falstaff,[17] and this is more
than comedy because she has exerted such a formative
influence on him. Binx must find his own place in life. He

17. The "fat-witted" remark is from Shakespeare, *Henry IV: Part One*, Act I,
Scene 2.

can escape his entrapment only by his own decisive act; he must choose for himself.

He agrees to return in one week, on his thirtieth birthday, presumably to inform her what he plans to do with his life, and Part One ends with Kate having a bad time. This first quarter of the novel constitutes a compact but leisurely beginning, introducing the main themes and characters, defining Binx's exile in Gentilly, and establishing the author's method. The pace now quickens. Less explication is needed, and for the rest of this antithesis phase I want to focus on the search and those elements most directly related to it.

Binx resumes his search with an excursion the next day, Thursday, to St. Bernard Parish. He wants to copy out a title from the courthouse and find a clue in the "doings" of his father, whose signature will be there. Another dream of war revives the "queasy-quince smell of 1951 and the Orient," and everything in the office smells of it except Sharon, his new secretary. Binx is in love with her, after his fashion, and describes her with curiously civilized male perception: "Her bottom is so beautiful that once as she crossed the room to the cooler I felt my eyes smart with tears of gratitude." She is one of those "rosy-cheeked Anglo-Saxon lovelies . . . commoner than sparrows in the South,"[18] and he stalks her with all the artifices culled from the movies, with "Gregorish Peckish" distances and nonchalance garnered from "the old Gable." The notion of taking Sharon along to St. Bernard Parish he terms "Gregorish Peckerish."

In Binx's explanation to Sharon about the hunting lodge, which was called Roaring Camp, we learn that his father had bought a telescope to explore a "fascinating scientific hobby" but then started reading Browning and "saw himself in need of a world of men." There is a connection here

---

18. And like sparrows they tend to disappear into their category of love-object. Binx tends to view them in the plural. He speaks earlier of settling down to raise a "flock" of Marcias and Sandras and Lindas of his own. The bird imagery in the novel is interesting. Even Emily had been a "bird" to her brothers before becoming the young prince.

with Binx's statement that his father was killed by romanticism and 1930 science. The father was an M.D. and, viewing himself objectively, felt he had to sleep a certain number of hours, keep regular, and have a "stimulating hobby (it was the nineteen thirties and everybody believed in science and talked about 'ductless glands')." What Binx jots in his notebook reflects Percy's own discovery: "Does a scientifically minded person become a romantic because he is a left-over from his own science?"

The idea grows out of Binx's explanation of the "vertical search," a term that gives us a good analogy for the ascent into abstraction. For years he conducted the search vertically, reading "fundamental" books like *A Study of History* or Shroedinger's *What Is Life?* The vertical search is scientific and objective, constantly unifying, understanding "more and more specimens by fewer and fewer formulae" and removing one further and further from concrete existence. After one particularly rewarding night reading *The Chemistry of Life,* Binx felt the main goals of his search had been reached. "The only difficulty was that though the universe had been disposed of, I myself was left over. There I lay in my hotel room with my search over yet still obliged to draw one breath and then the next." This tremendous predicament demonstrates the failure of abstraction, the "world-historical oversight" noted by Kierkegaard. Binx then took up the horizontal search, which is existential and addressed to the concrete realities of existence. The only book now in his library is *Arabia Deserta.* "Before, I wandered as a diversion. Now I wander seriously and sit and read as a diversion."

Jews are his "first real clue." Since the search made its reappearance he has become acutely aware of Jews. A person lost in everydayness notices nothing in passing a Jew on the street. A scientist or artist sees only another specimen like himself for study. But when a man alive to the possibility of the search meets a Jew in the street "he is like Robinson Crusoe seeing the footprint on the beach." Binx is "more Jewish than the Jews" he knows. They are "more at home than I am. I accept my exile." Jews are now a clue to him because he now recognizes that he too is a castaway, an exile like them.

Nell Lovell, Binx's cousin and Eddie's wife, exemplifies the person lost in despair. "For some time now," Binx says, "the impression has been growing upon me that everyone is dead." He meets Nell on the street. She and Eddie have just "re-examined" their values and found them "pretty darn enduring." They both have the same life goal and she is not reticent about stating it: "To make a contribution, however small, and leave the world just a little better off" (101). Here it is, the tribal cliché of Aunt Emily. Binx is embarrassed, and we get a singular demonstration of his dexterity in playing the expected role while guarding the integrity of his inner thoughts. "That's very good," he says, and she tells how she and Eddie have given the television to the children and now sit by the fire and read *The Prophet* aloud. "I don't find life gloomy!" she cries. "To me, books and people and things are endlessly fascinating. Don't you think so?"

"Yes." A rumble has commenced in my descending bowel, heralding a tremendous defecation.

Nell goes on talking and there is nothing to do but shift around as best one can, take care not to fart and watch her in a general sort of way: a forty-year-old woman with a good open American face and another forty years left in her; and eager, above all, eager, with that plaintive lost eagerness American college women get at a certain age. I get to thinking about her and old Eddie re-examining their values. Yes, true. Values. Very Good. And then I can't help wondering to myself: why does she talk as if she were dead? Another forty years to go and dead, dead, dead.

The reader has a picture not only of Binx shifting uncomfortably but also of this woman casting about for meaning in her inarticulate despair, which is unlikely ever to surmount the vague yearning for "books and people and things."

Percy's portrait of Nell is empathetic and comical. His humor often shows this kind of incongruity. He is harsher with Nell's sort of positive thinking when it operates in the realm of thought. He satirizes the radio program "This I

Believe," to which Binx is a devoted listener: "Monks have
their discipline. I have This I Believe." And Binx does have
a monkish devotion to irony. He once prepared a tape of
his own for submission: "Here are the beliefs of John Bicker-
son Bolling, a moviegoer living in New Orleans. I believe
in a good kick in the ass. This—I believe."

On Friday a request from Uncle Jules invades Binx's life
in Gentilly like a thunderbolt. Binx is to leave next Tuesday,
the very morning of Mardi Gras, for a convention in Chicago.
"Chicago. Misery misery son of a bitch of all miseries," Binx
thinks to himself. Uncle Jules could never understand, but
such a trip is "no small thing" to Binx, who has the "fortune
and misfortune to know how the spirit-presence of a place
can enrich a man or rob a man but never leave him alone,
how, if a man travels lightly to a hundred strange cities and
cares nothing for the risk he takes, he may find himself No
one and Nowhere." He consents to go, "looking pleased as
punch" but thinking, "Oh sons of all bitches and great beast
of Chicago lying in wait. There goes my life in Gentilly, my
Little Way, my secret existence among the happy shades in
Elysian Fields."

The loss of self involved in becoming a "no one" is a form
of abstraction, and consists of being uprooted from time and
place to become anyone anywhere, and Binx, in his passionate
horizontal search, is afraid of it.[19] When he goes to a movie,
especially in a strange place, he makes it a point to talk to
the ticket seller or the owner. Otherwise, he says, "I should
be seeing one copy of a film which might be shown anywhere
and at any time. There is a danger of slipping clean out
of space and time" (75).

If Binx fears becoming an anyone, Kate strives for it. She
longs for an escape from her predicament. A full analysis
of her condition is beyond the scope of this book. What is
important here is the way in which her predicament and

19. Percy himself travels a good deal, I might add, lest we confuse the author
with his creation. Through Binx Bolling he is probing the roots of the malaise,
not pouring out his soul.

outlook mesh with Binx's. During their first conversation in the novel Binx remarks, "Her voice has suddenly taken on its 'objective' tone." The objective tone goes with her social work, in which she "recites case histories in a kind of droning scientific voice: '—and all the while it was perfectly obvious that the poor woman had never experienced an orgasm' " (44–45). Kate's objectivity is that of the amateur-analyst-expert and perilously close to that of the patient Percy has written of who "does not conceive a higher existence for himself than to be 'what one should be' according to psychiatry." Kate is pursuing a kind of vertical search, seeking a summit from which she can look back upon herself abstractly without being obliged to experience her life.

She walks a "tight rope" suspended over an abyss. The terms is hers from the first time she was "sick." As a child with her mother still living, she had felt that everyone stood on solid ground, but now it seemed that everybody had become aware of "the abyss that yawned at their feet even on the most ordinary occasions—especially on the most ordinary occasions." A family party or luncheon club holds far greater terrors for her than does the middle of no man's land. The accident in which her fiancé had been killed had, by her own account, given her her life (58). Now she has broken her engagement with Walter.

Friday night, in the middle of a storm, she leaves the Iberia ball early and alone, coming to Binx several hours later with a discovery: "I am free. After twenty-five years I am free" (114). The realization had come to her at the psychiatrist's office but was too simple to believe: "My God, can a person live twenty-five years, a life of crucifixion, through a *misunderstanding?*" The psychiatrist, she recognizes, could not have told her. "How strange that you cannot pass along the discovery." And it truly is a discovery. Human existence does not lend itself to the summitry of a vertical search. One can escape into abstraction only by foregoing one's life. The "misunderstanding" is the metaphor in which one is imprisoned—his view of himself or the world, which is so obvious to him and so incomprehensible to others. The psychiatrist might in fact have been able to "tell" Kate, to inform her objectively where her exit into a full existence may lie, but he cannot exit for her. She must discover her way out existentially. She has tried inauthentically to be the "joyous and creative person" her psychiatrist recommended. Now she realizes that it is not good enough. "I had something better. I was free."

Binx, who has been thinking of building a service station near his basement apartment, recognizes that she is overtaking herself, already "laboring ever so slightly at her exaltation." Taking her cold hands, he tells her his idea: "We could stay on here at Mrs. Schexnaydre's. It is very comfortable. I may even run the station myself. You could come sit with me at night, if you liked. Did you know you can net over fifteen thousand a year on a good station?" "You sweet old Binx!" Kate says. "Are you asking me to marry you?" "Sure," he says, watching her uneasily. That is his proposal. She accepts in a rapture and leans over hugging herself, suddenly terribly afraid. "What am I going to do?" she asks. "You mean right now?" he says. "Yes." They will go down to the French Market, he says, and then home. "Is everything going to be all right?" "Yes," he says. "Tell me. Say it." "Everything is going to be all right."

So ends Part Two. Percy has circumvented the clichés about proposals and we know the marriage is going to balance on the edge of an abyss.

Part Three is built around a rotation with Sharon, a trip to the Gulf Coast in Binx's little red MG. It is an entertaining section, particularly when Binx is slightly injured in an accident and is able to play the modest hero over his war wound: "O Tony. O Rory. You never had it so good with direction." The accident is a true rotation because it comes uncalled for and brings its bonus: "the experiencing of the new beyond the expectation of the experiencing of the new." But all this is more distraction, part of his Little Way, "not the big search for the big happiness but the sad little happiness of drinks and kisses, a good little car and a warm deep thigh." His search advances only in their visit to the fishing camp of the Smiths, which they drop in on unannounced and find "ablaze like the *Titanic*."

The *Titanic* image is suggestive. For one thing Binx discovers that his old place at the camp has been "used up by rotatory and repetitive use" and is now in the grip of everydayness: "The everydayness is everywhere now, having begun in the cities and seeking out the remotest nook and corners of the countryside, even the swamps." His old strategies for defeating it are breaking down; life on the aesthetic plane is losing its savor, as it must for every Don Juan. Another thing at which the *Titanic* image hints is the precariousness of his mother's "canny management of the shocks of life." She is wary of good fortune, immured against bad. In her first marriage she lost Scotty, Binx's older brother. More recently a child of her second marriage had drowned. "Losing Duval, her favorite, confirmed her in her election of the ordinary. No more heart's desire for her, thank you. After Duval's death she has wanted everything colloquial and easy, even God." She refuses to acknowledge that anything new is wrong with Lonnie, Binx's paraplegic half-brother, who looks "terrible" to Binx. "That child won't drink his milk!" she explains.

In a conversation with her as she fishes, Binx gets some clues to his father. For one thing the elder Bolling had conducted a kind of a search of his own. Mile after mile he would ramble along the levee on "his famous walk," she tells Binx. And twice in his life he had simply quit eating: "It was like he thought eating was not—*important* enough." What was wrong with him? Binx wants to know. He was "overwrought," she says at once "in her mama-bee drone," and again he disappears into her emblem of him. The first time he had quit eating and lost thirty pounds, she had hit upon the idea of feeding him herself while she read him a book called *The Greene Murder Case*. He would get angry if she stopped reading. Evidently he too was a kind of moviegoer.

The next time he quit eating, the treatment had failed. It was like horse serum, he said; "you could use it only once." What rescued him was the catastrophe of war, which revived him instantly. He packed his suitcase and went to New Orleans to see the Canadian Consul. By the time he left in the blue uniform of an RCAF flight surgeon he had gained thirty pounds, the "best looking man I ever saw in my life. And so—cute!" Of course he was cute, Binx reflects. "He had found a way to do both: to please them and please himself. To leave. To do what he wanted to do and save old England doing it. And perhaps even carry off the grandest coup of all: to die."[20] In Binx's reflection here we can feel the immense weight of his inheritance. Moved by this clue to his own indentity, he tries to explore it: "Then before that he was lazy too." "He was not!" she cries, and failing to fit the disinclination into her familiar category of laziness, Binx then relates an experience of his own in the hope of making the connection with his father, a state of mind that had come over him during the retreat from the Chongchon River, when "nothing seemed worth doing except something I couldn't even remember," no prize satisfying because "it wasn't good enough for me." But his mother passes the experience off with a joke, reincorporating it into the familiar. Even her fondness for Binx is "a fondness carefully guarded against the personal, the heartfelt, a fondness deliberately rendered trite." He cannot really talk to her because she refuses to leave the domain of the ordinary.

With Lonnie, Binx has a special relationship. Lonnie is his favorite and a moviegoer. They are good friends because Binx does not feel sorry for him. Lonnie "has the gift of believing that he can offer his sufferings in reparation for men's indifference to the pierced heart of Jesus Christ," and

20. For what it is worth, Will Percy seems to have experienced the war as a lark. Looking back on it, he wrote, "And now a bit wizened, like picked chickens, I suppose,... our exploits forgotten except by us, our world slipping away, we hear the younger generation demanding peace and isolation and we feel sorry for them, knowing they missed a lot of fun and a lot of grief that was better than fun" (*Lanterns on the Levee*, 183).

Binx would not mind trading places with him: "His life is a serene business." Binx takes Lonnie to see *Fort Dobbs* at the Moonlite Drive-In. Sharon goes along but misses the secret shared by Binx and Lonnie, which is "that Sharon is not and never will be onto the little touches we see in the movie and, in the seeing, know that the other sees—as when Clint Walker tells the saddle tramp in the softiest [*sic*] easiest old Virginian voice: 'Mister, I don't believe I'd do that if I was you.' " This is the shared secret that is the mainspring of intersubjectivity; and Binx, who says he would jump into the bayou if any of the other Smiths tried to speak to him of God, has a serious and completely unselfconscious discussion about religion with Lonnie.[21] A devout Catholic, Lonnie has been fasting in the attempt to "conquer an habitual disposition," his joy at the death of his brilliant older brother, Duval:

> "Are you still worried about that? You accused yourself and received absolution, didn't you?"
> "Yes."
> "Then don't be scrupulous."
> "I'm not scrupulous."
> "Then what's the trouble?"
> "I'm still glad he's dead."
> "Why shouldn't you be? He sees God face to face and you don't."
> Lonnie grins at me with the liveliest sense of our complicity: let them ski all they want to. We have something better. (163)

Their games are the games of love, and the reader senses that Lonnie, the knight of faith, is going to die.

Part Four involves the rotation to Chicago. This rotation with its return is highly symbolic; and as Binx had feared at the first mention of Chicago, it hastens the destruction of the Little Way he leaves behind. For Kate it defines what could be the final swing of her dialectic. She has swung from

---

21. Perhaps this is because the passions of humor and irony, as Kierkegaard said, "are essentially different from the passion of faith" and "belong in the sphere of the infinite resignation" *(Fear and Trembling,* 62). Binx, who normally lives on the plane of irony, easily drops irony in the presence of Lonnie, the knight of faith. Binx speaks the truth in saying he has "entered the argument as a game played by [Lonnie's] rules."

father to stepmother and back again, with false starts in the
direction of Lyell Lovell and Walter Wade. Now in Part Four
she voices her hesitation over marrying Binx.

The first section of Part Four shows events closing in on
Kate, forcing her to a choice. Binx returns from his outing
on the Gulf Coast to find that she has taken a heavy dose
of sleeping pills. Sam Yerger, a novelist of sorts and friend
of the family, has arranged for Kate to see "one of those
fabulous continental geniuses" named Étienne Suë, a high-
powered New York psychiatrist. She is to stay with an old
woman called the Princess, who after Emily is the "most
charming, the wittiest and wisest woman" Sam has ever
known. The Princess will be Kate's companion and keep her
occupied. The plan tells us much about Sam and something
about what lies in store for Kate if she decides not to marry
Binx.

The ploy of the moment calls for Binx to appear looking
for her, knowing nothing, and bring her down to dinner.
She declines dinner, and we have instead a well-wrought
scene in which conversation of Binx and Kate upstairs is
counterpointed against the dinner talk below, a scene that
demonstrates that like Hemingway's Frederic Henry and his
Catherine the two of them are "alone against the others."
As Percy satirizes the conversation below, which revolves
around clichés like "the mind of the South" and "es-
chatological thrill"[22] anecdotes about so-and-so just back from
Geneva, Kate and Binx sit talking in a mezzanine above.
Kate tells Binx she had no desire to die when she took the
capsules, six or eight of them. She had become frightened
and everything had just seemed so "no 'count"; she only
wanted to "break out, or off, off dead center." She announces
that she is going with him to Chicago, that they can go by
train that very night. The swiftness with which she brings
this about suggests how things are closing in; she fears to
be with anyone but Binx.

22. The phrase is from Percy, "The Man on the Train," 482.

The train carries Binx far from his Little Way. He can never return. Kate has discovered she cannot live as a "neat little person like Della Street"; Binx, through the search, has lost the pleasure of his "tidy and ingenious life in Gentilly." He finds himself sitting next to a man with a "neat and well-ordered life" who clips articles with his pocket scissors-knife and underlines passages in his newspaper. One phrase Binx can make out over the man's shoulder triggers a waking dream that prepares the way for what is to follow. "In order to deepen and enrich the marital—" Binx reads in a counseling column. Subsequently he experiences a "waking wide-eyed dream" about Dr. and Mrs. Bob Dean, an "oldish couple" autographing copies of their book *Technique in Marriage*. As he reads from the book lying open on the counter he finds it "impossible not to imagine them at their researches, as solemn as a pair of brontosauruses, their heavy old freckled limbs twined about each other, hands probing skillfully for sensitive zones, pigmented areolas, out-of-the-way mucous glands, dormant vascular nexuses." This daydream is Percy's harshest comment on scientific humanism in the novel, a portrait of two "scientists" experimenting on each other, self-consciously transforming the act of love into a horror of abstraction.

Kate is "shaking like a leaf because she longs to be an anyone who is anywhere and she cannot." She leaves the compartment. Binx locates her in her roomette, hugging herself. She feels it is too late for marriage, which Binx could only carry off as one of his "ingenious little researches"; she has had enough of his "death house pranks." She is not up to "having a little hubby." Suicide is the only thing that keeps her alive. "But if I could *not* kill myself—ah then, I would." Binx, who listens to her voice more than to what she says, notes that her tone is more cheerful than her words and is not seriously concerned: she is talking it out. He keeps urging her to marry him. Finally she says there is only one way she could live, by his telling her what to do: "I am a religious person. What I want is to believe in someone com-

pletely and then do what he wants me to do." Will he tell
her what to do? "Sure." "You can do it," she says, "because
you are not religious. You are the unmoved mover. You
don't need God or anyone else—no credit to you, unless
it is a credit to be the most self-centered person alive. I don't
know whether I love you, but I believe in you and I will
do what you tell me."

That is the closest we come to a definition of their relationship. Kate becomes frightened again and they go to his
roomette. She wants no talk of love, but rests a hand on
him heavily like an "old buddy" and makes him a proposition.
The "researches" of Dr. and Mrs. Bob Dean have set the
scene and labor though he may, Binx is not equal to the
task. He confesses to his movie idol: "I'll have to tell you
the truth, Rory, painful though it is." He wishes he had *either*
tucked Kate in like Debbie and retired to his sofa in the
living room *or* "dispatched" her, Rhett Butler fashion, into
sweet sleep. Alas, he did neither. They both languished in
a limbo between the ethical and the aesthetic. Binx was
"frightened half to death by her bold (not really bold, not
whorish bold but theorish bold) carrying on," and like the
alienated commuter reading about his mental health, they
both "shook like leaves": "Flesh poor flesh failed us. The
burden was too great and flesh poor flesh, neither hallowed
by sacrament nor despised by spirit . . . but until this moment
seen through and canceled, rendered null by the cold and
fishy eye of the malaise—flesh poor flesh now at this moment
summoned all at once to be all and everything, end all and
be all, the last and only hope—quails and fails." This "latter-
day post-Christian sex" is a sickness. To be neither Christian
nor pagan, but marooned in the "cult of the naughty nice
wherein everyone is nicer than Christians and naughtier than
pagans"—that is the sickness. What should deliver them from
the malaise only plunges them into it more deeply than ever.[23]

23. This limbo is explored in *Love in the Ruins* as an almost general condition.
My interpretation of this scene is revised in the light of what Percy recently told
John Carr. Along with most readers I had assumed that some kind of ghastly

Chicago justifies all Binx's misgivings as its genie-soul "flaps down like a buzzard" and perches on his shoulder. The anonymity of the place is lethal. "Nobody but a Southerner knows the wrenching rinsing sadness of the cities of the North," Binx says. In Chicago "the Lake is the North itself: a perilous place from which the spirit winds come pouring forth all roused up and crying out alarm." The city recalls a painful memory of the summer Binx had come there with his father after his brother's death, his father "staking his everything on a perfect comradeship" between them now, and Binx, "through a child's cool perversity or some atavistic recoil from an intimacy too intimate," had turned away from "the terrible request" he saw in his father's eyes, "requiring from me his very life." The father had tried to live through the son, and the boy had "refused him what I knew I could not give."

This guilt-ridden repetition exposes Binx to the assaults of the convention, with its "good fellow" society into which Binx fits himself so easily on the surface and in which he is so desperately lost. He retreats with Kate into "the perilous out-of-doors" and finds "the tiniest bar in the busiest block of the Loop," where in his desperate alienation, he remarks, "I see her plain, see plain for the first time since I lay wounded in a ditch and watched an Oriental finch scratching around in the leaves." That Korean ditch was the place where he had first felt the contingency of his existence and where the idea of the search had occurred to him. The veil of everydayness has been ripped and Binx, now the Wandering Jew feeling his exile from all mankind, sees in Kate "a quiet little

---

consummation took place, but further consideration confirms Percy's statement: "It didn't come off. That's what happened." This is the most misread of all scenes in the novel insofar as literary interpretation is concerned, and the difficulty is something more than the frame of expectation the reader brings to it. One clue that misleads is this remark from Binx: "I never worked so hard in my life, Rory. I had no choice: the alternative was unspeakable." The alternative Percy had in mind was evidently that Kate would feel rejected or that Binx would appear unequal to the Real Right Thing. The scene clearly succeeds in turning Freud upside-down, as Percy likes to do, in using sex as "a symbol of failure on the existential level." See Carr (ed.), "Rotation and Repetition," 53.

body . . . a tough little city Celt; no, more of a Rachel, really, a dark little Rachel bound home to Brooklyn on the IRT."

A visit to his only friend in the Middle West, Harold Graebner, who saved Binx's life in Korea and consequently loves him, succeeds in undoing Harold, who is lost in a suburban nowhere. It is too much for Harold, this "sudden confrontation of a time past, a time so terrible and splendid in its arch-reality; and so lost—cut adrift like a great ship in the flood of years." Binx and Kate withdraw to an "Aztec mortuary" of a movie house to watch *The Young Philadelphians*, which Binx sums up in two sentences: "Paul Newman is an idealistic young fellow who is disillusioned and becomes cynical and calculating. But in the end he recovers his ideals." Kate wails as they leave the theater and "creep home to the hotel, sunk into ourselves and with no stomach even for hand-holding": something bad is about to happen. And it does. A note awaits them asking Binx to call New Orleans. "This I accordingly do, and my aunt's voice speaks to the operator, then to me, and does not change its tone." No one had thought to tell Emily that Kate was going with him to Chicago. The police had found her car at the terminal. Binx cannot explain why he had not informed her.

We know there is to be a reckoning as Binx and Kate catch the midnight bus for New Orleans. Their Mardi Gras is spent on the bus. When they arrive in New Orleans that evening the street cleaners are sweeping confetti into heaps in the gutters. "The cold mizzling rain smells of sour paper pulp." The carnival has ended. Ahead lies Lent.

SYNTHESIS: THE LEAP

"I am not saying that I pretend to understand you," says a voice we recognize as Aunt Emily's. It is next morning, Ash Wednesday. She addresses Binx with a "rare and ominous objectivity." For several thousand years men have conducted themselves in certain recognizable ways, well or badly, she observes, but Binx has discovered something new. "One may simply default. Pass. Do as one pleases, shrug, turn on one's heel and leave. Exit. Why after all need one act humanly? Like all great discoveries it is breathtakingly simple."[24] Emily this morning is no longer the young prince but "erect and handsome as the Black Prince," and the scene is a classic confrontation between generations. It opens the synthesis phase of Binx's life.

Emily applies the *coup de grâce* to his Little Way, but note how carefully Percy has prepared for the leap Binx is about to make. The renewed possibility of the search has opened the way. The weight of the inheritance threatens the integrity of his Little Way; the meeting with Holden and the other incidents discussed earlier leaves him vulnerable; and the talk with Lonnie, a true knight of faith, invades the sanctity of his aesthetic sphere with ultimate questions. His involvement with Kate in her predicament prompts him to offer marriage, though he still hopes to incorporate her into his Little Way. But the fiasco on the train, the desperation of Chicago, and his recognition of her as Rachel foreclose on that false hope. Now Emily has her turn.

While she castigates him with "the old forms of civility and even of humor," interspersing her criticisms of him with lamentations over the low estate to which American society has fallen, Binx listens mutely, struck dumb by his inability to formulate a protest, even to find "a recognizable, a right form of wrongness" for her consideration. The clash of aristocratic and existential perspectives is most clearly focused in the question of his relations with Kate:

"Were you intimate with Kate?"
"Intimate?"

24. Much of the fan mail Percy receives on the novel is from businessmen who heartily agree with Aunt Emily and take it for granted the author stands with them in condemning Binx. Percy takes such compliments with good-natured irony, saying in effect, "Well, she's right, of course, in a way." The Faulknerian tone in Emily's remarks is unmistakable. Perhaps it is the tone that goes with a world in decline. Even Kierkegaard strikes a "Faulknerian" tone in describing the leveling process. See Søren Kierkegaard, *The Present Age,* trans. Alexander Dru (New York, 1962), 83, for an example.

"Yes."
"Not very."
"I ask you again. Were you intimate with her?"
"I suppose so. Though intimate is not quite the word."
"You suppose so. Intimate is not quite the word. I wonder what is the word."

She speaks the language of forms, by which Binx was unsuccessfully intimate with Kate, but Binx, viewing the episode existentially, denies that it was "very" intimate. The euphemism is remarkably ill-chosen on Emily's part: the "intimacy" was a despairing exercise in alienation.

The impasse is total. Emily is a strong character, stronger in will than Faulkner's Dilsey, though unlike Dilsey she has history against her and her world can only decline. Subtly Percy comments on her as she talks. While she goes on and on about a civilization that enshrines mediocrity and prides itself on commonness, she toys continually with a sword-shaped letter opener. She seems not to have noticed that years ago Binx had bent the tip of it trying to open a drawer. She makes reference to a black chimney sweep as "your prize exhibit for the progress of the human race in the past three thousand years" while the sweep replies from the street: "*R-r-r-ra-monez la cheminée du haut en bas!*" The implication is clear. She who has taken up the bent sword of the Bollings[25] lacks the awareness even to observe its present shape, while the black man in the street, speaking for the mute scion who bent it, calls for a thorough cleaning of the chimney, top to bottom.

One further quality of the scene deserves comment, one that emerges in their final recorded exchange in the novel:

"Don't you love these things? Don't you live by them?"
"No."
"What do you love? What do you live by?"
I am silent.
"Tell me where I have failed you."
"You haven't."

---

25. The symbolism here is more than sexual, of course. Note the contrast with "the old broadsword virtues" of the Stoics, as Percy once called them (Walker Percy, "The Failure and the Hope," *Katallagete*, I [1965], 19).

"What do you think is the purpose of life—to go to the movies and dally with every girl that comes along?"
"No."

Binx so despairs of communicating with her that he has not even told her he plans to marry Kate. His silence here resembles that of Meursault in Camus's novel *The Stranger* as Meursault tries to explain why he killed the Arab. It was because the sun, Meursault says, but that sounds nonsensical, and anyway he is "morally guilty of his mother's death."[26] Binx tells his aunt: "My objections, though they are not exactly objections, cannot be expressed in the usual way. To tell the truth, I can't express them at all." There is not the slightest chance Emily will comprehend his "objections." She says, "Well," closing the ledger on his account, and dismisses him, looking past him, without addressing him by name: "I do thank you so much for coming by." The Stranger has arrived in America.

The outburst beginning "Today is my thirtieth birthday" shows Binx's predicament as he sits on the ocean wave in the school yard. Already he had rejected what Emily represents. The tradition she offers him, noble though it may be, has become irrelevant. It cannot fathom Kate's difficulties, only intensify them; Kate is unafraid with Binx because he has rejected it. And it has nothing at all to say concerning the new wine of Binx's search except that the old bottles are better. After Emily's withering assault he must face the world to whose mercies he is left by the destruction of his exile in Gentilly. If, as I suggested earlier, he passed through doubt in rejecting his inheritance and immersed himself in sensuality, metamorphosed into a Faust and then into a Don Juan, he now becomes an Ahasuerus as he confronts his despair. On his thirtieth birthday, wayfarer that he is, he must recognize the bankruptcy of his life without the Little Way, in his "dark pilgrimage." He has nothing to show for

26. Albert Camus, *The Stranger*, trans. Stuart Gilbert (New York, 1946), 128, 130.

thirty years but the nose for *merde* that is his true inheritance from his father. Swamped in inauthenticity and the abstraction of a behaviorism that reduces love to mechanical ritual, he feels the loss of self at the heart of the approved "warm and creative person." The dung beetle which had witnessed the beginning of his search in 1951 returns as the anyone prospering on the excrement of contemporary despair.[27] Everyone is a humanist, none a seeker, and all have become the anonymous dead under the fallout of the malaise, where the unspoken fear is that the bomb will *not* fall. Binx himself knows nothing and feels only desire.

Ultimately this recognition of despair catapults him out of his exile, but the immediate effect of Emily's tongue-lashing obscures the response. His search has been abandoned as "no match for [his] aunt, her rightness and her despair." Desire comes "howling down Elysian Fields like a mistral." His first thought is to go back to where he was: he tries to call Sharon. "It is certain now that my aunt is right and that Kate knows it and that nothing is left but Sharon." But Sharon is not in the office. Has she quit? He has yet to realize it is Ash Wednesday and the office is closed. He calls her apartment to learn from her roommate Joyce that Sharon is now engaged. Without hesitation he decides to be "frank." "Old confederate Marlon Brando—a reedy insinuating voice, full of winks and leers and above all pleased with itself." But that phase is past and he cannot go back; his own facility trips him up. "What a shock. On and on it goes."[28] Round and round goes the ocean wave as he tries to wangle a date with Joyce, painfully aware of the rotational pit into which he has stumbled, and the place names reflect the change: "Elysian Fields glistens like a vat of sulfur; the playground looks as if it alone had survived the end of the world."[29]

27. The dry husk of Gregor Samsa swept out by the charwoman in Kafka's "The Metamorphosis" is referred to by her as a dung beetle.

28. This "shock" is connected to his comment earlier, upon learning from his mother that her father had loved pretty girls to his dying day. "Does it last that long?" (155) Binx asks, in what sounds rather like despair.

29. A conclusive note from Kierkegaard's *Concluding Unscientific Postscript* on

The only thing that can rescue him is his own decisive act. At first glance his decision seems purely fortuitous as Kate pulls up just then in her car. She sits there "like a bomber pilot... looking sideways at the children and not seeing, and she could be I myself, sooty eyed and nowhere." Is it possible? he wonders. "Is it possible that—it is not too late?" Too late for the survivors to "discover themselves to be themselves and live as merrily as children among the viny ruins"? Binx can no longer bear to go round and round like the ocean wave creaking on the schoolground. "May I bring along my own fiancee, Kate Cutrer?" he asks Joyce, his decision evidently made.

Kate is pleased by his performance of the morning, convinced that his refusal to inform Emily they are to be married was a "grand stoic gesture, like a magazine hero." Binx is to see his aunt that afternoon, as promised, to tell her his plans. "What do you plan to do?" Kate asks. His response is the most important passage in the novel: "I shrug. There is only one thing I can do: listen to people, see how they stick themselves into the world, hand them along a ways in their dark journey and be handed along, and for good and selfish reasons. It only remains to decide whether this vocation is best pursued in a service station or—" Here his new awareness of the world, a religious awareness born of his despair, surfaces for a moment. His vocation is listening to people, handing them along and being handed along. Binx is a wayfarer to whom the question of what to "do" professionally is of secondary importance. He is quite willing to go to medical school, if his aunt wishes, having no desire to give unnecessary pain. That is the nature of the return

---

the aesthetic sphere from which Binx is being forcibly ejected: "It is an imagination-existence in aesthetic passion, and therefore paradoxical, colliding with time; it is in its maximum despair; it is therefore not existence but an existential possibility tending toward existence, and brought so close to it that you feel how every moment is wasted as long as it has not come to a decision." Quoted in translator's preface to *Either / Or*, I, xi.

he makes to Emily's values. He will put on the outward forms, which are trivial. The inner content will be his own.

The leap he makes is evident in the conversation that follows, where we can watch Binx becoming a knight of faith. Marriage, Kate says, seems "the wildest sort of thing to do." He agrees. "We had better make it fast," she then urges fearfully; it would help if she could be sure he knew how frightened she was:

> "I am frightened when I am alone and I am frightened when I am with people. The only time I'm not frightened is when I'm with you. You'll have to be with me a great deal."
> "I will."
> "Do you want to?"
> "Yes."
> "I will be under treatment a long time."
> "I know that."
> "And I'm not sure I'll ever change. Really change."
> "You might."

Kate is his princess, and he accepts her in the full knowledge that she is unlikely to change, that the sword of a severe disturbance will always hang over his beloved. In putting herself in his charge Kate renounces herself, becoming in a strange sense a knight of infinite resignation; but Binx, knowing the impossibility, embraces the paradox in faith and proposes "to live joyfully and happily every instant by virtue of the absurd, every instant to see the sword hanging over the head of the beloved, and yet not to find repose in the pain of resignation, but joy by virtue of the absurd."[30]

His leap of faith is the leap no dancer can make, and in making it he vaults over the ethical stage altogether and lands in a definite posture in the religious. That is to be his synthesis phase.[31] His dialectic merges with Kate's as the

---

30. Kierkegaard, *Fear and Trembling*, 61. See my discussion of the infinite passion in Chapter Two.

31. Percy corroborates this leap into the religious sphere: "But in the end—we're using Kierkegaardian terminology—in the end Binx jumps from the aesthetic clear across the ethical to the religious. He has no ethical sphere at all. That's what Aunt Emily can't understand about him. He just doesn't believe in being the honor-

commitment lightly made earlier, his "proposal" involving the service station, is now solemnized. Kate is plucking shreds of feathered flesh from her thumb. Binx takes her hand, kissing the blood.[32] "But you must try not to hurt yourself so much." "I will try! I will!"

Now, in his characteristic way, Percy sets the final scene of this decisive week off against the visit of a respectable middle-class Negro to the church next door. Binx cannot say why the black man is here. "Is it part and parcel of the complex business of coming up in the world? Or is it because he believes that God himself is present here at the corner of Elysian Fields and Bons Enfants? Or is he here for both reasons: through some dim dazzling trick of grace, coming for the one and receiving the other as God's own importunate bonus?" Because of the man's "ambiguous sienna color" it is impossible even to know whether he has received ashes. In the aftermath of Aunt Emily's remarks this ambiguous Negro seems to show that Emily is now at two removes from reality: the first being that her aristocratic world is gone, the second that the black man is already falling victim to the snares of the world that has succeeded it. Binx and Kate, having learned something of those snares, have some hope of evading them.

An epilogue moved forward a little more than a year suggests how things stand at that time. A good deal is conveyed in the tone. Kate and Binx are now married and Binx is in medical school. Jules is dead and Lonnie has succumbed to a massive virus infection. Emily has accepted the demise of her expectations for Binx and patronizes him fondly: "As soon as she accepted what she herself had been saying all those years, that the Bolling family had gone to seed and

---

able man, doing the right thing, for its own sake" (Carr [ed.], "Rotation and Repetition," 49). Lewis A. Lawson suggests provisionally that Binx moves to the ethical sphere, but I think the evidence clearly supports Percy's own view. See Lawson, "Walker Percy's Indirect Communications."

32. His gesture is clearly a kind of Eucharist, a celebration of the holy intersubjective communion into which he now enters with Kate.

that I was not one of her heroes but a very ordinary fellow, we got along very well." Both women find him comical. To Emily he is still Falstaff, but it is clear that this ordinary fellow who married his Kate is more than a clown, if not quite Henry V.

As for his search, Binx has little inclination to speak. "For one thing, I have not the authority, as the great Danish philosopher declared, to speak of such matters in any way other than the edifying. For another thing, it is not open to me even to be edifying, since the time is later than his, much too late to edify or do much of anything except plant a foot in the right place as the opportunity presents itself—if indeed asskicking is properly distinguished from edification." It is not merely that he lacks the authority to speak. If the authority were his he would still be unable to relay the message, which cannot pass through the barrier separating the religious realm from the ethical. Only faith can part that barrier. And the reference to "asskicking" is important, referring to the comments on "This I Believe"; it is part of the negative mold of the novel. The hour is far too late for moralizing about how men should live. One can only plant a foot occasionally in the appropriate place.[33]

As for Binx, he now expands into the full house instead of confining himself to the basement. The nature of its upper stories is suggested implicitly in the final scene, which jumps back a bit to the day before Lonnie's death. Kate has taken it into her head to visit Lonnie. Binx has his doubts about her notion, but it strikes her as the thing to do "under the circumstances if one is the sort of person who etc etc." She is still playing out her roles. Kate is unprepared for Lonnie's physical deterioration. His condition is not presented directly but reflected in her response afterwards: "Oh my God, how

---

33. Kierkegaard discusses the ethical question of keeping silent in Problem III of *Fear and Trembling*. One sentence from a complicated analysis: "Ethics is a dangerous science, and it might be possible that Aristophanes was determined by purely ethical considerations in resolving to reprove by laughter his misguided age" (117).

dreadful"; Lonnie is so "hideously thin and yellow, like one of those wrecks lying on a flatcar at Dachau." When Binx tells her she is "very good-looking today," she is horrified: "There is something grisly about you." In her eyes Binx is callous. She does not live in the infinite passion and cannot grasp his paradoxical religiousness, nor does she perceive her own identity in the Jewishness of the Dachau image. In reality Binx is caring for the children, Lonnie's brothers and sisters, with the surest delicacy of feeling. When they ask him if Lonnie is going to die, he says yes. "But he wouldn't want you to be sad. He told me to give you a kiss and tell you that he loved you." The children are not sad, nor are they being treated to the masking of death that denies authentic being to children and adults alike. "This is a very serious and out-of-the-way business." They cast about for ways of prolonging "this game of serious talk and serious listening." Lonnie will be resurrected on the last day just like them, Binx tells them; he will be able to ski. "Hurray!" cry the twins.[34]

Binx decides to take them for a ride on the Audubon Park train, but first he returns to ask a favor of Kate. She is to go downtown to pick up some documents. Just how little she has progressed is apparent in her uneasiness. In something like posthypnotic suggestion he tells her exactly what to do and where to go, even where to sit on the streetcar, and picks a cape jasmine for her. This is how Percy ends the novel:

> "I've got to be sure about one thing."
> "What?"
> "I'm going to sit next to the window on the Lake side and put the cape jasmine in my lap?"

34. Percy says this was a salute to Dostoevski, specifically to *The Brothers Karamazov*. Kate misses the import of what he does, but Binx is not joking: "Like Alyosha he tells the truth . . . One of the kids [in Dostoevski's novel] says, 'Is it true we're all going to rise on the last day and be together?' A little boy named Kolya had just died. And so Alyosha said, 'Yeah, that's true. We're really going to be there.' And the kids say, 'Hurrah for Karamazov!' " (Carr [ed.], "Rotation and Repetition," 50).

"That's right."
"And you'll be thinking of me just that way?"
"That's right."
"Good by."
"Good by."
Twenty feet away she turns around.
"Mr Klostermann?"
"Mr Klostermann."
I watch her walk toward St Charles, cape jasmine held against her cheek, until my brothers and sisters call out behind me.

Kate is mortally fearful and dependent as Binx returns to help his half-brothers and -sisters through their brother's death. All his flippancy is gone. There is no trace of self-consciousness, and much is left unsaid. The continuing motion of the novel suggests the continuing quality of his life with Kate, who will remain a cripple. For the house he has chosen to live in, we know that Binx has found a place suitable for the wayfarer who knows that he must hand people along and be handed along in turn. The half-brothers have become brothers. Binx has found his vocation. He inhabits the full house now and it is his.

Percy suggests this without moralizing and without grandiose claims, by his elliptical approach and the language of understatement. The reader can accept it or not, as he prefers. There is no attempt to force it down his throat. To me that is why *The Moviegoer* is a moving novel and no small achievement.

4

Ground Zero to Santa Fe

The Last Gentleman is a more ambitious novel than *The Moviegoer* and a more spacious one. In his second novel Percy has moved out in a number of ways from the confines of his first. The physical scope alone suggests the difference. Where *The Moviegoer* is intensive, centering closely on New Orleans, with a couple of excursions along the Gulf Coast and a sojourn to Chicago, *The Last Gentleman* is extensive and moves from New York through the Deep South to the Southwest. Along the way it develops an amplitude the earlier novel lacks. And Percy makes a minor stylistic breakthrough in capturing a supple American rhythm and tone that in retrospect give *The Moviegoer* the slightest trace of a European accent. The protagonist of *The Last Gentleman* breaks out of his underground existence as a humidification engineer in Macy's basement and makes a journey that takes him across country and out of time, from the contemporary "fallout" of American life to a realm beyond the reach of time.

Simultaneously a shift of emphasis takes place. *The Moviegoer* probes the malaise of American life and records, almost in passing, the death of the narrator's half-brother, Lonnie Smith. *The Last Gentleman* by contrast is structured on the impending death of Jamie Vaught, and Percy climaxes the novel with a powerfully rendered account of the event itself. Clearly *The Moviegoer* did not offer him sufficient latitude to explore the fact of death, the uniquely personal "I and my death" of the existentialists. Its reality permeates *The Last Gentleman*. And the death of Jamie Vaught is set off against a peculiarly modern kind of death-in-life.

The novel describes a pilgrimage, but it is a pilgrimage unlike any other because Will Barrett is a new kind of pilgrim. He suffers a postmodern incapacity. What is it to be a pilgrim if you are blind to signs along the way and deaf to the messages? That question underlies the novel. Will's journey takes place in a world denied grace by an affliction Kierkegaard saw in the making. Percy explores its lethal complications in being, choosing for the purpose a young man whose malady disqualifies him as pilgrim while it qualifies him admirably as protagonist.

Will Barrett qualifies as protagonist in that he suffers from amnesia and from time to time lapses into fugue states following which he can recall nothing of what has transpired. Even between spells he is shaky about what is what. "Much of the time he was like a man who has just crawled out of a bombed building," Percy says. But such a predicament is not altogether bad: "Like the sole survivor of a bombed building, he had no secondhand opinions and he could see things afresh."[1] This fresh vision of things is combined with a sentience, a supersensitive radar, which enables him to receive the signals others are transmitting along with, or in spite of, their words. Lacking secure memory, he cannot make logical or temporal connections; possessing acute sensibility, he can perceive the sense of a situation through all the nonsense of its words. He thus serves the author as an instrument for taking a fresh look at the American scene. The novel attempts a clear phenomenological look at American life in the 1960's, unobscured by the clouded lenses of fashionable opinion.

Reinforcing this primary qualification of Will Barrett's is another. Until the moment the novel opens he has lived in

1. Walker Percy, *The Last Gentleman* (New York, 1966), 11. Page references in the text are to this original hardcover edition.

a state of "pure possibility, not knowing what sort of man he was or what he must do, and supposing therefore that he must be all men and do everything" (4). He is as undefined at the outset as the world he inhabits. Near the end of the novel his sense of possibility receives a jolt that marks the beginning for him of "what is called a normal life" (374) when Sutter Vaught informs him bluntly that he, Sutter, will not be around after Jamie's death. Will cannot understand why. Sutter, who is planning to kill himself with a Colt pistol, says in exasperation: "What in Christ's name do you think I'm doing out here [in New Mexico]? Do you think I'm staying? Do you think I'm going back [to Alabama]?" The stark elimination of alternatives finally astonishes Will for the first time in his life, after which he takes shape as a normal person. But in the meantime his sense of limitless possibility combines with his amnesia to facilitate a fresh look at the current scene as events drive him closer and closer to a final choice.

What disqualifies him as a pilgrim is an incapacity we need to define at the outset. It is more than an incapacity of will, to make the obvious pun, and is related to one of his quirky notions: "that 'It' had already happened, the terrible event that everyone dreads" (45). With his amnesic spells Will is peculiarly vulnerable to such a notion, since the disaster might have occurred during one of his fugues. His shakiness leaves open the question whether "It" has already taken place and what "It" can be if not the blowing up of the world, which manifestly has not happened yet. And indeed "It" has happened, a terrible catastrophe that Will cannot possibly see because it consists in large measure of the way he has come to look upon himself.[2]

Will is a true descendant of Descartes, and the mind-body rift that takes place with Descartes has been fatally widened in Will's case by his veneration of science. The question will be taken up more fully along the way. In a sense Will's creed

---

2. This "condition" is more easily seen after a reading of *Love in the Ruins*. I prefer not to anticipate here, but to approach more stealthily, hoping to discern the outlines of it as Percy seems to have discovered them in his fiction.

is: I think, therefore I *am* not. It may have been such a fact of consciousness that Kierkegaard had in mind when he noted in his journal: "It is the grace of God that he wishes to be personal in relation to you; if you throw away his grace he punishes you by behaving objectively towards you." Will lives in a state without grace because he has come to view himself objectively. He takes "an objective attitude to his own personality," as Kierkegaard said of Socrates in danger.[3] If we translate Kierkegaard into our own terms and define grace here as subjectivity or inwardness,[4] Will's condition begins to make sense. He is denied grace because he has abdicated himself. He lives not in the infinite passion but in a shadowy objective remove that denies him access to his own inwardness.

The Last Gentleman is the pilgrimage of an incapacitated pilgrim. The physical movement of the novel is a direct analogue for his pilgrimage, and I will follow the chapter divisions in my discussion as we move in five stages from Ground Zero to Santa Fe.

CHAPTER ONE: A SHELTER FROM THE FALLOUT

Early in the novel the author gives us a glimpse of a period in Will Barrett's New York life in which he takes up with some Ohioans. He has been keeping company with a brunette named Carol Schwartz who is "long of leg and deep of thigh" and has a habit of cooing to cats. Once at a ski lodge near Bear Mountain she leaned over him as he lay with his head on her thigh and said: "I'm a people-liker and I think you're my kind of people. Are you a people-liker?"

> His knee began to jerk involuntarily and at the first opportunity he extricated himself and rushed out of the lodge. Outside, he ran through the snowy woods and threw himself into a brierpatch like a saint of old. Shivering with pain and cold, he gazed up at the shadowy knoll associated by tradition with Mad Anthony Wayne. He muttered

3. Søren Kierkegaard, *The Journals of Kierkegaard*, trans. Alexander Dru (New York, 1959), 250, 248.
4. In *Concluding Unscientific Postscript* Kierkegaard says *truth* is subjectivity (*A Kierkegaard Anthology*, ed. Robert Bretall [New York, 1946], 210–26).

to himself: "Barrett, you poor fellow, you must be very bad off, worse than you imagined, to have gotten things so mixed up. Here you are lying in a brierpatch when you could be lounging with young people like yourself, people against whom no objection can be raised, your head pillowed in the lap of a handsome girl. Is it not true that the American Revolution has succeeded beyond the wildest dreams of Wayne and his friends, so that practically everyone in the United States is free to sit around a cozy fire in ski pants? What is wrong with that? What is the matter with you, you poor fellow?" (21)

The trouble with Will Barrett is that this consumer's paradise yields inauthenticity in myriad forms along with material wealth, and as Brer Rabbit knew,[5] the brier patch may be a distinct improvement over previous circumstances—the world in this instance of "people-likers."

Percy's starting point in the novel is the consumer's paradise of contemporary America, which more than satisfies the officially defined "needs" of most people but produces a menacing fallout or malaise as well.[6] Like Binx Bolling, Will Barrett has reached an accommodation with circumstances in finding himself a fallout shelter as a humidification engineer for Macy's, three floors below ground. Again Percy houses his hero significantly, and again in a house without a beloved. Will's expertise in the matter of atmosphere recalls something from Marcel that seems fundamental to *The Last Gentleman*. Speaking of the need for transcendence, Marcel likens experience to a chemical solution receptive to various degrees of saturation. He then asks "whether the urgent inner need for transcendence might not, in its most fundamental nature, coincide with an aspiration towards a purer and purer mode of experience."[7] Though I very much doubt that Percy had

5. Br'er Rabbit, a creation of Joel Chandler Harris, was trapped by Br'er Fox through the agency of the Tar Baby, but managed to hoodwink Br'er Fox into casting him into the brier patch, from which he made his exit with considerable cheer.

6. One of Percy's working titles for the novel was *The Fallout*.

7. Gabriel Marcel, *Mystery of Being*, trans. G. S. Fraser (2 vols.; Chicago, 1960), I, 68. Curiously, on the following page Marcel mentions the "distorting spectacles" of preconceived ideas that tend to obstruct our vision when we travel in a strange country. This notion coincides with Percy's choice of an amnesic for his tour through the strange country of contemporary America.

Marcel's metaphor in mind, the image of experience as a solution receptive to different degrees of saturation reflects the progression of the novel. The atmosphere of *The Last Gentleman,* gaseous rather than liquid, undergoes a transcendent change from the noxious urban smog of "ravening particles" described in this opening section to the purer air of the American Southwest, where the novel ends.

The first chapter depicts Will Barrett's life under the fallout. The precise quality of the New York atmosphere is most clearly seen from a Southern vantage point later in the novel, somewhat in the same way Chicago is presented in *The Moviegoer.* It is a peculiarly Northern atmosphere, and Will feels good in it because everyone else feels bad:

> True, there was a happiness in the North. That is to say, nearly everyone would have denied that he was unhappy. And certainly the North was victorious. It had never lost a war. But Northerners had turned morose in their victory. They were solitary and shut-off to themselves and he, the engineer, had got used to living among them. Their cities, rich and busy as they were, nevertheless looked bombed out. And his own happiness had come from being onto the unhappiness beneath their happiness. It was possible for him to be at home in the North because the North was homeless. (177)

The homeless North is populated by "good steady wistful post-Protestant Yankees," and Will is at home in it because he too is lost. The New York depicted in the novel corresponds to what Percy has called the "notion of the American city as an alien place." It is a good jumping-off place because as he says the "lostness of the American in America is a paradigm of the existentialist or even the Christian view."[8] Percy's Ground Zero is an appropriate place from which to begin a postmodern pilgrimage.[9]

"One fine day in early summer," the novel begins, "a young man lay thinking in Central Park." Immediately we note several things. The character is presented in a prone position, and he is thinking, not acting. For another thing, Percy has shifted from the dramatized first-person narration of *The*

---

8. Brown, "An Interview," 9.
9. Another working title for the novel was *Ground Zero.*

Moviegoer to an omniscient point of view; *The Last Gentleman* is the only novel of Percy's to date that is not narrated by the central character. And with the shift in narrative point of view comes a certain distancing and new possibilities for dramatic irony. The introduction of Will Barrett as "a young man" says a good deal. He materializes as an anyone, and the various designations with which Percy tags him dramatize his condition. Kierkegaard long ago described the pure possibility that is Will's mode of existence: "Possibility then appears to the self ever greater and greater, more and more things become possible, because nothing becomes actual. At last it is as if everything were possible—but this is precisely when the abyss has swallowed up the self . . . [and] the individual becomes for himself a mirage."[10]

Will has become just such a mirage to himself. It is instructive to watch how the author refers to him through the first chapter. Here in this homeless place he is presented as "a young man." More frequently the designation is simply "he," but in this first chapter Will's specific designations alternate between "the young man" and "the Southerner." In the office of Dr. Gamow, his analyst, he becomes "the patient" or "the other." Once he is described, in the analyst's eyes, as a "Southern belle . . . light on his feet and giving away nothing." The changing designations reflect the reality because here in New York he is a chameleon, indentified by successive functions, changing color protectively to conform to his surroundings: these are his roles. Percy weaves "the engineer" in unobtrusively a dozen times by way of preparation and

10. The balance of the passage: "Every little possibility even would require some time to become actuality. But finally the time which should be available for actuality becomes shorter and shorter, everything becomes more and more instantaneous. Possibility becomes more and more intense—but only in the sense of possibility, not in the sense of actuality; for in the sense of actuality the meaning of intensity is that at least something of that which is possible becomes actual. At the instant something appears possible, and then a new possibility makes its appearance, at last this phantasmagoria moves so rapidly that it is as if everything were possible—and this is precisely the last moment, when the individual becomes for himself a mirage" (Søren Kierkegaard, *The Sickness unto Death*, trans. Walter Lowrie [New York, 1954], 169).

actually names him Williston Bibb Barrett just before he identifies him permanently as "the engineer." Because it is important here to maintain a critical distance from the author,
I will refer to the engineer simply as Will.

Will's amnesia allies him in an odd way with Faulkner's
Benjy Compson, though he is by no means an idiot.[11] His
time sense is almost as dislocated as Benjy's, but the sound
and fury he experiences belong to an abstract postmodern
world shorn, like Benjy's, of the benefits of the past. Will
is assaulted by noxious particles, the weight of evidence for
which suggests "his own deteriorating condition," Percy
observes; for if there were "any 'noxious particles' around,
they were, as every psychologist knows, more likely to be
found inside his head than in the sky." The author's mention
of this likelihood leads us to suspect the contrary, that the
particles are really there; and Percy has written that Will's
symptoms can be interpreted merely as evidences of "personality disorder and maladaptation of organism to environment," or seen as "more or less appropriate reactions to a
new order of things, an as yet unnamed era which may have
begun without his even being aware of it."[12] Will's affliction
is clearly more general than it first appears to be. His amnesia
cannot be altogether accounted for scientifically, Percy has
said,[13] and there is substance in Will's suspicion "that the
world catastrophe which everyone fears might happen has
in fact already happened," though Percy adds that the suspicion "can be read, if one prefers, as a delusion."[14]

The novel's epigraph from Romano Guardini confirms that
the "as yet unnamed era" of which Percy speaks is the postmodern, post-Christian era in which, says Guardini, the
unbeliever will emerge from the fogs of secularism [and]
cease to reap benefit from the values and forces developed

11. He has much in common with Dostoevski's Prince Myshkin in *The Idiot*.
Percy speaks of a "conscious kinship" (Brown, "An Interview," 6).

12. From Percy's prefatory remarks for *"The Last Gentleman:* Two Excerpts from
the Forthcoming Novel," *Harper's*, CCXXXII (1966), 54.

13. Brown, "An Interview," 5.

14. Percy, *"The Last Gentleman:* Two Excerpts," 54.

by the very Revelation he denies."[15] By whatever name we call it, this period comes to us through Will Barrett as a time wrenched out of joint and subject to peculiar bombardment. What its sound and fury signify is the subject of the book.

The novel opens with Will's discovery of Kitty Vaught, but the momentous event of the first chapter is his cutting of ties with "sweet mother psychoanalysis," his leave-taking from Dr. Gamow, his analyst. For five years Will has been engaged with Dr. Gamow in what can only be described as mock-therapy, a daily fifty-five minutes that altogether have cost him about eighteen thousand dollars. Will is the incarnation of the naïve secular faith in psychoanalysis. He understands that "it is people who count, one's relations with people, one's warmth toward and understanding of people," and has often achieved his goal of "cultivating rewarding interpersonal relationships with a variety of people." Nor does he turn up his nose at religion in the fashion of "old-style scientists," for he knows from reading modern psychologists "that we have much to learn from the psychological insights of the World's Great Religions." The irony is unmistakable, if we needed it for a clue to add to the author's inane repetition of "people." What is wrong with these admirable goals? What is Percy carping about now?

The answer is suggested in his comment that Will Barrett at his best is "everything a psychologist could have desired him to be." Like Kate Cutrer in her "objective" moments, he is able to dissociate himself from himself in the most exemplary way, and he is so very modern that he knows the World's Great Religions have yielded great psychological insights. What he misses is that they are indeed *in*-sights, not *out*-sights

15. The complete epigraph: "... We know now that the modern world is coming to an end ... at the same time, the unbeliever will emerge from the fogs of secularism. He will cease to reap benefit from the values and forces developed by the very Revelation he denies ... Loneliness in faith will be terrible. Love will disappear from the face of the public world, but the more precious will be that love which flows from one lonely person to another ... the world to come will be filled with animosity and danger, but it will be a world open and clean."

viewed from some transcendent objectivity, and as Kierkegaard insisted, they can only be seen inwardly.[16] From
the limbo of his objectivity Will cannot really *see* what is there.
Percy has provided a clue in saying that Will has eliminated
Christianity as a viable possibility: "That is gone. That is
no longer even to be considered. It's not even to be spoken
of, taken seriously, or anything else."[17] Will is a postmodern
citizen who has no truck with antiquated hypotheses. He
thus eliminates himself from the body of those receptive to
any news from across the seas.

His trouble, we are told, comes from groups. At first glance
that seems strange, inasmuch as he has sharpened his "group
skills" in years of group therapy. "So adept did he become
at role-taking, as the social scientists call it, that he all but
disappeared into the group" (19). That is just the trouble.
He can play any role for which the need arises—"young man,"
"patient," "Southerner." What he cannot do is say what he
is, or define himself more clearly than a chameleon can define
its color. He cannot choose. Percy turns this adeptness of
Will's to satirical purposes by allowing him naïvely to bring
a friend from his interracial group in the Village to the meeting he is attending simultaneously with a group of nostalgic
expatriate Southerners. But Will's role-playing dexterity is
best illustrated in his final call on Dr. Gamow.

For five years the two have been stalemated while Will
squanders his inheritance symbolically in fees. Perhaps this
prodigality is a form of the forgetting prescribed in the epigraph from Kierkegaard,[18] an irony-laden rejection of what
has been handed down. Certainly as described it amounts
to selling one's birthright for a mess of pottage, and carries

16. In "The Message in the Bottle" (425) Percy defines the uniqueness of the
Christian message—that which distinguishes it rather than which it possesses in
common, say, with Buddhism—as being "not a teaching but a teacher, not a piece
of knowledge *sub specie aeternitatis* but a piece of news, not a member in good
standing of the World's Great Religions but a unique Person-Event-Thing in time."
    17. Carr (ed.), "Rotation and Repetition," 51.
    18. "If a man cannot forget, he will never amount to much." See Bretall (ed.),
A Kierkegaard Anthology, 27.

echoes of the sale of Benjy's pasture to send Quentin Compson to Harvard. Just how valuable the therapy has been to Will is indicated by their probings of his feelings about sex. It is Dr. Gamow's theory "that one's needs arise from a hunger for stroking and that the supreme experience is sexual intimacy" (215), and Will worries about whether a nervous condition can be caused by not having intercourse. Yet in five years he has never told the analyst whether he has had sexual relations with girls: "It was none of his business." Dr. Gamow has an "ambiguous" chair in his office, intended to provide clues from the patient's posture. "It was characteristic of the engineer that he sat in the ambiguous chair ambiguously, leaving it just as it was, neither up nor down, neither quite facing Dr. Gamow nor facing away."

During this final visit Percy shifts the point of view to Dr. Gamow in order to reconstruct the history of their strange marathon:

> For the first year the analyst had been charmed—never had he had a more responsive patient. Never had his own theories found a readier confirmation than in the free (they seemed to be free) associations and the copious dreams which this one spread out at his feet like so many trophies. The next year or so left him pleased still but baffled. This one was a little too good to be true. At last the suspicion awoke that he, the doctor, was being *entertained,* royally it is true and getting paid for the privilege besides, but entertained nevertheless. Trophies they were sure enough, these dazzling wares offered every day, trophies to put him off the scent while the patient got clean away. (31)

It is in the course of the last year that Dr. Gamow has decided his patient is a "Southern belle . . . a good dancing partner, light on his feet and giving away nothing." The Southern belle image is a good one, for the dance Percy presents is hilariously funny once the intellectual perspective becomes clear, and the author is satirizing more than the analysis cult. As Will mimics Dr. Gamow's "mebbe's" and parries the analyst's stereotyped interpretations of his Freudian slips, we catch a glimpse, under the patient's presumably tender epidermis, of the hard-rock Southerner, secure in his inner redoubt, mocking the baffled Yankee. Like Mark Twain's innocents abroad, this innocent is having his fun at the expense of the natives in that strange foreign country, the North.

Inasmuch as a major portion of the novel involves a return to Will's Southern roots, the background Percy gives us on Will Barrett in this first chapter is important. Will comes from a family that has "turned ironical and lost its gift for action," a bit of information that helps to clarify things at times when the author himself seems in danger of becoming swamped in irony. Since Will is identified in the title as the *last* gentleman, it is important to trace the succession of that species and to follow its decline:

> It was an honorable and violent family, but gradually the violence had been deflected and turned inward. The great grandfather knew what was what and said so and acted accordingly and did not care what anyone thought. He even wore a pistol in a holster like a Western hero and once met the Grand Wizard of the Ku Klux Klan in a barbershop and invited him then and there to shoot it out in the street. The next generation, the grandfather, seemed to know what was what but he was not really so sure. He was brave but he gave much thought to the business of being brave. He too would have shot it out with the Grand Wizard if only he could have made certain it was the thing to do. The father was a brave man too and he said he didn't care what others thought, but he did care. More than anything else, he wished to act with honor and to be thought well of by other men. So living for him was a strain. He became ironical. For him it was not a small thing to walk down the street on an ordinary September morning. (9)

Along with the decline of the heroic virtues we recall from Aunt Emily's lectures and know so well from popular mythology, we can see here the insidious growth of hyperconsciousness described by Kierkegaard and Dostoevski.[19] The

19. Compare this process with that culminating in Dostoevski's Underground Man, "the hyperconscious man, who has come, of course, not out of the lap of nature but out of a retort . . . [and] is sometimes so nonplussed in the presence of his antithesis [the man of action] that with all his hyperconsciousness he genuinely thinks of himself as a mouse and not a man" (Fyodor Dostoevski, *"Notes from Underground" and "The Grand Inquisitor,"* trans. Ralph E. Matlaw [New York, 1960], 9–10).

scene almost seems to have been set here for Kierkegaard's
The Present Age.

"As for the present young man," Percy says, "the last of
the line, he did not know what to think. So he became a
watcher and a listener and a wanderer." As the scion of this
distinguished line, he is in a quandary—a peculiarly Southern
quandary, as Percy presents it: "Like many young men in
the South, he became overly subtle and had trouble ruling
out the possible. They are not like an immigrant's son in
Passaic who decides to become a dentist and that is that.
Southerners have trouble ruling out the possible." Whatever
Will's personal idiosyncrasies, Percy clearly intends him to
represent an element in the South. With his *déjà vus* and
his obsession with noxious particles, Will is a post-Faulknerian
Quentin Compson, quartered in the Manhattan YMCA
instead of the Harvard Quad, burdened with the weight of
the Southern past even while he endures the bombardments
of modern urban America.

Will has had a go at Princeton, where he occupied the
same room his grandfather has used in 1910—the same year,
curiously, in which Quentin Compson committed suicide at
Harvard.[20] It turned out to be a "sad business . . . this business
of being a youth at college, one of many generations inhabit-
ing the same old buildings, joshing with the same janitors
who had joshed with the class of '37." Here in this very Percyan
sentence conveying a world view in a few words, we see Will's
temperamental affinity with Binx Bolling. Half a paragraph
later comes an even clearer echo of *The Moviegoer* as Will
groans about his good fortune in good old Lower Pyne: "Here
I am surrounded by good fellows and the spirit of Old Nassau
and wishing instead I was lying in a ditch in Wyoming or
sitting in a downtown park in Toledo."

Will withdraws to New York, where he finds his exile in

20. This coincidence suggests that Quentin, the Compson heir, has since become
a progenitor to the contemporary young aristocratic Southerner, who is now
estranged even from this archetypal figure who so vehemently denied he hated
the South. Where Quentin was decisive enough to drown himself, Will escapes
by forgetting. It is a moot question which shows greater courage.

a landscape bombarded by everydayness and inauthenticity and devitalized by abstraction. Only in ordeal does life revive. Will has the impression that people feel better in hurricanes, a desperate thesis to account for desperate circumstances. The Metropolitan Museum of Art suffers a peculiar malady. Ravenous particles are "stealing the substance from painting and viewer alike"; Will finds the paintings "encrusted with a public secretion." Only the fortuitous collapse of a skylight, which leaves a workman prostrate in front of him, "laid out and powdered head to toe like a baker" in powdered glass, is able to restore the paintings to visibility: "It was at this moment that the engineer happened to look under his arm and catch sight of the Velázquez. It was glowing like a jewel!" The following morning he takes corrective action. Exhausting his bank account, he buys a $1,900 telescope, a German product operating on a "new optical principle," a thing of "magical properties" crafted by "gnomic slow-handed old men in the Harz Mountains. [Its] lenses did not transmit light merely. They penetrated to the heart of things." And his first trial of the instrument confirms what he has suspected, "that bricks, as well as other things, are not as accessible as they used to be. Special measures are needed to recover them." His $1,900 has been well invested: "The telescope recovered them."

Armed with his powerful telescope, and having for five years been, as he tells Dr. Gamow, "an object of technique," Will decides that maybe he should "go over to the other side, become one of them, the scientists."[21] Dr. Gamow is on the right track in asking Will if he intends to become a "see-er"; Will is out to see what there is. After cutting himself adrift from his "alma mater, sweet mother psychoanalysis," he reflects: "I am indeed an engineer . . . if

21. Note the reversal of what Percy said of himself ("From Facts to Fiction," 28) regarding what happened when he had to quit studying the scarlet tubercle bacillus under the microscope and join the patients: "Now I was one of them." It is worth noting, incidentally, that the Greek root of "aesthete," Kierkegaard's category of the noncommitted inhabitant of the aesthetic sphere, means a person who perceives.

only a humidification engineer, which is no great shakes as a profession." But he has deeper plans: "I shall engineer the future of my life according to the scientific principles and the self-knowledge I have so arduously gained from five years of analysis." The irony is almost shrill. What is an engineer, after all, if not a man who manages things objectively, without the mess and bother of one compelled to *experience* his life? In assigning Will Barrett, here in this euphoric state at the end of the first chapter, his permanent designation of engineer, Percy suggests his failing: he wants to *engineer* his life on the soundest "scientific" principles rather than to commit himself to the vexatious and sovereign task of living it.

CHAPTER TWO: A SIGN AT GROUND ZERO

Will's point of departure is his recognition that he cannot "be all men and do everything," that he is "not destined to do everything but only one or two things." Like so many young Southerners, he has "had to know everything before he could do anything," but now he receives a sign. As with the mass of men lost in everydayness, who "do not know what to do and so live out their lives as if they were waiting for some sign or another," he is ready: "If a total stranger had stopped him this morning on Columbus Circle and thrust into his palm a note which read: *Meet me on the NE corner of Lindell Blvd and Kings Highway in St. Louis 9 A.M. next Thursday—have news of utmost importance,* he'd have struck out for St. Louis (the question is, how many people nowadays would not?)" (6).

The instrument of his deliverance is the telescope, a "brilliant theater" of lenses so powerful that it virtually "create[s] its own world." Its magnification is such that he cannot be sure which building the cornice he is observing belongs to; he cannot relate the "insight" to its background. The world of the telescope is a spatial analogue for his own world of time, a thing sharply observed but severely dislocated. He has taken to watching a peregrine falcon that preys on the fat pigeons in Central Park. "Down it would come smoking, at two hundred miles an hour, big feet stuck out in front like a Stuka, strike the pigeons in mid-air with a thump and a blue flak-burst of feathers." Quite apart from the extraordinary vividness with which Percy describes it, this falcon, like Will, is a peregrine—a pilgrim or traveler. We learn later that notwithstanding his vacillation, Will harbors the instinct to plunder women sexually. The falcon has "abandoned its natural home in the northern wilderness and taken up residence on top of the hotel." And Will himself is not so far from the wilderness. His great difficulty, we learn much later, is that for years he has had a "consuming desire for girls, for the coarsest possible relations with them, without knowing how to treat them as human beings" (370). He is a casualty of civilization who cannot resolve this dilemma, cannot "relate" properly; so he withdraws to observe the deadly strikes of his feathered counterpart. The unerring falcon is a good foil for the gentleman-voyeur, foreshadowing with the greatest subtlety an essential part of Will's pilgrimage, his attempt to reconcile these opposing impulses.[22]

The event that is to change his life comes about purely by chance. Loosening the thumbscrew, he lowers the telescope's barrel to the horizontal. A final glimpse catches a woman sitting on a park bench. He reads from her newspaper: "... parley fails." Speech fails, a slogan for the times. Percy's description of the concrete bench is memorable: "A sad yellow 1901 concrete it was, enough to strike a pang to the heart." The Handsome Woman, as Will thinks of her, hides a note in an ornamental scroll of the bench and departs. Will promptly hunts down the note, a love verse, and returns to his vigil. Percy's presentation of Kitty Vaught typifies much in these early chapters:

> His heart gave a leap. He fell in love at first sight and at a distance of two thousand feet. It was not so much her good looks, her smooth brushed brow and firm round neck bowed so that two or three ver-

22. Along with Sutter he also prefigures what Percy in *Love in the Ruins* calls angelism-bestialism.

tebrae surfaced in the soft flesh, as a certain bemused and dry-eyed expression in which he seemed to recognize—himself! She was a beautiful girl but she also slouched and was watchful and dry-eyed and musing like a thirteen-year-old boy. She was his better half. It would be possible to sit on a bench and eat a peanut-butter sandwich with her and not say a word.

To turn Percy's own words against him, he was Will and Kitty "meeting cute"—that is, accidentally, Hollywood style[23]—and rather straining at it. But the conclusion of the passage strikes the authentic Percyan note and we are back on the track: the perfect test of one's "better half," somehow, would be to sit with her on a bench and eat a peanut butter sandwich without saying a word.

The meeting comes to Will as a sign, one that becomes more fateful when he learns that the bench is located exactly at ground zero. It is illuminating to see how Percy prepares for this revelation. Will continues his vigil for a couple of weeks, emerging directly from his night's work in Macy's sub-basement to keep watch for his love, who does not reappear. The land at Nedick's corner, he learns, is the most "valuable spot on the entire earth," recently appraised at ninety dollars per cubic inch. "It gave him pleasure to stand in Nedick's and think about the cubic inch of space at the tip of his nose, a perfect little jewel of an investment." The humor prepares us for a hallucination he experiences recurrently on these mornings:

> Now, as he stood in Nedick's, it seemed to him that the scene which took place before his eyes was happening in a time long past. The canyon of Seventh Avenue with the smoking rays of sunlight piercing the thundering blue shadow, the echoing twilight spaces as dim and resounding as the precipice air of a Western gorge, the street and the people themselves seemed to recede before his gaze. It was like watching a film of bygone days in which, by virtue merely of the lapsed time, the subject is invested with an archaic sweetness and

23. Percy, "The Man on the Train," 485: "When the Bomb falls and the commuter picks his way through the rubble of Fifth Avenue to Central Park, there to take up his abode in an abandoned toolshed à la Robert Nathan, everything depends upon his meeting *her* and meeting her accidentally (or, as they say in Hollywood, meeting cute. . . .)" Kitty obviously is *her*.

wholeness all the more touching for its being exposed as an illusion. People even walked faster, like the crowds in silent films, surging to and fro in a wavelike movement, their faces set in expressions of serious purpose so patent as to be funny and tender. Everyone acted as if he knew exactly what he was doing and this was the funniest business of all. (43)

This remarkable vision is reminiscent of the vision of Long Island with which Fitzgerald concludes *The Great Gatsby*, "a fresh, green breast of the new world."[24] And it parallels Binx Bolling's visit to a dreary "historic site" on the Gulf, which has a far less pungent "smell of history" than a yellowed scrap of newspaper he finds there that recounts a Biloxi election of 1948: "1948. What a faroff time."[25] The *Moviegoer* parallel contrasts chronological with existential time; the *Gatsby* one simply projects the reader back into historical time. The passage quoted above likewise has the effect of suspending our customary time perspective and subjecting the everyday scene to another light. But there is something else involved.

The reference to "lapsed time" is a clue. We have seen the phrase in *The Moviegoer*. Will's hallucination is a "re-enactment of past experience" that isolates the "lapsed time" and permits it to be "savored of itself," unadulterated by events.[26] We can see the scene for what it is. And what do we see? Masses of people surging through the street in a "wavelike movement," jerkily as in silent films, their faces set in "serious purpose" in this scene invested with an "archaic sweetness and wholeness all the more touching for being exposed as an illusion." A very touching illusion indeed; and

24. "And as the moon rose higher the inessential houses began to melt away until gradually I became aware of the old island here that flowered once for Dutch sailors' eyes—a fresh, green breast of the new world. Its vanished trees, the trees that had made way for Gatsby's house, had once pandered in whispers to the last and greatest of all human dreams; for a transitory enchanted moment man must have held his breath in the presence of this continent, compelled into an aesthetic contemplation he neither understood nor desired, face to face for the last time in history with something commensurate to his capacity for wonder" (F. Scott Fitzgerald, *The Great Gatsby* [New York, 1925], 182).
25. Percy, *Moviegoer*, 129–30.
26. *Ibid.*, 79–80.

the "funniest business of all" is that everyone acts "as if he knew exactly what he was doing." What is this illusion, and what does it mean?

What Will sees in his hallucination, I think, is a vision of *modern* life. What invests it with "archaic sweetness and wholeness" is that he is viewing it from a *post*modern vantage point in time. His amnesia, Percy has said, "suggests a post-Christian shakiness about historical time," accentuated by his transplantation to New York City and his night work in Macy's sub-basement; he becomes "almost Oriental in his abstraction from time."[27] Looked upon from this postmodern, post-Christian perspective with which he emerges from his underground redoubt into the light of day, the whole scene has a most illusory and archaic sweetness and wholeness. The view is backward in time to the period before the Western world view had been totally shattered. This modern world had a sweet wholeness about it, illusory or not, even if it was living off the diminishing capital of the Christian faith—"reap[ing] benefit," as Guardini puts it, "from the values and forces developed by the very Revelation" it denies. Authority was still there, beleaguered though it was, and one could be a liberated modern rebelling against superstition even while secure in the warmth of one's faith in "science." Men knew what they were about. From a postmodern perspective, with the "fogs of secularism" dissipated, this world can only evoke the repetitive nostalgia of an old silent film. How quaint that everyone seems to know what he is doing! A funny business indeed!

Will's hallucination is a brilliant phenomenological rendering of future consciousness in which we can see Percy moving ahead in time toward his next novel. Here it foreshadows what Will is about to recognize as a sign. As he continues his vigil the sky grows "more paltry" every day and the raven-

27. Brown, "An Interview," 6–7. Will's disorientation about time is connected, Percy says here, with a theory of Eric Voegelin's in *Order and History* (Baton Rouge, 1956) contrasting the unhistorical cyclical time of Greece and the Orient with historical time, which began with the emergence of Israel.

ing particles bolder. "Museums become uninhabitable. Concerts were self-canceling. Sitting in the park one day, he heard a high-pitched keening sound directly over his head" and looked up "through his eyebrows" only to find that the "white sky was empty." That same night, sitting at his console three stories underground he comes upon something in the Sunday *Times:*

> There on the front page of an inner section was a map of Greater New York which was overlaid by a series of concentric circles rippling out to Mamaroneck in the north, to Plainfield in the south. He picked it up. It was one of those maps illustrating the effects of the latest weapon, in this case some kind of nerve gas. The innermost circle, he noted idly, called the area of irreversible axon degeneration, took in Manhattan Island and Brooklyn as far as Flatbush, Queens as far as Flushing, and the lower Bronx. The next circle was marked the zone of "fatty degeneration of the proximal nephrone," and the third that of "reversible cortical edema." (45)

Seated before the "flickering lights of the console," Will frowns and wonders. "Was it possible, he wondered, that—that 'It' had already happened, the terrible event that everyone dreaded." But no: he smiles and thumps his head; "he was not yet so bad off as to believe that he was being affected by an invisible gas."

Invisible gas, no; but that something has already taken place becomes portentously clear when after ten minutes of studying the map Will's heart gives a "big bump" in his neck: "Like a funnel, the circles carried his eye plunging down into the heart of Manhattan Island to—there, just inside the southeast corner of Central Park; there the point of the compass had been struck while the pen swiveled, there just north of the little amoeba of the Pond. The bench, where the Handsome Woman had sat, was exactly at ground zero" (45). Will's sign emanates from ground zero. That is the starting point for the pilgrimage of this incapacitated pilgrim. His journey will carry him from the hallucinatory postmodern world, which in fact is the present world shorn of illusion, back through the modern world to the South, both new and old, in search of roots and meaning. The sign at ground zero leads him straight to the Vaughts, who will lead him the rest of the way.

Once this action begins, the pace picks up. Will follows Rita, the Handsome Woman, to a hospital in Washington Heights, where he is taken for a member of the staff and promptly runs into Poppy Vaught, patriarch of the clan and owner of the world's second largest Chevrolet agency. The old man is "too fond of everyone"; someone in the family must be seriously ill. The "sentient engineer" catches a whiff of "fresh cotton-and-ironing-board" in the old man's seersucker suit, the "iron-washpot smell" that "no machine in the world had ever put . . . there and nobody either but a colored washwoman working in her own back yard and sprinkling starch with a pine switch." He detects a "lilt in the old man's speech, a caroling in the vowels which was almost Irish." "Excuse me, sir, but are you from Alabama?" he asks, and quickly narrows it down:

> "From North Alabama?"
> "I was." [The old man's] yellow eye gleamed through the smoke. He fell instantly into the attitude of one who is prepared to be amazed. There was no doubt in his mind that the younger man was going to amaze him.
> "Birmingham? Gadsden?"
> "Halfway between," cried the old man, his eye glittering like an eagle's. "Wait a minute," said he, looking at the engineer with his festive and slightly ironic astonishment. "Don't I know you? Aren't you—" snapping his finger.
> "Will Barrett. Williston Bibb Barrett."
> "Over in—" He shook his head toward the southwest.
> "Ithaca. In the Mississippi Delta."
> "You're Ed Barrett's boy."
> "Yes, sir."

In the space of a moment the abstract postmodern world becomes concrete and personal with the intimacy of the Southern community, and this shock of recognition between Southerners in the North galvanizes the action in what has been up to now a very leisurely getting under way.

The encounter dramatizes Will's sentient nature, his keen perception of sense data and the fine receptivity of his "antennae," which pick up the signal through all the static of the words.[28] The fateful magnetism between him and the Vaughts owes something to the manner of their meeting. Percy shifts the narrative point of view to demonstrate how each of the Vaughts in turn takes to Will. He feels himself "molt," under Mrs. Vaught's eyes, from "a Southerner in the North, an amiable person who wears the badge of his origin in a faint burlesque of itself, to a Southerner in the South, a skillful player of an old play who knows his cues and waits smiling in the wings." She immediately recognizes that he is "nice." "There was a lightness in him: he knew how to fool with her. They could even have a fuss."[29] Poppy sees Will as "a stout Southern lad in the old style, wellborn but lusty as anyone, the sort who knows how to get along with older men." Jamie considers him "a fellow technician, like himself an initiate of science, that is, of a secret, shared view of the world, a genial freemasonry which sets itself apart from ordinary folk and sees behind appearances."

Kitty, his love, makes her appearance in a manner reminiscent of Kate in *The Moviegoer*. She is simply there, in the scene around Jamie's bed: "As the engineer looked at [Rita] he became aware of a radiance from another quarter, a 'certain someone' as they used to say in old novels." She is indeed a "certain someone," meaning no one in particular, as we see in Percy's tone: "Again a pang of love pierced his heart. Having fallen in love, of course, he might not look at her." The author encases her in clichés. Something is vaguely wrong with Kitty, as we already suspect from the secret passing of notes, and she feels safe with Will because something—amnesia—is wrong with him too. We get a firmer sense of what is wrong with Kitty as we come to know the woman who is passing her notes, Rita Vaught.

28. Percy usually reserves this highly developed radar to the Negro, who having by necessity been "other-directed" in the past, possesses it to an almost singular degree.

29. Will's chameleonlike mutability serves Percy effectively in such relations and is always convincing. The rather cozy chauvinism that often envelops such situations can become tiresome to an outsider, but even he can recognize, almost touch, this notion of a "fuss." Percy has a gift for such palpability.

Rita comes across as one of the most unpleasant dogooders I have met in fiction. Witness the way she breaks the news about Jamie to Will:

> Rita was smoothing out her skirt until it made a perfect membrane across her thighs. "Our Jamie is not going to make it, Bill," she said in a low thrilling voice and with a sweetness that struck a pang to the marrow.
>
> There passed between them the almost voluptuous intercourse of bad news. Why is it, thought he, hunkering over and taking his pulse, I cannot hear what people say but only the channel they use?
>
> "So it's not such a big thing," she said softly. "One small adolescent as against the thirty thousand Japanese children we polished off."
>
> "How's that?" said the engineer, cupping his good ear.
>
> "At Hiroshima and Nagasaki."
>
> "I don't, ah—"
>
> "But this little guy happens to be a friend of mine. And yours. He has myelogenous leukemia, Bill." (89–90)

Rita is patronizing and meddlesome, and Percy captures it all perfectly in her speech. She is the kind of ally who can damage a good cause more than a dozen enemies. To Kitty she is a saint. "You hear about people being unselfish," Kitty tells Will. "She actually is—the only one I know." Rita knows how to induce guilt, and people are constantly in her debt. "For one thing, Rita has done so much for us, for me," Kitty says, "and we have done so badly by her." The two of them share a "charming cottage in a mews stuck away inside a city block in the Village" where Will is surprised to discover they have "gotten round" the ravening particles by making things "small and bright and hiding them away in the secret sunny center of a regular city block." The relationship is at least latently lesbian, and Rita's jealousy of Will surfaces clearly at times, but this minor theme leads away from the central theme of the book.

Rita, who is Southern-born, can toss around the jargon with the best of the Yankees. Simpleminded Kitty echoes her in explaining that Rita's marriage with Sutter went wrong because Sutter developed "abnormal psychosexual requirements." Will reacts to such talk like a Southern gentleman: "He didn't much like her using the word 'psychosexual.' It reminded him of the tough little babes of his old therapy group, who used expressions like 'mental masturbation' and 'getting your jollies.' It had the echo of someone else. She was his sweetheart and ought to know better."[30]

Will's concern with what it means to be a gentleman is important to the book, as the title makes clear, and influences his decision to return to the South. A scene with Poppy Vaught throws some light on his decision. When Will tells Poppy he is a Presbyterian and went to Princeton, Poppy replies that there is nothing wrong with him. "No sir," says Will, thinking that if there is nothing wrong with him there must be something very wrong with the world. "However, I do have a nervous condition—" he begins. "Nervous!" Poppy breaks in. "Hell, I'd be nervous too if I lived up here with all these folks. All huddled up in the Y in the daytime and way up under a store all night. And peeping at folks through a spyglass. Shoot, man!" This colloquial, commonsense summary of Will's condition establishes a recognizable norm for him: "It mightn't be a bad idea to return to the South and discover his identity, to use Dr. Gamow's expression." He returns to the business maxims he gleans from *Living*[31] and determines to straighten out his life:

> You do things by doing things, not by not doing them. No more crazy upsidedownness, he resolved. Good was better than bad. Good environments are better than bad environments. Back to the South, finish his education, make use of his connections, be a business or professional man, marry a wife and live him a life. What was wrong with that? No more pressing against girls, rassling around in elevators and automobiles and other similar monkey business such as gives you stone pains and God knew what else. What was wrong with a good little house in a pretty green suburb in Atlanta or Birmingham or Memphis and a pretty little wife in a brand-new kitchen with a red dress on at nine o'clock in the morning and a sweet good-morning kiss and the little ones off to school and a good old mammy to take

30. If anyone wanted to make out a case against Percy for misogyny, *The Last Gentleman* would be the place to start. There is no woman in the book who appears in a really favorable light, as Aunt Emily does in *The Moviegoer*. This phenomenon seems to go with a general depreciation of woman in a landscape denuded of good men—as it might be seen by any gentleman who found himself last.

31. *Living* is Will's variation on Binx's "This I Believe."

care of them? The way to see Kitty is not to see her but to see her. (85)

This long passage demonstrates just how entangled Will is in the clichés by which he tries to live. He lacks the irony of Binx Bolling and, living as he does in pure possibility, sees charm in the notion that he might "marry him a wife and live him a life." His problem is how to live. The sign at Ground Zero brings him out of his underground shelter and delivers him into the hands of the clan of Vaught.

Kitty, his "certain someone," is a dud. She may be his "better half," as he reflects upon first sighting her through his telescope, but the novel is good evidence that these two halves do not constitute a whole.[32] Her position is that of a woman in an arranged marriage, someone with whom to perform certain rites during and after the ceremony, with the difference that she is too busy playing inauthentic roles to benefit by the security of such a traditional relationship. The girl who looks so substantial to Will is in reality a shadowy succession of rehearsals for an approved role. The scene in the park, which if anything is more self-conscious than its counterpart in *The Moviegoer*, makes clear how lost she is. Kitty offers herself to Will as The Thing to Do. He responds courteously, knowing her concern for "passing her test," even though she refers to herself in the third person, talks Rita talk ("you big geezer"), and breathes "Dearest" and "My precious" at him in the most nullifying way. The scene has redeeming humor as the "engineer" swings her "forty-five degrees in the dust," and the "cops and the Negroes" shoot it out in Harlem through the whole charade, providing a real, hot-blooded backdrop for this pallid "experiment by Kitty for the benefit of Kitty." The scene is more painful than the episode in *The Moviegoer* because it is dramatized, and Percy demonstrates convincingly that sex functions here as "a symbol of failure on the existential level."[33] "Darling,"

32. Brainard Cheney aptly refers to them as " 'complementary' defectives" ("Secular Society as Deadly Farce," *Sewanee Review*, LXXV [1967], 346).
33. Percy in Carr (ed.), "Rotation and Repetition," 51.

Will says, shaking his head with bewilderment. "Was this it at last, the august secret of the Western world?" It was not. Chalk up two more for the malaise.

The important thing to emerge from this fiasco is Will's intense interest in Sutter. Kitty, now dressed and "hugging her decent skirted knees like a proper Georgia coed," recounts the disintegration of everything the previous summer at Rita's place in Tesuque and Rita's attempt to instill Ahaiyute myths in the young Indian boy Carlos. *"What did Sutter say?"* Will wants to know—in Percy's italics. Sutter's response to everything becomes tremendously important. Kitty feels the real trouble all along between Sutter and Rita is that "Rita did all the giving and Sutter did all the taking. Do you know what he said to me? 'Blankety-blank on unselfishness,' said he. 'I agree with Val and the Christers, it's a fornication of spirit.'" *"Blankety-blank?"* Will inquires. "Crap," Kitty says. *"Don't talk like that,"* he says, and from this point on Will's interest in Sutter intensifies with his belief that Sutter has some secret to tell him. Sutter is the expert who can tell him how to live.

It becomes clearer and clearer that what Will is searching for is a father figure more than a "certain someone." The choice confronting a gentleman comes into focus tentatively in the first of a number of memories in flashback of his own father. The memory is prompted by the warm smells of summer and the discovery of a quotation from Montaigne hidden in the park bench; his father had quoted Montaigne on summer nights. The reader knows the father is dead but has yet to learn he died by his own hand. In Will's memory his father is pacing up and down under the water oaks while the boy Will tends the record player pouring out Brahms from old 78 discs. His father is angry about the whites fornicating in cars on the levee to the west. He continues his lament while the "Great Horn Theme [goes] abroad, the very sound of the ruined gorgeousness of the nineteenth century, the worst of times." The Negroes fornicate, the preacher best of all, he says; but now the whites "fornicate too and in public and expect *them* back yonder somehow not to notice. Then they expect their women to be respected." Each will pick up the worst of the other and lose the best of himself. "One will learn to fornicate in public and the other will end by pissing in the street." The boy listens respectfully. "Go to whores if you have to, but always remember the difference," his father says. "Don't treat a lady like a whore or a whore like a lady. . . . If you do one, then you're going to be like them, a fornicator and not caring. If you do the other, you'll be like them, fornicator and hypocrite" (97).

Will loses the recollection at this point: *"Then what happened after that? After he—"* That is all; memory is blocked out by what follows, but the dilemma is sharply posed: either be a gentleman or be a fornicator, not a gentleman who fornicates. Either the ethical sphere or the aesthetic. Will's effort shortly thereafter to meet Kitty's expectations in the park shows gentlemanly manners enlisted in an ungentlemanly cause. His father was right: Kitty makes a better lady-coed than she does a whore. The chapter ends on a missed connection between Will and the departing Vaughts, an error arranged by Rita which leaves Will standing on the highway in New Jersey with a sign reading "PRINCETON STUDENT SEEKS RIDE SOUTH." In identifying himself as a Princeton student in yet another of his impersonations, this gentlemanly wayfarer reveals just how dislocated he is. He escapes the fallout by thumb-power, heading home.

CHAPTER THREE: LEVITTOWN AND POINTS SOUTH

The third chapter contains Percy's broadest satire to this date and some of the funniest episodes in contemporary fiction. The author hits a new and more resilient stride in the opening paragraph as he describes Will's first ride: "A bottle-green Chevrolet, an old '58 Junebug, passed and hesitated, the driver's foot lifting and the carburetor sucking wind, speeded up and hesitated again. As the engineer watched politely lest he presume upon fortune, the Chevrolet pulled off the highway and sat interestingly on the shoulder a good hundred yards to the south" (119). The driver, a "light-colored high-stomached Negro dressed in a good brown suit," proves to be a white man heading south to crack the "cotton curtain." This man, who evokes recollections of John Howard Griffin, turns out to be Forney Aiken, a name aptly suggesting illicit intercourse. Forney has his conclusions all in readiness, even the title for the book he will write once he collects the proper evidence: *No Man an Island.*

A stop at Forney's stone cottage in Bucks County, Pennsylvania, where he has a "firkin factory" with about eight thousand unsold firkins in residence, brings about a swimming pool romp between Will and the only other young person around, Forney's college-girl daughter Muzh. She talks on and on about the fascinating people in attendance at Forney's party:

> On she went about the guests in her rapid, cataloguing voice, bent toward him, the waterline at his mouth, while he grew even fainter with hunger and more agitated. As her knees brushed against his and she spoke of having transcended Western values, he seized her through the thick parts, fell upon her as much from weakness as desire, fainted upon her, the fine brown berry of a girl she was. "Zut alors," she cried softly, and now perfunctorily, unsurprised, keeping herself flexed and bent away from him, she asked him about the transvaluation of values. (129)

That the humor has a connection with Will's pilgrimage becomes evident when Forney explains to him that Mort Prince's latest novel *Love,* a "deeply religious" book, is by the author's own admission "about —ing." Will groans. "What the devil does he mean telling me it's about —ing? Is —ing a joking matter? Am I to understand I am free to ———— his daughter?"

Mort Prince inspire's Percy's satire. Mort is "our kind of folks," Forney assures Will. His credo is simple: "saying Yes to Life wherever it is found." His novel *Love,* which is delivered to Will in his bed by Muzh wearing a shorty nightgown, is about "orgasms, good and bad, some forty-six," and ends on what passes for a religious note: " 'And so I humbly ask of life,' said the hero to his last partner with whose assistance he had managed to coincide with his best expectations, 'that it grant us the only salvation, that of one human being discovering himself through another and through the miracle of love.' " The satire accomplishes two things here. It demonstrates how such writers can be, like Rita, the thieves of virtue, the "goody-goodies" Confucius spoke of[34] who by occupying defensible positions render them indefensible. And by contrast it heightens the value of being a gentleman.

When Will actually meets Mort Prince he likes him at once, "perceiving that he [is] not the mighty fornicator of his novels but a perky little bull-shooter of a certain style, the sort who stands in the kitchen during parties, suspended from himself so-to-speak, beer can in hand and matter forming at the corner of his mouth, all the while spieling off some very good stuff and very funny."[35] The visit to Mort's place in Levittown provides a good glimpse of Northern neighbors enforcing the American way of life. They fancy themselves to be defending their homes against "block-busting" real estate men. Mort's house, which has a cathedral entrance, serves as a shrine of property rights, which are sacred and segregated, though Mort himself indignantly defends his right to sell to anyone. Things become very sticky until Forney saves the day by showing his white patch, which easily patches over the difficulties. The episode dramatizes a suspicion Percy voiced in 1957 that perhaps "the best imaginable society is not a country-wide Levittown in which everyone is a good

34. "The goody-goodies are the thieves of virtue," Confucius is supposed to have said. Mencius wrote in explanation: "You want to criticize them and they seem so perfect; you want to lampoon them, and they seem so correct; they fall in with the current conventions and thoroughly identify themselves with the ways of the times. In their living, they seem so honest and faithful, and in their conduct they seem to be so moral. Everybody likes them and they are quite pleased with themselves. But it is impossible to lead them into the ways of the Emperors Yao and Hsun." See Lin Yutang (ed.), *The Wisdom of China and India* (New York, 1942), 835–36. The term *hsiangyuan* more nearly means respectable people, Yutang says. Rita is the respectable emancipated female.

35. Presumably any resemblance to Norman Mailer is purely coincidental, though I once spent most of the interval between an Iowa dusk and dawn watching Mailer perform similarly in a kitchen.

liberal ashamed of his past, but a pluralistic society, rich in regional memories and usages."[36] The scene is enough to nourish similar suspicions in any reasonable mind. Mort is still angry on principle: "If there is any one thing that pisses me off, it's bigotry." His anger is "a special delayed Hemingway writer's sort of anger," and it is embarrassing. "This was the age of embarrassment, thought the engineer, of unspendable rage. Who to hit? No one." For Will the time has come to move on.

"Fetching his firkin," he takes his leave. He comes to himself after an amnesic spell one misty morning in Virginia, "experiencing the interior dislocations which always afflicted him on old battlegrounds." Percy simply drops him in the South, in the vicinity of Richmond, which sets Will to musing how Richmond might be today if the war had turned out differently:

> Perhaps Main Street would be the Wall Street of the South, and Broad might vie with New Orleans for opera and theater. Here in the White Oak Swamp might be located the great Lee-Randolph complex, bigger than GM and making better cars (the Lee surpassing both Lincoln and Cadillac, the Lil' Reb outselling even Volkswagens). Richmond would have five million souls by now, William and Mary be as good as Harvard and less subverted. In Chattanooga and Mobile there would be talk of the "tough cynical Richmonders," the Berliners of the hemisphere. (144)

A fine Confederate fantasy, and one with which even a Yankee can empathize after the Levittown encounter. On the author's part it is quite a coup. Percy has left the postmodern and modern worlds behind and leapt back into the past; and through Will's shakiness about time he has jarred loose the hold that history has upon us, rendering the North-South reality fluid and thus revivifying his phenomenological approach as we enter the old Confederacy. The reader is obliged to share this gap in Will's memory. With this final jump Percy has shifted dramatically from the abstracted post-

---

36. Percy, "A Southern View," 429. At first reading, this scene struck me as overdrawn. The news I have heard since that time has persuaded me that Percy's satire is on target.

modern urban world, future-oriented and bombarded by noxious particles, to the nostalgia-laden and immanent South awash in memory.

Will's return to the South is a vital part of the Return, as Percy calls it, the search for an answer to the question, Who am I? Will's Return is a response to the nameless instinct that draws him back to the house of his childhood where he can recover himself. His journey back into the South is accompanied by *déjà vus*, most of them beautifully done, and an often ecstatic rediscovery of the familiar. He overtakes the Vaughts at Williamsburg, where they share a joyous reunion not in Old Williamsburg but in the Coach-and-Four Motel on the outskirts. Will learns how adroitly Rita had cut him from the herd back in New York when Poppy tells him, "Rita said she asked you to come with us and you refused." Rita holds Will off by calling him Lance Corporal, "skirting with him the abyss within himself" in the knowledge that he cannot be sure he did not simply forget the alleged conversation.

The Trav-L-Aire is important. Rita, who owns it, has christened it Ulysses because it is meant "to lead us beyond the borders of the Western world and bring us home" (92). Coming from Rita, such a notion is suspect, and in fact Percy presents the Trav-L-Aire in the most American context. "She was all she might be, a nice balance of truck heaviness, steel and stout below and cabined aluminum lightness above," a well-crafted piece of work like the new school Binx admires in *The Moviegoer*. Inside was the "coziest little caboose imaginable, somehow larger inside than out, yet all compact of shelf, bunk, galley and sink": "Now here surely is a good way to live nowadays, said he and sat down on the firkin: mobile yet at home, compacted and not linked up with the crumby carnival linkage of a trailer, in the world yet not of the world, sampling the particularities of place yet cabined off from the sadness of place, curtained away from the ghosts of Malvern Hill, peeping out at the doleful woods of Spotsylvania through the cheerful plexiglass of Sheboygan" (147). The

Trav-L-Aire combines the best of two worlds. Its true identity stands revealed in the light of what Percy wrote ten years earlier: "The road is better than the inn, said Cervantes—and by this he meant that rotation is better than the alienation of everydayness." Mark Twain hit upon an "admirable rota-tion" in *Huckleberry Finn:* "A man who sets out adrift down the Mississippi had thrice over insured the integrity of his possibility without the least surrender of access to actual-ization—there is always that which lies around the bend. He is, to begin with, the random on the mobile; but most impor-tant, he is on the Mississippi which, during the entire journey, flows *between* states: he is neither in Illinois or Missouri but in a privileged zone between the two."[37] One has only to compare the two quotations to recognize the Trav-L-Aire as Huck Finn's raft on wheels, with a few gadgets to bring it to date.

The Trav-L-Aire affords Will and Jamie the luxury of being able to step ashore when they please and to withdraw as they choose, a beautiful way to sample the wares without buying. This perfect vehicle for rotation combines in Will's case with amnesia, which Percy says is the perfect device of rotation,[38] to provide a truly "privileged zone," the best condition imaginable for a rotation. So for Will the return by Trav-L-Aire amounts to an existential repetition with rota-tional dividends, which amounts to a spectacular circum-stance. From time to time Percy has Will and Jamie "stepping down from the zone of the possible to the zone of the realized," the actualized South.

Sometimes his tone becomes a bit cozy, as in his account of the "complex Southern tactic of assaying a running start, a joke before the joke, ten assumptions shared and a common stance of rhetoric and a whole shared set of ironies and opposites. He was home" (154). One does not have to be a Southerner, presumably, to possess subtlety of mind, and

37. Percy, "The Man on the Train," 484.
38. *Ibid.,* 486.

such passages highlight an occasional contrast between the fiction artist in Percy and the rhetorician. When he is dramatizing, the effect can be awesomely real; when he begins rhapsodizing on the same theme it can go hollow without advance notice. He seldom yields to this temptation that so often undoes Faulkner, and it could be that on occasion the looseness of his third-person narration taps a vein of suppressed orotundity.[39]

Frequently this looseness serves him well indeed. In the Quality Court scene it enables him to present the courting of Will and Kitty with cool detachment. They have been avoiding each other like strangers. Will collides with Kitty one evening at the motel ice dispenser. She fills her pitcher and waits, stooping to see the full moon "through the cloister of the Quality Court." He asks her to go for a walk along the beach. Things are uneasy because Kitty has been clinging to Rita. Each now feels the other has changed. The conversation is forced. Finally, Will tells Kitty he loves her. "Why did this not sound right, here on Folly Beach in old Carolina in the moonlight?" When he kisses her he gets an inkling of what is wrong: "She was too dutiful and athletic. She worked her mouth against his (is this right, she as good as asked). 'Wonderful,' she breathed, lying back. 'A perfect setting.'" The pain of it is almost suffocating. The setting is right; what can be wrong? They are like tourists unhappy in Taxco. The distance Percy maintains is effective here, and he goes on to show the disjunction between Will's expectations of her as a woman and Kitty's expectations of herself:

> If he loved a girl and walked with her on Folly Beach by moonlight, kissed her sweet lips and held her charms in his arms, it should follow that he would be simply he and she she, she as complete as a camellia with her corolla of reticences and allurements. But she, Kitty, was no such thing. Love, she, like him, was obliged to see as a naked

39. Such occasions demonstrate, I think, that Henry James was fallible in his judgment in the preface to *The Ambassadors* that "the first person, in the long piece, is a form foredoomed to looseness." The first-person narration seems to have kept a tight rein on Percy in *The Moviegoer*. Perhaps the third-person here has "foredoomed" him by its looseness to certain excesses.

garden of stamens and pistils. . . . he saw that she was out to be a proper girl and taking every care to do the right wrong thing. There were even echoes of a third person: what, you worry about the boys as good a figure as you have, etc. So he was the boy and she was doing her best to do what a girl does. (160)

That is just the trouble: it should follow but does not. Kitty is no camellia complete with her "corolla of reticences and allurements." The whole scene is a desperately inauthentic playing of roles. To this Southern lady, love has become a "naked garden of stamens and pistils." Even as Will resolves to "court her henceforth in the old style" it seems to be "his duty now to protect her non-virtue" as best he can. Courting among the "quality" in old Carolina has come to this.

When desire catches him "like a mighty wind" back at the water cooler, he takes her into the service room. Immediately the door opens opposite them to disclose Rita, one specter haunting their relationship. "There you are," she says. The chapter ends with a storm, but the description of Will's departure from the scene here strikes the final note: "And off he went, bereft, careening down the abstract, decent, lewd Quality corridor." Sexual roles are as muddled among the Southern quality as anywhere. The malaise is everywhere.

CHAPTER FOUR: THE NEW SOUTH

"The South he came home to was different from the South he had left," the next chapter begins. "It was happy, victorious, Christian, rich, patriotic and Republican." The new South "throb[s] like a diesel," and Will finds it disconcerting despite its impressive happiness:

The happiness of the South was very formidable. It was an almost invincible happiness. It defied you to call it anything else. Everyone was in fact happy. The women were beautiful and charming. The men were healthy and successful and funny; they knew how to tell stories. They had everything the North had and more. They had a history, they had a place redolent with memories, they had good conversation, they believed in God and defended the Constitution, and they were getting rich in the bargain. They had the best of victory and defeat. Their happiness was aggressive and irresistible. He was determined to be as happy as anyone, even though his happiness before had come from Northern unhappiness. If folks down here are happy and at home, he told himself, then I shall be happy and at home too. (178)

This panegyric, even though we know it describes Will's rediscovery of the South, seems a preposterous picture of a society undergoing profound racial turbulence. Is Percy telling it "straight"?

It is easy to conclude that he is, despite the obvious exaggeration. But a closer look at the new South he portrays in the novel shows it to be an impressive façade behind which lie agonizing difficulties. We know that for Percy man is not at home in the world and that for Will to be "happy and at home too" would be delusive, which is why this pilgrim cannot stop here. And the author soon confirms this: "Nothing was wrong, but he got worse anyway. The happiness of the South drove him wild with despair." Percy's best symbol of this new South is the Vaught family residence, a "castle fronting on a golf links."[40] The Vaughts are at home there, where Poppy is rich enough to give each of his children a check with a "row of odd Q-shaped zeroes march[ing] to the east" (80): one hundred thousand dollars, to be precise. "Money is a great joy," as Binx Bolling would say.[41] Still, it is not quite the old South, either. As the football crowd is leaving for the game and the three servants stand waving farewell on the back steps, Lamar Thigpen remarks, "There's nothing like the old-timey ways!" But Percy adds a note: "The Vaught retainers seemed to remind Lamar of an earlier, more gracious time, even though the purple castle didn't look much like an antebellum mansion and the golf links even less like a cotton plantation" (262).

The Vaughts have risen in the world along with this new South, though Mrs. Vaught was already an Episcopalian. One casualty of their ascent in status, Sutter points out, is Jamie, who has never been baptized. The situation dramatizes a

40. Recall Percy's unpublished apprentice novel *The Charterhouse*, in which the country club displaces the cathedral.
41. Percy, *Moviegoer*, 94.

profound conflict of interest. At Jamie's birth, Poppy was a Baptist, and so it was postponed; then Poppy became an Episcopalian too and Jamie's baptism "got lost in the shuffle." It is one thing for the parents to be at home in this purple castle, and another for Jamie, who is going to die. One scene unveils Jamie's predicament. Kitty, Jamie, and Will have been attending classes at the university nearby, but Jamie is sick of it: "I've got to go." He wants to move, to get on the road and out of town.

There is a long scene during which Jamie endures angrily what everyone else is doing, a scene which in the light of his imminent death subjects their everyday lives to a searching existentialist light. Kitty, now a Chi Omega, is excited about the Tennessee game and the Pan-Hellenic dance. Son Junior, a "pale glum fornicator, the type who hangs around the men's room at a dance, patting himself and talking about poontang," is trying to persuade Will to join the Phi Nus and represent the pledge class at their national leadership conference, where the theme will be "Christian Hellenism." Mrs. Vaught runs on about the Bavarian Illuminate, a group representing "European and Jewish finance [that] had sold out the Confederacy" (63). She urges a book expounding this theme upon Will, but in a rather different approach to the fate of the Confederacy, Will is reading a book entitled *R. E. Lee* which keeps him "moving his shoulders in the old body-English of correcting the horrific Confederate foul-ups." Rita busily patronizes Jamie, ruffling his hair, patting him, and calling him Tiger while offering superficial explanations for his ill humor.[42] She suspects it comes from listening to the Thigpens' "infinitely dreary amalgam of Fundamentalism and racism." "What do I care about that? That's not it," Jamie groans, glaring at her angrily. "This is all irrelevant. I just don't care about that." It certainly is irrelevant to him. He

---

42. One of her explanations is that his sister Val, who has become a Catholic, had upset him with her talk of baptism: "a rather stupid Irishman in a black shirt pour[ing] water over his head while uttering words in a dead language" (223). Rita is incapable of grasping anything beyond the compass of her own certainties.

cannot explain what he wants, but Will senses it: "Jamie wants to get away. He would like to spend some time in a new place and live a simple life without the old associations—such as, for example, parking the camper on a stretch of beach."

Jamie announces one morning on the way to class that he wants to "quit school and go out west. Or rather transfer" (237). College has become a bore;[43] he needs to go, and soon. Kitty, who holds the world literature anthology on her lap like a typical college cheerleader and understands its contents equally as well, cannot understand his urgency: after all, the Tennessee game is set for the following day. "I have never in my life," she says when Will makes immediate plans to accompany him. Jamie is not interested in seeing the Tennessee game or in "Chem 2 or 3 or 4"; he knows he will never be a scientist. What follows opens the way for the death scene at the end:

> "I-ah. I just want to take this trip. No, to tell you the truth I'm going to transfer. I've already spoken to—it can be done."
> "Transfer! Where? Where're yall going to live—in the camper?"
> "I know this boy who goes to school in Albuquerque. In fact I heard from him yesterday. I correspond with him quite a bit. I could live with him, in fact." After a moment he added: "His father has a shop of some sort. Out on the highway." (240)

This passage can be read on the plane of religious symbolism, with the boy in Albuquerque as Jesus. For one thing Jamie has settled the question of his "transfer" but neglects—rather pointedly, it seems—to mention with whom he has conferred.[44] And Jamie has been corresponding with this boy—in fact could live with him. Another hint comes at the end:

43. To Will college has "nothing whatever to do with life": "From the anthology there arose a subtler smell, both exotic and businesslike, of the poet's disorder, his sweats and scribblings, and of the office order of the professor and the sweet ultimate ink. By contrast, everything else seemed untidy, the summer past, the ruined garden, one's own life. Their best hope lay in the books themselves, the orderly march of chapter and sub-heading, the tables, the summaries, the index, the fine fat page of type" (192). This passage echoes the theme of Sartre's *Nausea*, particularly Roquentin's description of the ordered library (76).

44. Rita has evidently inquired about this transfer earlier (234), but the author's way of presenting the information makes sense to me only on the basis of such an interpretation.

the father's shop on the highway. Dropping the clue as an afterthought makes the point more subtly, while lending it emphasis. Jamie follows these remarks with an account of a Russian novel he has read that in this context illustrates the power of hope;[45] and as if to underline his own hope he decides to take his Freylinghausen star charts along: "I understand the atmosphere is a great deal clearer in New Mexico."

We are thus prepared for the transcendent move to the Southwest in which the book culminates; but some unfinished business remains, here in the South. For one thing, Kitty has now "arrived." She has become a cheerleader and has found her role. No longer a "changeling," a girl "not absolutely certain of her sex," she is "flushed and high-colored now just because she [has] found out what she [is]—a bride." Will has been ensnared by the Vaughts; and Kitty, who is "house-minded," wants to cage him in Cap'n Andy's house. Percy sums up this package deal in one of his capsule statements: " 'Do you mean you want to come back here and live?' he asked her at last, looking around at the ferny Episcopal woods and the doleful view and thinking of feeding the chickadees for the next forty years."

Will has decided to go with Jamie. If Kitty will come along, fine; otherwise he will share the Trav-L-Aire with Jamie. Then Rita complicates his problem by persuading Jamie to delay his trip, shattering the plan, which by now Will needs almost as much as Jamie. "What he could not tell Kitty was: if I can marry, then you can travel. I can even stand this new horsy conjugal way, this sad poilu love with you, if you will hit the road with me. Jamie is dying, so he needs to go. But I need to go too. Now the pantry's got us, locked in, with a cold potato love, and you the chatelaine, with the keys at your belt" (246). Rita, who wants Kitty for her own,

45. The novel, which Jamie considers the best he has ever read, is about a prisoner crossing Siberia in a crowded boxcar who is miraculously supplied with blueberries and fresh warm milk by peasant women along the route: "even though he knew no one and the train only stopped for a few minutes at a time, somehow news of this young man traveled ahead of the train and they expected him" (241).

knows perfectly well what a threat this "cold potato love" is to Will. He suddenly recognizes the risk as she explains why it is best to "live with" decisions for a while, to see if "perhaps they can be lived with": *"She was daring him.* Very well, said the fine-eyed expression and the quirky (yes, legal) eyebrow. Let us see what we shall see. . . . Let us see if you can do what you say you want to do, stay here and get married in the regular woman's way of getting married, marry a wife and live a life" (250). She forces the dilemma upon him: either be a pilgrim and go off with Jamie, or marry Kitty and feed the chickadees. And Will cannot move to such a decisive act; he cannot choose. In a contest of wills with Rita he is unable to pry Kitty, his "lordly lioness" who has been "turned into a twittering bird-girl with little bitty legs," away from her "teacher." His failing is summed up in Poppy Vaught's comment about some of his "colonels" selling Chevrolets: "They can't close." Nor can Will, who lacks will.

Sutter comes to his rescue. The "faint sexual reek" of the "used, almost comfortable malice" between Sutter and Rita is well evoked as Sutter contends with her for Jamie. Sutter is a pivotal figure in the novel. An assistant coroner who lives in a "relic of the baronial years of the twenties" called the Kenilworth Arms, Sutter is a complicated figure who demands a chapter to himself. His outlook is suggested by his driving an Edsel "to remind him of the debacle of the Ford Motor Company and to commemorate the last victory of the American people over marketing research and opinion polls" (180). It is as if all the dialectical ironies of Percy's books had been concentrated in one man. What Binx and Will perceive, Sutter *enacts.* He carries irony into action. His presence becomes crucial because Will is a good man of curtailed awareness and Sutter provides an alternative view as the novel develops a dual center of consciousness.

Sutter's liability insurance has been canceled since he hit upon a rather Percyan notion: "putting well people in the hospital and sending the truly sick home." The idea has its merits, as demonstrated in the case of an executive who was

"cheerful and healthy and open-handed" and whose only
difficulty was that he could not stop screaming, "his mouth
forming a perfect O" while his children "peep[ed] out from
behind the stereo." Sutter prescribed the terminal ward for
him and in two weeks he was "right as rain." The terminal
ward of course would assure the patient of an appropriate
existentialist shock. The story fascinates Will. But when he
approaches Sutter, his "expert," to ask him whether he has
seen "many cases" of amnesia, Sutter asks: "Do you regard
yourself as a case?" That is the pertinent question, because
in fact what Will hopes to become is just that: "what one
should be" according to psychiatry.[46] Sutter knows that Will
cannot really be helped until he is "Will-ing" to take charge
of his own existence. "I can't help you," he tells Will angrily.
"Fornicate if you want to and enjoy yourself but don't come
looking to me for a merit badge certifying you as a Christian
or a gentleman or whatever it is you cleave by" (216). Sutter
knows his man. No expert can "help" Will by telling him
how to live. That is up to him.

Sutter does help him out of the impasse of the moment.
He tells Will to go to his room and sleep for nine hours.
Something will happen when he gets up that will help him
decide what to do, though he may have a difficult time for
a few days. "Now I shall not tell you what to do," Sutter
says in a kind of posthypnotic suggestion similar to those
Binx gives Kate, "but I will tell you now that you will be
free to act" (261). In effect Sutter puts Will on the road
he must travel alone. Will is to hunt Sutter up, wherever
he is, in case he finds himself in a "tight spot." Sutter's injunc-
tion later proves to be the slim thread that persuades him
to continue his pilgrimage. Will awakes from his deep sleep
to find that Sutter has spirited Jamie away, presumably having
left town to avoid prosecution for hanky-panky with an on-
duty nurse. Will keeps a rendezvous with Kitty to look at
Cap'n Andy's house. His hope has been that they get married

---

46. See my discussion of inauthenticity in Chapter 2.

and head out west to find Jamie, then "park the camper in an arroyo or dry wash and attend the University of New Mexico since there is bound to be such a place"; Kitty's hope is to return to play her role as bride in these "ferny Episcopal woods."

The final scene in this chapter makes another comment on the new South in which Kitty sees her place so hopefully. The night after the Tennessee game they return to the campus to get their books. Something is amiss. Will picks up signals, a "queer greenish light flicker[ing] over the treetops" along with "flat popping noises, unchambered, not like a shotgun but two-syllabled, ba-*rop*, ba-*rop*." As Kitty heads for the Chi Omega house, three men who are not students but look like "the men who hang around service stations in south Jackson" plunge into the woods bearing shotguns. The scene suggests the arrival of James Meredith at "Ole Miss." Will encounters a group of students bearing a flagstaff. Led by Bubba Joe Phillips, one of Kitty's acquaintances, they are bent on vindicating their white manhood. Will Barrett, this last Southern gentleman who in his Princeton days "blew up" a Union monument and is "by no means a liberal, but rather so mystified by white and black alike that he could not allow himself the luxury of hatred,"[47] is caught by the butt of the flagstaff and slammed into the "old pocked Vermont marble" of the Confederate monument. Before he succumbs to unconsciousness, he feels himself at the "dawn of discovery" and, raising a forefinger, asks aloud: "But why is it—?"

The question remains unanswered. The last gentleman seems to have happened upon one of those tribal secrets "closest to one and therefore most inaccessible," which are so absurd when viewed from a state of innocence. This use of Will's forgetting surprises a fine moment as he raises a forefinger in puzzled protest before subsiding into the void.

47. A view of "racial questions" appropriate to a man coming to himself in a strange place as a castaway.

Chapter Five: On the Road to Santa Fe

At this point Will takes his leave of Kitty and sets out on his pilgrimage to the Southwest. We know that as a pilgrim he must somehow do this, but his necessity presents the author with a serious difficulty: how to head Will in the right direction, and do so convincingly, when he is manifestly weak-willed and is now entirely on his own. The artistry Percy brings to this problem is worth looking at. Sutter was right in saying that something would free Will to act, though it is uncertain whether it was the blow on the head from the Confederate monument that freed him or just another fugue. At any rate amnesia is the agent. "What is this place? Where am I going?" Will asks himself, touching his bruised head. "Where am I bound and what is my name?" he groans aloud, sitting on a picnic bench.

Once again we have Percy's castaway, coming to himself with only a bizarre casebook and a map for clues. His reaction, uncolored by memory, to Sutter's casebook is "My God, what is all this stuff?" But the map has a penciled line on it; at least he is "on course." Something tugs at him, "as unfinished and urgent a piece of business as leaving the bathtub running." The author breaks in to comment upon what Will cannot remember: "No wonder he was confused. He had forgotten Kitty . . . and now remembered nothing more than that he had forgotten"; he felt only the "nameless tugging" pulling him back. "But he had also forgotten what Sutter told him the night before—*come find me*—and recorded only the huge tug forward in the opposite direction." Percy uses Will's amnesia to shear away distracting elements and present the simple alternatives. Will decides not to go back because he has been there. "There was nothing to do but go about his business."[48] So he cooks breakfast and hits the road, following the vague instinctive tug of a pilgrim.

---

48. The phrasing echoes Jesus' question to Joseph: "Wist ye not that I must be about my father's business?" (Luke 2:49).

The first item of business, laid out on his map by Sutter, is a visit to Val. The Trav-L-Aire affords him such episodes in much the same way Huck Finn's raft gives Huck glimpses of the Grangerfords and the Phelpses. When he finds her among surplus army buildings in what looks like a "lunar installation," he is still in an amnesic state, memory tugging at him with a "terrific claim," and cannot say her name. Val is feeding entrails to a cooped-up hawk that seems to underline how little her own predatory instincts have been affected by her conversion to Catholicism.[49] As a pilgrim, or peregrine, she is not on the way so much as caged up in herself. But through her fascination with linguistics she has found satisfaction in teaching culturally deprived black children who literally cannot speak because they are brought up in silence. "When they do suddenly break into the world of language, it is something to see. They are like Adam on the First Day."[50] Astonishingly enough, they are receptive to the good news of Christianity: "They believe me. I'm not sure anybody else does now."[51]

In his casebook Sutter accuses Val of canceling herself out. He can accept "the Scandalous Thing, the Wrinkle in Time, the Jew-Christ-Church business," but not the Southern businessman as the "new Adam." "You reversed your dialectic and cancelled yourself"; at least, he says, "have the courage of your revolt." Whatever the merits of Sutter's criticism, Val plays a key role in charging Will with Jamie's salvation. Earlier, at the Vaught castle, she had told him she did not want Jamie dying an "unprovided" death: "I don't want him to die without knowing why he came here, what he is doing here, and why he is leaving." It might fall to Will to tell

49. "That's what I don't understand, you know: that I believe the whole business: God, the Jews, Christ, the Church, grace, and the forgiveness of sins—and that I'm meaner than ever.... I still hope my enemies fry in hell" (289). Her name is ironic: Valentine.

50. "In the joy of naming," Percy says, "one lives authentically" ("Naming and Being," 153). The connection with Percy's writings on language is evident.

51. Sutter predicts in his casebook that after ten years the good news will mean nothing even to Val's "little Tyree dummies" (296).

him about "the economy of salvation." She was concerned about the "guff" Jamie was reading, the "book about radio noise from the galaxies, noise which might not be noise"; it was "usually a bad sign when dying people [became] interested in communication with other worlds" (202). Now she conveys the message to Will that Sutter and Jamie have been there and are headed for Santa Fe. She asks Will to pray for her to receive the grace "not to hate the guts of some people, however much they deserve it," and goes back to her hawk.

Now Will is off again in the Trav-L-Aire, this time heading home, without knowing it, to stand before the house of his father. But first, in a comic interlude, he runs into Forney Aiken and crew, now in trouble in his native Ithaca. Mort Prince had been unable to make the trip, but Forney has the company of a black playwright. Their guitarist friend Bugs Flieger is in jail, and they are in imminent danger of arrest, holed up in the Dew Drop Inn, the playwright incredulous and overjoyed at "seeing life unfold in the same absurd dramatic way as a Broadway play." The moment of truth arrives when two policemen Will knows break in. The cruel one, Beans, snaps Will on the fly with a finger, presumably for complicity with the strangers, and a good repetition results: "Had this happened to him as a boy, getting snapped on the fly? The humiliation was familiar." The incident invokes the spirit of Will's grandfather and father, who had fought the same battles with the same people, and Will, who can never get the straight of things, recovers from his nausea and plants himself solidly: "For once in his life he had time and position and a good shot, and for once things became as clear as they used to be in the old honorable days. He hit Beans in the root of his neck as hard as he ever hit the sandbag in the West Side Y.M.C.A." For once Will does not have to know everything before he can act; he knows enough. And it is a good scene, worthy of Mark Twain, as he sweet-talks his way out of a tight spot with old football-huddle tactics while his companions make their escape in the Trav-L-Aire.

The purpose of his return is not to slug Beans in the neck, and yet the encounter provides a fitting entry to his hometown, for Will has come back to recover himself, and the repetition in the blow he delivers opens the way for the Return as he homes in on the reality he must confront: his father's suicide. "Every man," Percy has quoted Kierkegaard as saying, "has to stand in front of the house of his childhood in order to recover himself,"[52] and the meaning of his act can be either aesthetic or existential: "one, as an occasion for the connoisseur sampling of a rare emotion, the other a question asked literally and seriously: what does it really mean?"[53] In Will's case the question could not be more existential. He has come back to Ithaca because he must fathom the meaning of his father's suicide and somehow deal with it before he can be free to become himself. His amnesia and even his deafness are related to what he is blocking out.[54]

Now the intermittent sieges of memory circle closer to the event as Will, who has become a fugitive in his own hometown, stealthily approaches, under cover of a "moonless overcast night," the scene of his childhood: "He stood in the inky darkness of the water oaks and looked at his house." The house itself is almost unchanged. There they are, the aunts, all six of them, sitting on the porch, "hearty as muzhiks," their husbands "dead and gone these forty years, pegged out so long ago that he could not remember anyone ever speaking of them." Three aunts are watching television, there

52. Carr (ed.), "Rotation and Repetition," 50. Whether or not this accurately represents Kierkegaard—and I have been unable to verify it—the interpretation certainly speaks for Percy.
53. Percy, "The Man on the Train," 490.
54. "Most cases of amnesia," says Lewis A. Lawson, "are caused by an unwillingness to face the present, but to face the present is often to face the past, and the particular homing pattern that Barrett evinces suggests that his primary problem is in accepting something that occurred in his past" ("Walker Percy's Southern Stoic," 22). Percy himself told John Carr: "So Barrett is obsessed with this thing that had happened, his father's suicide. And the whole first two-thirds of the book is going back to this thing that had happened, which actually had shocked him so much he'd almost become a hysteric. He was deaf in one ear" (Carr [ed.], "Rotation and Repetition," 50).

on the front porch of his father's house, and Percy sets the inanities of "Strike It Rich" off in counterpoint against the remembered tragedy of Will's father's death.

The father had long made his nightly stroll under the water oaks because he liked to hear Brahms outside. The boy had felt a sense of dread about the strolls because men had sworn to kill his father. "Do you want them to kill you, Father?" he had asked. "I'm going to run them out of town, son, every last miserable son of a bitch" (228), his father had replied.[55] Will's anxiety surfaces in a scene following this memory as he awakes in the night to "the silence of a time afterwards" (228) and goes into the Vaught castle looking for a room closed off from the rest of the attic, an episode foreshadowing, in Will's recollection, his father's suicide. Now, as Will stands before his house, he recalls the night, just such a night as this, on which his father had killed himself. It had been a "night of victory" on which the father had learned all his enemies had left town. They no longer had to stay: "We haven't won, son," he said. "We've lost." The father scarcely answered the boy's questions; already he was withdrawing into his "wintry kingdom of self."[56] "The mellowness of Brahms had gone overripe, the victorious serenity of the Great Horn Theme was false, oh fake fake. Underneath, all was unwell" (317). "Why do you like to be alone?" the boy asked. "In the last analysis you are alone," his father replied, turning into the "darkness of the oaks." *"Don't leave,"* the boy pleaded, as the man turned into the

55. He is referring to Klansmen and racists, the political descendants of the old Vardaman regime once fought by Percy's great-uncle.

56. The phrase is Percy's, but for its use in this context I am indebted to Lewis A. Lawson's article "Walker Percy's Southern Stoic." The nobility of Aunt Emily and Will's father, Percy says, is the Stoic's "stern inner summons to man's full estate, to duty, to honor, to generosity toward his fellow-men and above all to his inferiors—not because they were made in the image of God and were therefore lovable in themselves, but because to do them an injustice would be to defile the inner fortress which was oneself." This Stoicism did not "wish to survive. Its most characteristic mood was a poetic pessimism which took a grim satisfaction in the dissolution of its values—because social decay confirmed one in his original choice of the wintry kingdom of self" (Percy, "Stoicism in the South," 343).

"darkness of the water oaks." "I'm not leaving, son," the father said. Then, "resting his hand on the other's shoulder so heavily that the boy looked up to see his father's face," he went into the house without saying anything and made his way to the attic with a double-barreled shotgun. "The sound came crashing through the music, louder than twenty Philcos, a single sound, yet more prolonged and thunderous than a single shot. The youth turned off the Philco and went upstairs."

"—and Anacin does not upset your stummick," Bill Cullen says to the aunts watching television on the front porch, as present time intrudes upon his memory.

"Wait," Will thinks, and the word has poignance from the fading memory of his earlier plea: *"Don't leave."* His fingers explore the juncture of iron and bark around the old hitching post. His father was wrong; he was looking in the wrong place. "It was not in the Brahms that one looked and not in solitariness and not in the old sad poetry but"—and here he "wrung out his ear" in a gesture that suggests a throwing off of the hysterical deafness connected with that thunderous crash. He seems on the verge of discovery. Not in the Brahms "but here, under your nose, here in the very curiousness and drollness and extraness[57] of the iron and the bark—he shook his head—that—" But the passage is broken in upon by one of Percy's best encapsulations: "The TV studio audience laughed with its quick, obedient laughter—once we were lonesome back home, the old sad home of our fathers, and here we are together and happy at last."

The conjunction brings a whole world into focus: the desperate inauthenticity of the TV laugh show audience, gone from the "old sad home of our fathers," being soaked up by these tough old women whose men, some of them, had

57. The "extraness" may be related to the "excess" Sartre encounters in *Nausea,* which is one translation of *de trop* (Jean-Paul Sartre, *Nausea,* trans. Lloyd Alexander [New York, 1964], 133). It certainly seems to divide the fact of existence from the "sad old poetry." I hear an echo too of Binx Bolling's discovery that he has been left over from his vertical search.

taken their own lives rather than accept the pass they found themselves in. The meaning of the moment has been captured by Lewis A. Lawson when he says Will must come back "to accept finally the fact that his Stoic father had adandoned him, would not wait for him, did not prepare him for the chaos that is life."[58] His father had in effect abandoned Will for his private solution in the kingdom of self; and until Will has confronted that stark fact he cannot hope to make his way through the droll disorder of his own existence. Will rejects his father's Stoicism, which tells him how to die but not how to live. That is why he is the *last* gentleman; the role is played out. Now he will become a pilgrim.

It is a good occasion for a summation of the present state of things between black and white. Earlier in the novel Percy remarks that the Southerner, who prides himself on knowing the Negro, only "looks at a Negro twice" and in fact knows less about Negroes than about Martians "because he knows that he does not know about Martians."[59] He comments too on "this awful vulnerability" of the blacks. "It's going to ruin us all, this helplessness." The innocence of some like the boy David is unfair to everyone. "They're going to violate you and it's going to ruin us all, you, them, us. And that's a shame because they're not that bad. They're not that bad" (189). Now, in the darkness under the water oaks, a young Negro comes whistling toward Will and stops just short of colliding with him. They look at each other:

> There was nothing to say. Their fathers would have had much to say: "In the end, Sam, it comes down to a question of character." "Yes suh, Lawyer Barrett, you right about that. Like I was saying to my wife only this evenin—" But the sons had nothing to say. The engineer looked at the other as the half second wore on. You may be in a fix and I know that but what you don't know and won't believe and must find out for yourself is that I'm in a fix too and you got to get where I am before you even know what I'm talking

58. Lawson, "Walker Percy's Southern Stoic," 29.
59. In an interview Percy expands on this by saying that almost every Southerner he has ever met claims to know "all there is to know" about Negroes, though he himself does not (Cremeens, "Percy, the Man and the Novelist," 277).

about and I know that and that's why there is nothing to say now. Meanwhile I wish you well. (319)

The white Southern gentleman, descendant of the racial moderate who once was almost the sole champion of the black man's rights in the South, now finds himself in a "fix" the black will have to understand before they can really speak to each other again. It is a painful recognition.

Having rejected the Stoic view, which cannot help him, and the new South, in which he can never be at home, Will is ready for the road. But first there is some unfinished business. He enters his house by the back door and climbs to the attic, to the "windowless interior room," that lofty kingdom of self, where his father had killed himself. Nothing has been touched; the bore of the shotgun is "still speckled with powder grains." He takes a collapsible boat he and his father had used for a duck hunt, has the faithful black cook fix him a big breakfast, and sneaks out before the first aunt comes downstairs in the morning. In the willows alongside the levee he assembles the boat and launches himself into the "privileged zone"[60] of the Mississippi. He glides downstream, neither in Mississippi nor in Louisiana, casting a neutral eye on the reprehensible activities at old Fort Ste. Marie, where civil rights activists are being held prisoner, like Huck Finn observing human malfeasance along the shore.

A visit to Uncle Fannin, the last of his father's generation, completes Will's Southern business and assesses the hope of the "old" South. In a very shut-off place called Shut Off,[61] the old racial ease still obtains but, upon closer inspection, seems to mean mostly that Uncle Fannin and his black subordinate vibrate to the same television programs. Upstairs in his old room, in a grotesque symbol of devotion to death

60. The reference is to Percy's article "The Man on the Train," 484. This episode is Huck Finn raised to the second power, in a sense, a rotation within a rotation, since the Trav-L-Aire is the original raft.

61. Earlier in the novel Percy describes Northerners as "solitary and shut-off to themselves" (177), morose in their victory over the South.

and the old days, Will sleeps alongside a skull that had belonged to his namesake, Dr. Williston Barrett, the "original misfit," who became "the only long-lived Barrett male." Next day he recovers the Trav-L-Aire, this time without Forney Aiken and crew, and is ready to roll.

The final move is to the "transcending Southwest," as Sutter calls it. The atmosphere is truly clearer, as Jamie had anticipated,[62] though the intellectual atmosphere becomes rather dense with ideas from Sutter's casebook, which sometimes rather jams the signal.[63] The casebook actually contributes a good deal if the reader does not stop to puzzle it out as he goes. It is imperative here to cut through to the essentials in this climactic phase of the novel, and I want to bypass the extraneous substance of the casebook and hold to the main line of the novel.

The action of this final phase takes place in and around Santa Fe, which of course means Holy Faith. Sutter's ranch hideout nearby is the "locus of pure possibility," Will discovers, his neck prickling. "What a man can be the next minute bears no relation to what he is or what he was the minute before." And as it happens, it is here in the Southwest that Will is finally to narrow his infinite possibilities and decide to do one or two things instead of all. But Sutter is not at

62. In Willa Cather's novel *Death Comes for the Archbishop*, Father Latour chooses to return to New Mexico from his native France to die. In New Mexico he "always awoke a young man" with a sense of the "light dry wind blowing in through the windows." Cather contrasts that air with the "moisture of plowed land, the heaviness of labour and growth and grain-bearing, [which] utterly destroyed it; one could breathe that only on the bright edges of the world, on the great grass plains or the sage-brush desert." The passage that follows makes an interesting comparison with Percy's treatment of the desert: "That air would disappear from the whole earth in time, perhaps; but long after his day. He did not know just when it had become so necessary to him, but he had come back to die in exile for the sake of it. Something soft and wild and free, something that whispered to the ear on the pillow, lightened the heart, softly, softly picked the lock, slid the bolts, and released the prisoned spirit of man into the wind, into the blue and gold, into the morning, into the morning!" (*Death Comes for the Archbishop* [New York, 1927], 275–76).

63. Percy once explained that the alternative to the casebook was "long Dostoevskian conversations" and he was "damned if [he would] do that" (Brown, "An Interview," 8).

his ranch, and Will locates him in the plaza at Santa Fe, coming out of an adobe Rexall. Will runs after him as Sutter moves on in his dusty Edsel:

> "Sir," said the courteous engineer, trotting along and leaning down to see the driver.
> "What?" But the Edsel kept moving.
> "Wait, sir."
> "Are you Philip?" asked the driver.
> "Eh?" said the engineer, cupping his good ear, and for a moment was not certain he was not.
> "Are you Philip and is this the Gaza Desert?" The Edsel stopped.
> "Do you have something to tell me?" (345)

Sutter's reference is to Philip the evangelist, who encountered the eunuch in Gaza and gave him the good news of Christ's coming.[64] We will soon see in just what sense Sutter is a eunuch and what news Will has for him.

Will's first duty is to be a faithful companion to Jamie, whose death is imminent. Percy's medical experience comes into play in this section, with its officious nurses and cavalier interns, and he captures perfectly the sustaining illusions by which we manage ultimate questions. Death seems far off as Will plays cards with Jamie. "How can anyone play a six of clubs one minute and die the next?" For several days they play: "It was understood that the universe was contracted to enclose the two young men. If it can be kept so, Jamie as good as said and the visitor agreed, a small sunny corner where we can play a game and undertake small tasks, nothing very serious can go amiss. . . . Time disposed itself in short tolerable stretches between the bright beads of the games" (351). Or sometimes Jamie prefers to be alone with his book: "The book was the safest sunniest most inviolate circle of all."

We know this inviolate circle will soon be broken in upon, but before that happens there are matters to be taken up between Will and Sutter. Sutter has arrived at a dead end

---

64. The story is found in Acts 8:26–39. Philip baptized the eunuch and went on to spread the good news until he arrived at Caesarea.

in a dude ranch on the road to Albuquerque. "We are doomed to the transcendence of abstraction," his casebook says. Sutter defines transcendence as the self-abstraction that can take place in science, elevating a person to "a posture over and against the world," which is thereby "demoted to immanence" (331). From his orbit of abstraction the only reentry he can find into immanence is sexual, which is why he is a "pornographer." "But entry doesn't avail: one skids off into transcendence."Sutter is in fact a eunuch because he is locked into his own egocentrism, as Marcel calls it; he cannot initiate the call to another that can bring about a true transcendence through intersubjectivity.[65] Intellectually he can see everything but his own failing. He cannot escape his imprisonment.

Will Barrett suffers an equally pernicious form of abstraction. The layman dispossessed by science is trapped in abstraction without realizing it. This is "something psychologically even more portentous," Percy has written, than the technological transformation of the world by science: "the absorption by the layman not of the scientific method but rather the magical aura of science whose credentials he accepts for all sectors of reality." In the lay culture of a scientific society nothing is easier than to "fall prey to a kind of seduction which sunders one's very self from itself into an all-transcendent 'objective' consciousness and a consumer-self with a list of 'needs' to be satisfied."[66] Sutter knows the phenomenon but Will does not. Sutter says of Will in his casebook that "his posture is self-defeating": he "wishes to cling to his transcendence and to locate a fellow transcender (e.g., me) who will tell him how to traffic with immanence (e.g., 'environment,' 'groups,' 'experience,' etc.) in such a way that he will be happy. Therefore I will tell him nothing" (339). Will is denied grace because he has abdicated himself. He has learned to view himself objectively.

65. Transcendence as I interpret it is not into abstraction, which is closed, but out of it, through the portal of one's unique self into the openness of the intersubjective communion—whether with God or with other men.

66. Walker Percy, "Notes for a Novel about the End of the World," *Katallagete*, (Winter, 1967–68), 12.

Will never does grasp this difficulty of his, but he recognizes that he cannot forever drift along on pure possibility. His recognition takes place after a two-hour phone call to Kitty in Alabama and is dramatized on the front porch of Sutter's dude ranch cottage. Will has been in touch with Kitty by telephone and decided to go back to Alabama. He will marry Kitty and become personnel manager for Poppy's Chevrolet agency. Will informs Sutter of his decision and in what amounts to a litany he spiels off a list of clichés that Binx Bolling has treated with irony:

> "It is better to do something than do nothing—no reflection, sir."
> "No reflection."
> "It is good to have a family."
> "You are quite right."
> "Better to love and be loved."
> "Absolutely."
> "To cultivate whatever talents one has."
> "Correct."
> "To make a contribution, however small."
> "However small."
> "To do one's best to promote tolerance and understanding between the races, surely the most pressing need before the country."
> "Beyond question the most pressing need. Tolerance and understanding. Yes." (369–70)

The "contribution, however small" is word-for-word what Nell Lovell says in *The Moviegoer*, and it is as if Binx were standing in Sutter's place, the echoes are so strong. I do not detect irony here. Will after all has been living in pure possibility. This recipe is at least concrete, and whatever his means of livelihood, it is his calling that matters. A pilgrim will encounter obstacles on any road.

The "moment of his first astonishment" lies just ahead. Sutter, whom Will comes to see as the "dismalest failure, a man who had thrown himself away," is at the end of his road. Having rejected the first two courses, "living like a Swede" or "as a Christian among Christians in Alabama,"[67]

---

67. Rather similar to the alternatives Kierkegaard spelled out in *Either / Or*—the aesthetic or the ethical—though it is an open question whether Sutter even envisions the possibility of moving to the religious sphere himself.

he is going to opt for the remaining alternative: "to die like an honest man." When Will fails to understand him, Sutter demands irritably: "What in Christ's name do you think I'm doing out here? Do you think I'm staying? Do you think I'm going back?" This moment of astonishment marks the beginning of Will's normal life: "From that time forward it was possible to meet him and after a few minutes form a clear notion of what sort of fellow he was and how he would spend the rest of his life." He has been jarred out of pure possibility.

Jamie's death is described in realistic detail in an extended scene of indelible power. Will is unprepared for death without the presence of women to cushion him from its reality, and Percy shows him reacting with a well-conditioned modern mentality: "It was the shame of it, the bare-faced embarrassment of getting worse and dying which took him by surprise and caught his breath in his throat. How is this matter to be set right? Were there no officials to deal with the shame of dying, to make suitable recompense?" Val, whose presence is felt, charges Will again by telephone with seeing to Jamie's baptism; it is his "unprovided death" that concerns her. And Sutter has still another concern. He had become depressed last summer upon first seeing Jamie's blood smear, "depressed not because he was going to die but because I knew he would not die well, would be eased out in an oxygen tent, tranquilized and with no sweat to anyone and not even know what he was doing" (358). Where Will would mask the fact of death itself, Val is concerned with the administration of sacraments and Sutter with Jamie's dying his own death, aware of what is happening.

Unless one takes an orthodox Catholic position (I am not competent to do so), it is difficult to know in just what sense Jamie is "saved." One interpreter sees the ending simply as "the drama of Jamie's redemption."[68] To me the administra-

68. Michel T. Blouin, "The Novels of Walker Percy: An Attempt at Synthesis," *Xavier University Studies*, VI (1968), 40.

tion of sacraments alone hardly satisfies the demands set up in the novel, and the evidence is rather mixed. We have an umpirelike priest administering baptism from a "clouded plastic glass" and holding Jamie's hand while awaiting his death with a "workaday five-o'clock-in-the-afternoon expression," which may stress the centrality of the rite over the instruments but is hardly a flattering view of the priest. We have the derisive brother standing by, denying Jamie the intravenous fluids that might prolong his life a few days, holding him strapped to the bed with a sheet as he draws his last breaths. And we have the innocent Will, who does not grasp what takes place but is able to interpret Jamie's last garbled words, even though he does not "know how he knew." Jamie certainly is in need of news relevant to his predicament, in Percy's terms from "The Message in the Bottle." Jamie seems to accept the credentials of the newsbearer, though he pulls down the corners of his mouth in a "sort of ironic acknowledgment" when the priest says Jamie should know the message is true because he, the priest, is here to tell him. A "Holsum bread" truck passes under the street light at this moment. As to the possibility of the news, Percy's third canon of acceptance, that is for each to judge for himself. The possibility can only be accepted by faith, as Kierkegaard defined it, as a movement by virtue of the absurd.

We might recall that earlier in the novel Will felt "it didn't make much difference, even to Jamie, whether he lived or died—if one left out of it what he might 'do' in [those] forty years, that is, add to 'science' " (231). Before he set out on this last journey, Jamie lived in self-abstraction. Now, at his death, he enters his life fully. Perhaps having made the leap of faith, he receives the repetition. It is well to remember Percy's statement that trial cannot be "re-presented" in literature; "Job's and Abraham's trial are lost in the telling."[69] And Kierkegaard insists that the sphere of religious transcen-

---

69. Percy, "The Man on the Train," 480.

dence cannot be grasped from the sphere of immanence. Perhaps Will's gift for transmitting garbled messages he cannot understand suggests a signal coming through. However we interpret this scene, it is clear that Jamie becomes a *sovereign* wayfarer, aware of his own death and in charge of his life.

Will and Sutter remain. In a sense each is incapacitated, Will by his veneration of the experts, Sutter by his inability to break out of egocentrism. What are we to make of the ending? The clue is in Sutter's quip about Philip in Gaza. The previous summer, shortly after he had learned of Jamie's illness, Sutter had taken Jamie camping in the desert, where they became lost for four days. The canteens were found "mysteriously emptied" (175) and they escaped only because a plane spotted them by chance.[70] Val had seen the ordeal as a religious experience. If we consider that Sutter emotionally has become a eunuch, we can speculate that he fled to the desert this time not only to let Jamie experience his own death but also in the hope that some kind of good news might yet reach him through the agency of Will—some fourth possibility to add to the alternatives with which he was to astonish Will. What kind of news could he expect to hear from Will?

Will is a witness to Jamie's death and salvation, but a witness in the objective sense, not as one in whom an event takes place but as an onlooker. He knows something is happening but cannot figure it out. As Percy says, he *misses* it.[71] The pilgrim misses the import of another's pilgrimage; it is the derisive Sutter who knows what is taking place. Will misses it because as a good postmodern he has eliminated Christianity from consideration. As Percy remarks, "That is gone. That is no longer even to be considered."[72] Will is the cat

70. If this account Rita gives is accurate, the possibility looms that Sutter had emptied the canteens in the hope of finding a religious exit for himself while assisting in Jamie's salvation.
71. Carr, "Rotation and Repetition," 51.
72. *Ibid.*

in Percy's cartoon who has run off the cliff and finds himself standing in air.[73] The Christian alternative is more obsolete to Will than Sutter's Edsel in a world of glittering Chevrolets. The irony of the ending is that the evangelist is without evangel—good news. Then what message can he possibly have for Sutter?

The epigraph from Romano Guardini suggests an answer. The modern world is coming to an end, and the postmodern world, with the fogs of secularism lifted, will be "filled with animosity and danger." "Love will disappear from the face of the public world, but the more precious will be that love which flows from one lonely person to another." The doctor in the case has a more desperate need than his patient. The ending dramatizes the reality. Sutter turns back. Will cannot read the signs or hear the message but he carries the good news of love; he can initiate the call. And Sutter still has some capacity to respond; he waits in his "fake Ford" as Will comes bounding after him with his "final question." His "I'll think about it" is a major concession.

One reason Sutter turns back in response to Will's expressed need may be that Will finally shows some sign of shouldering the burden of his existence. Perhaps he Will Bear-It. If he leaves off calling the experts of the world "sir," there is a possibility he may yet become sovereign. In the end, as the strength "flowed like oil into his muscles and he ran with great joyous ten-foot antelope bounds" after the waiting Edsel, like Philip after the eunuch in his chariot, he was bearing a kind of good news. Maybe he can survive the hazards of promoting Chevrolets in Poppy's agency and feeding the chickadees with his certain someone. We have to give him an outside chance, for up to now Will's whole life has been a postulate to him, the good news a tune played to the deaf. Perhaps the grace of inwardness will now enter his life and he will hear.

73. Percy, "The Culture Critics," 250. See the discussion of man as wayfarer in Chapter 2.

It is a long way from Ground Zero to Santa Fe, and there is no resting place yet. We cannot be sure that Sutter has really turned back, or that Will's hope will not become mired in the "ferny Episcopal woods" of Alabama. All we know for sure is that the engine is running.

5

The Ruins of Consensus

Percy's third novel is his most ambitious and demands consideration as a major work. In his earlier novels he probes the malaise intensively or traces a pilgrimage from the dislocated postmodern world back into the ancestral past and on to a transcendent timelessness. But times have gone from bad to worse all the while, and Percy, surveying the ruins-in-the-making of contemporary America, now leaps boldly into futuristic satire. What he attempts in *Love in the Ruins* is a comic synthesis of modern thought, like Dante's comedy in his time,[1] and one addressed to the realities of the day. Its scope extends to the borders of the republic and beyond. Like Dante he writes in the aftermath of an Event, but in this case the Event is followed by an Eclipse. The landscape of *Love in the Ruins* lies deep in the shadow of that Eclipse, in the eerie twilight of a double vision that it will be my task to bring into focus. In such a complex book it is easy to become lost. My aim here is to make out the principal guideposts and thereby keep to the way.

Love in the Ruins is Percy's most comprehensive diagnosis of the malaise. Underlying the novel is a question that has haunted the minds of many: how to account for the "mon-

1. Percy described his intention to me in almost these words. His impression, based on the novel's reception, was that the comedy had succeeded but the synthesis had failed. Personally I think it is too early to judge.

strousness which the twentieth century let loose upon the world," as he once put it, "not the bomb but the beastliness"? Or to narrow the question as Percy does, "why does humanism lead to beastliness?"[2] The novel suggests some answers. If we contemplate the scene he lays before us, we can see that his figures languish in the ruins of a consensus. "The terror that confronts our age," says the anthropologist Loren Eiseley, "is our own conception of ourselves."[3] And it is just such an urgency—our conception of ourselves—that informs Percy's novel, the ruins of which are built on what he has referred to as a "consensus anthropology."[4]

This consensus anthropology gives *Love in the Ruins* a blurred background that often lends it a peculiar comic quality. An example should clarify what I mean. In the climactic showdown in The Pit, midway in the novel, Dr. Thomas More, Percy's narrator, meets Dr. Buddy Brown in a contest for the welfare of an old man named Mr. Ives. The patient has gone mute and taken to antisocial acts such as defecating on Flirtation Walk in the Senior Citizens Settlement. He sits in his robe, "head jogging peacefully, monkey eyes gone blank," while his fate is being decided. Dr. More's status is ambiguously patient-staff, since he has yet to be officially released from the mental hospital to which he voluntarily committed himself. While Dr. More admires the beauty of his own hand and the medical students in the amphitheater contribute whoops and yells to the proceedings, Dr. Brown makes the conventional case for shipping Mr. Ives off to the Happy Isles Separation Center for a painless termination. Buddy Brown reads from the medical chart:

" 'Despite extensive reconditioning in the Skinner box, the patient continued to exhibit antisocial behavior. This behavior,' " Buddy hastens to add, " 'occurred before his stroke last month.' "

2. Walker Percy, "Hughes's Solipsism Malgré Lui," *Sewanee Review*, LXXII (1964), 492, 495. This is a review of Richard Hughes's *The Fox in the Attic* (New York, 1962).
3. Loren Eiseley, "The Uncompleted Man," *Harper's*, CCXXVIII (1964), 54.
4. Walker Percy, "Walter M. Miller, Jr.'s *A Canticle for Leibowitz*," in David Madden (ed.), *Rediscoveries* (New York, 1971), 264.

"If he had a stroke," I say.

"If he had a stroke," Buddy allows gravely. "Well, Doctor?"

"Well what?"

"What would you do with him?"

"Discharge him."

"To suffer another thirty years?" asks Buddy, smiling. "To cause other people suffering?"

"At least he'd have a sporting chance."

"A sporting chance to do what?"

"To avoid your packing him off to Georgia, where they'd sink electrodes in his head, plant him like a carrot in that hothouse which is nothing more than an anteroom to the funeral parlor. Then throw the Euphoric Switch—"

"Doctor!" interrupts the Director sternly [as he looks on].

"Aaah!" The students blush at the word *funeral*. Girls try to pull their dresses down over their knees.

Buddy flushes angrily.

The Director is angrier still.

"Doctor!" He levels a quivering finger at me, then crooks it, summoning me. Craning down, he croaks into my ear. "You know very well that the patient is present and that there is no guarantee that he cannot understand you."

"Excuse me, sir, but I hope—indeed I have reason to believe—that he does understand me."[5]

What accounts for the humor of this passage? Do we detect anomalies in the proceedings, or is everything quite in order?

If everything is as it should be, then Percy is too late and we have already arrived at our destination in the strange new world he paints for us. But if we still have eyes to see, what we see here is blurred, "a double vision of man," to use Percy's phrase, "like watching a ghost on TV."[6] Note the general response in the amphitheater. No one seems shocked at the prospect of exterminating an old man who is no threat to anyone; propriety consists in not speaking plainly about it in his presence. The obscenity is not in the act but in the unmasking of it. Aside from the embarrassing presence of the old man himself, the only discordant note is struck by Dr. More, who insists the patient know what fate is being prepared for him. What we have is a war between

5. Walker Percy, *Love in the Ruins* (New York, 1971), 224. Subsequent page references will be given in the text.

6. Percy, *"A Canticle for Leibowitz,"* 265.

conventional propriety and the bizarre notions of an eccentric psychiatrist on "patient-staff" status who insists on flouting convention.

A closer look at this conventional propriety gives rise to "eerie neck pricklings," as Percy once described his response to a science fiction novel.[7] The Director who presides over convention here is a behaviorist, like Buddy Brown, both of them scientific humanists who insist on the supremacy of human values. "Tom, you and I don't disagree," Dr. Brown tells Dr. More before the encounter, and as Dr. More listens skeptically Dr. Brown runs through his litany: what counts is the "quality of life," the "right of the individual to control his own body," above all "a man's sacred right to choose his own destiny and realize his own potential." They both "believe in the same things, differing only in the best way to achieve them" (197–98). What Dr. Brown recites is the consensus anthropology of which Percy has spoken, which he says might be called "the Western democratic-technological humanist view of man as higher organism invested in certain traditional trappings of a more or less nominal Judaeo-Christianity."[8]

Juxtapose Dr. Brown's views with what Percy has written elsewhere about the "standard intellectual baggage" most of us carry:

> Do you really mean that God made man in His image? Well, hm, it is a manner of speaking. If He didn't and man is in fact an organism in an environment with certain needs and drives which he satisfies from the environment, then what do you mean by talking about the "freedom and sacredness of the individual"? What is so sacred about the life of one individual, especially if he is hungry, sick, suffering, useless? Well, hm, we are speaking of "values"; we mean that man has a sacred right and is free to choose his own life or, failing that, a creative death. And suppose he is incompetent to do so, may we choose it for him? Well—[9]

Quit stalling, Percy seems to say. It is one or the other: either

7. *Ibid.*
8. *Ibid.*, 264.
9. *Ibid.*

a child of God, free and sacred, or an organism in an environment, whose sufferings can be terminated with impunity.
It cannot possibly be both. And the "eerie neck pricklings"
one often feels in reading *Love in the Ruins* arise when the
incoherence of this consensus is revealed. Percy has set out
to destroy the middle ground of the consensus; he wants
to sharpen the focus. Either / or, in effect: you cannot have
it both ways.[10]

The instrument of his explorations is Dr. Thomas More,
the eccentric "patient-staff" narrator, who flouts propriety
by uttering words like *funeral* in public places. And just as
The Last Gentleman moves into territory foreshadowed in *The
Moviegoer*, the stark landscape of personal death, *Love in the
Ruins* moves on to explore terrain tentatively staked out in
The Last Gentleman, the land that lies in twilight under an
Eclipse, plagued by the modern Black Death of the spirit.
But Dr. More is no Will Barrett, disoriented and unable to
assemble the pieces of his world. He is quite clear on what
is what, and his diagnosis shows the monstrousness loosed
upon the world by the twentieth century to be rooted in
a strange new malady.

The condition he finds is a rift in the humanity of men.
He calls it More's syndrome: "chronic angelism-bestialism
that rives soul from body and sets it orbiting the great world
as the spirit of abstraction whence it takes the form of beasts,
swans and bulls, werewolves, blood-suckers, Mr. Hydes, or
just poor lonesome ghost locked in its own machinery" (383).
The rift involves more than the traditional mind-body split,
as I will undertake to explain. What we must keep in mind
is the narrator's identity, for the novel has numerous literary

---

10. Percy has confirmed to me—if the novel were not enough evidence—that
it was his intent to destroy the middle ground. He explained to an NBA press
conference that he set out to rock the boat until it swamped: "I wanted to explore
how the boat could go under while we are still using words like 'the dignity of
the individual' and 'the quality of life.'" The meanings of such words have slipped
their moorings. "It is the job of the satirist to detect these slips and to exaggerate
them so that they become known to everybody" ("The Authors That Bloom in
the Spring," *Publishers' Weekly*, CXCIX [1971], 23).

and mythic parallels to confound the unwary, most conspicuously a suburban Paradise that is unspeakably lost and a Faustus who does more than wonder at unlawful things. The parallels are by turns amusing, illuminating, and exasperating; they cannot bear the weight of the novel. The key lies in the loyalties and allegiances of a latter-day Thomas More.

Dr. Thomas More, collateral descendant of the original, presides over Percy's comic synthesis. Unlike his distinguished forebear, Percy's narrator is not projecting Utopia but fighting a rearguard action against it. Like Sir Thomas he refuses allegiance to the new order: that is the central fact in the novel. Dr. More challenges a consensus anthropology that draws its rhetoric from one source and its operating assumptions from another. His loyalty is to a conception of man that goes back through Marcel to More and Aquinas: *homo viator*, or man as wayfarer. In the sixteenth century, the time of Thomas More, says Hallett Smith, man occupied a unique position: "God had made three kinds of creatures: the angelical, who were pure intelligence; the brutal, who were pure 'sense' or instinct, without 'discourse of reason'; and the human, who had some attributes of both." Man's position midway between angel and beast was precarious. He could ascend gradually to the angelic level, but since the Fall it had become more likely that he would incline toward the condition of beast. "There was available to him, however, Divine Grace, by means of which he could, if he would, reverse the effects of the Fall."[11]

The novel describes a new Fall in which man has become lost to himself, even to his sins. It takes place in the twilight of an Eclipse that will be discussed presently. Dr. More has invented an "ontological lapsometer," a device to measure the depth of this new Fall scientifically. With the aid of his lapsometer he can diagnose and even cure the ills of man— psychological, political, philosophical. The lapsometer thus

11. Hallett Smith, "The Sixteenth Century: Man and Society," in M. H. Abrams and others (eds.), *The Norton Anthology of English Literature* (rev. ed.; New York, 1968), 401.

becomes the key to Percy's synthesis. His chief diagnostician is the middle-aged psychiatrist Dr. Thomas More. Since the doctor's diagnosis must stand or fall on its own merits—and because I feel more comfortable doing so—I will refer to Dr. More simply as Tom. And with that introduction we are ready for a look at the novel to see what is what in Paradise after the new Fall and what forms of grace are available to those destined to become its exiles.

THE POLARIZATION OF PARADISE

The novel opens on the Fourth of July as Percy jumps directly into the middle of the action. But the USA whose birth is commemorated on this day is neither the New Canaan envisioned by the early Puritans nor the shining republican haven for the Rights of Man, but a decaying mock-Paradise beginning to sprout vines. Something awful has gone wrong. "Undoubtedly something is about to happen," Tom informs us at the outset. "Or is it that something has stopped happening?" Is it that God has removed his blessing from the USA or simply that our luck has run out? Either way, that "felicitous and privileged siding" so long and joyously occupied by the United States of America is no more; the clanking old historical machinery of the "roller-coaster" chain has taken hold and now carries us "back into history with its ordinary catastrophes." Tom More, still another of Percy's castaways, comes to himself in these "dread latter days of the old violent beloved U.S.A. and of the Christ-forgetting Christ-haunted death-dealing Western world" and asks himself if it has happened at last. Carbine across his lap, he occupies the southwest cusp of the cloverleaf on a decaying interstate, surveying the ruins of our civilization.

That is the predicament into which Percy drops us in his opening pages. He moves along at a good clip, alternating present action with accounts of the recent past and with Tom's personal confessions and judgments and his prophecies uttered in the spirit of John the Baptist. Given the pace of the narrative, we need to get the lay of the land before we proceed.

The geography of this fallen paradise reveals its underlying divisions. On the extremes lie the town and the swamp. The town where Tom maintains an office has become a refuge for "all manner of conservative folk, graduates of Bob Jones University, retired Air Force colonels, passed-over Navy commanders, ex–Washington, D.C., policemen, patriotic chiropractors, two officials of the National Rifle Association, and six conservative proctologists" (16). To this culture the Honey Island Swamp is counterculture, a vast wilderness serving as both refuge and guerrilla base for "forays against outlying subdivisions and shopping plazas." Where the population of the town is ideologically homogeneous, the inhabitants of the swamp are a wild aggregation of the disaffected; and as Percy calls the roll the authentic kaleidoscopic color of our contemporary culture is on parade: "Bantu guerrillas, dropouts from Tulane and Vanderbilt, M.I.T. and Loyola; draft dodgers, deserters from the Swedish army, psychopaths and pederasts from Memphis and New Orleans whose practices were not even to be tolerated in New Orleans; antipapal Catholics, malcontented Methodists, ESPers, UFOers, Aquarians, ex–Ayn Randers, Choctaw Zionists who have returned from their ancestral grounds, and even a few old graybeard Kerouac beats, wiry old sourdoughs of the spirit who carry pilgrim staffs, recite sutras, and leap from hummock to hummock as agile as mountain goats."

Between these two extremes lies that "oasis of concord in a troubled land" where Tom makes his home, Paradise Estates. In Paradise conservative Christian businessmen live peacefully alongside liberal unbelieving scientists. They grumble of "atheism and immorality" or "outworn creeds and dogmas," respectively, but there is little difference. Conservative housewives, picking up their faithful black mammies in Happy Hollow, carry them in the back seat, old style, while liberal housewives require theirs to ride alongside of them in front. Both agree that other blacks are mostly trifling and no-account. Northerners by now outnumber Southerners, equaling them in enthusiasm for mint juleps and hushpuppies. Readers who know Percy will recognize Paradise Estates as a haven for the despair which is unaware of itself. This paradise is no melting pot, but the mushy suburbia of modern society. Between town and swamp it lies, this oasis; between the orthodox and the disaffected, a sweet concord of the unaffected. Everything is either polarized or pulped.

Still there is "hope," for just beyond the hump of the interchange where Tom keeps watch is Fedville, the federal complex that stands as a monument to man's resolve to better his condition. Its monoliths house the hospital and medical school, NASA, the Behavioral Institute, the Geriatrics Center, and the Love Clinic. Fedville is the latter-day Crystal Palace to which Tom is destined to play Underground Man. The presiding spirit is that of B. F. Skinner, with his enlightened behaviorism. It is Skinner's new order, more than anything else, to which Tom refuses allegiance, and it is here at Fedville that this latter-day Thomas More is fated to undergo his public trial.

This brief sketch of the novel's geography should make clear that the southwest cusp of the interstate alongside a ruined motel is a more fitting place for the modern wayfarer than the false paradise Tom has left behind. We can reenter the landscape at that point now as the novel gets under way.

"Two more hours should tell the story," Tom remarks in the second paragraph, coming to himself as Percy introduces an element of plot interest in this most suspenseful of his novels. "One way or other. Either I am right and a catastrophe will occur, or it won't and I'm crazy. In either case the outlook is not so good." A strange predicament, on this late afternoon of the Fourth of July. Is the end of the world at hand? Why is the narrator sitting here in a pine grove? *Three* girls? Why the wacky tone if catastrophe looms and God has removed his blessing from the USA? The first page raises these questions; and Percy, juggling assorted elements of present, past, and future, proceeds in this opening section to demonstrate just what a pass Tom and the others have come to.

The times, we are told, are bad. But the man who pronounces the judgment is broken out in hives from drinking gin fizzes and somehow involved with three girls at once, and the antic quality of the second little scene qualifies the mention of "evil particles" in the third: "Principalities and powers are everywhere victorious. Wickedness flourishes in high places." The tone belongs to John the Baptist, but the spirit is something else—Tom the Baptist, perhaps, a new kind of prophet seeking to reconcile man to his sins. And as he goes on to speak of a catastrophe whose cause, effects, and prevention are "known only to me," he sounds like a bookie with an inside tip, an impression confirmed when he produces his invention: "Here in my pocket is the very means of inoculating persons against such an eventuality or of curing them should it overtake them" (5). This kind of introduction, from a writer with Percy's control of tone, is a clue to the role of the lapsometer. Tom's invention is no technological miracle for which the science-worshiping public should hold its breath, but a focusing device introduced to dramatize the condition for which it is designed.

The comic perspective established in these first three sections holds as Percy goes on to juxtapose a page on the fragmentation of the church with three lines on buzzards. The Catholic Church, like everything else, has split into factions, the American schismatics enshrining property rights and the Dutch relevance. The Roman Catholics have become a scattered remnant, the one priest faithful to Rome reduced to moonlighting as a fire-watcher, keeping an eye out for brushfires below and signs and portents above. As for Tom, the bad Catholic of the novel's subtitle, he all but boasts of his degeneracy: "I believe in God and the whole business but I love women best, music and science next, whiskey next, and my fellowman hardly at all" (6). What lies behind such a confession? For one professing Christianity it seems a peculiar thing to banter about. We might do well to recall that Sir Thomas More, Tom's sainted ancestor, was famed for his humor, remarking to the sheriff's officer as he climbed to the gallows, "I pray you, Master Lieutenant, see me safe up, and for my coming down let me shift for myself."[12] Kierkegaard called humor "the last stage of existential inwardness before faith,"[13] and in fact Tom is dwelling in the comic religious mode of Kierkegaard, where "a man stands up and says the right thing... and so has understood it, and then when he has to act does the wrong thing... and so shows that he has not understood it."[14] Tom acknowledges he may be a liar: "Nevertheless I still believe." A thoroughly fallen-in and decadent state, it seems, both for Tom and for the Church, a sort of spiritual carrion. Percy then interposes three lines: "A couple of buzzards circle the interchange a mile high. Do I imagine it, or does one cock his head and eye me for meat? Don't count on it, old fellow!" The spirit of this rejoinder permeates the book: not just yet, old fellow!

The Dr. Faustus theme is sounded in a section on the vanity of scientists. Tom's greatest worry is not the catastrophe he fears but the possibility that it will overtake them before his discovery can create a sensation in the world of science. His invention could save the world or destroy it, "and in the next two hours will very likely do one or the other." A most dangerous thing "in the wrong hands," as we know from recent history. But Percy is not ready to introduce his Mephistophilis. Having embraced science and music as sec-

12. *Ibid.*, 403.
13. Søren Kierkegaard, *Concluding Unscientific Postscript to the "Philosophical Fragments*," trans. David R. Swenson and Walter Lowrie (Princeton, N. J., 1941), 259.
14. Søren Kierkegaard, *Fear and Trembling* and *The Sickness unto Death*, trans. Walter Lowrie (New York, 1954), 222. "It is infinitely comic," Kierkegaard says, "that a man can understand the whole truth about how wretched and petty this world is, etc.—that he can understand this, and then cannot recognize again what he understood; for almost in the same moment he himself goes off and takes part in the same pettiness and wretchedness, takes glory in it and receives glory from it, that is, accepts it."

ond in his scheme of values, just behind women, Tom now cautions the reader against "the layman's canonization of scientists." He drives home his point with the scientist's prayer: "Lord, grant that my discovery may increase knowledge and help other men. Failing that, Lord, grant that it will not lead to man's destruction. Failing that, Lord, grant that my article in *Brain* be published before the destruction takes place" (7–8). By this fine bit of satire Percy dramatizes a cogent point, one he has repeatedly made, and prepares the reader to view science as well as society from a critical vantage point.

The scientific vogue clearly has not eradicated superstition, nor have the standard home remedies prevented disintegration. The Rotary banner, split down the middle, still hangs in the dining room of the burnt-out Howard Johnson, asking pathetically: "Is it the truth? Is it fair to all concerned? Will it build goodwill and better friendships?" Superstition thrives, in altered forms. People ignore the true omens, the vines sprouting everywhere, five years after the Christmas riot. Barry Bocock, an engineer who is Tom's neighbor, bristles when Tom notes that the vines are cracking the slab under his house: "That'll be the day." He prefers to speak of the latest mysterious atrocity. "The work of a madman!" he says ritualistically, banishing the specter with a magic word that explains nothing.

Having established the comic tone and perspective, given direction to the narrative, and introduced some of the principal elements, Percy now slows his pace to sketch in the geography. Certain details deserve note. The old St. Michael's Church in the plaza is deserted, but the television tower looming over Tom's house in Paradise is busily transmitting. "By a trick of perspective," Tom observes, the tower seems to rise from St. Michael's "dumpy silo." Beyond the abandoned silo of the church the cubes and loaves of new houses are scattered among the pines of Paradise Estates: the empty storage bin of the church contrasts with the abundant material loaf of secular society. It was not always so with Tom, who recalls how in the best of the old times he used to eat Christ in Communion. The church is named after St. Michael, who is represented in art bearing a lance and shield. In this suburban paradise St. Michael's lance has been transformed into a television tower.

The politics of Paradise reflect its general condition. Both major parties have changed their names. The Grand Old Party is now the Knotheads, so named from the remark of a detested "Eastern-liberal commentator" who noted that CCCP, the initials for the proposed Christian Conservative Constitutional Party, corresponded to those worn by Soviet cosmonauts—"the most knotheaded political bungle of the century." The old Democrats are now the Left Party, or LEFTPAPASANE, which according to the Knotheads (who supplied the name) stands for Liberty, Equality, Fraternity, The Pill, Atheism, Pot, Anti-Pollution, Sex, Abortion Now, and Euthanasia. Both parties have had their "triumphs." The Lefts were able to remove "In God We Trust" from pennies; the Knotheads pushed through a law requiring compulsory prayer in black public schools and provided funds for birth control in Africa, Asia, and Alabama. The war in Ecuador has dragged on for fifteen years.

"The center did not hold," Tom notes laconically, borrowing from Yeats. "However, the Gross National Product continues to rise." These two one-line paragraphs convey something of the mad surrealism of contemporary life, but readers seeking literal prophecy in this novel are apt to be disenchanted.[15] Percy is not attempting to project current trends into the future literally, but to exaggerate them with the satirist's aim of creating awareness, to "prophesy in order to be wrong," as he remarked to a press conference shortly before the book came out. "In fact," he said, "my book could be

---

15. An unnamed reviewer in the London *Times Literary Supplement*, October 1, 1971, faults the book for having failed to "present a credible projection of the actualities of the current American crisis" and asks in plaintive exasperation, "Is there no draft then?" The reviewer becomes so befuddled that by the end of his article he is referring to the author as "Mr. Walker."

described as entertainment for Americans who are thinking things over in a period of eerie tranquility."[16]

The narrator who supplies this entertainment is an alcoholic psychiatrist who compares himself to "old Doc" in Western movies: "if you catch old Doc sober, he's all right, etcetera. In fact, he's some kind of genius, I heard he went to Harvard, etcetera, etcetera." Like Percy's other protagonists, Tom inherits a tradition. The Mores come of a long and rare tradition: a line of Anglo-Saxon Catholics who remained steadfastly Catholic among Protestants and Mediterranean or Irish Catholics alike. "Wanderers we became, like the Jews in the wilderness." They settled in Louisiana, "where religious and ethnic confusion is sufficiently widespread and good-natured that no one keeps track of such matters—except Baptists, who don't like Catholics no matter what." Tom's father was a "failed physician who also drank," a man so "overwhelmed with longing" that he was unfitted for anything but building houses for martins; his mother supported the family by selling real estate. Tom himself, who has the good fortune to have been left forty thousand shares of Reynolds aluminum by his faithless wife, carries on the tradition of his father by a life of longing, "longings for women, for the Nobel Prize, for the hot bosky bite of bourbon whiskey, and other great heartwrenching longings that have no name." He laments his failure to emulate "that great soul, the dearest best noblest merriest of Englishmen," his ancestor. "Sir Thomas was right, of course, and I am wrong. But on the other hand these are peculiar times. . . ."

For all his failings, Tom is a "genius nevertheless who sees into the hidden causes of things and erects simple hypotheses to account for the glut of everyday events." At twenty-six he stumbled upon a scientific discovery and gave promise of adding luster to the family name for the first time since Sir Thomas. Assigned to a team of physicists working on

16. "The Authors That Bloom in the Spring," 23.

the "secret Vieux Carré project under the Sugar Bowl," he discovered in the aftermath of a nuclear mishap that radiation from Heavy Sodium and Heavy Chloride had a tendency to unhinge people who were exposed to it. Patients got better; psychiatrists got worse. Superstition had it that "the yellow cloud had driven the demons out of the mad patients and into the doctors." Tom found through blood chemistry that both had significant elements of Heavy Sodium and Chloride in their blood.

What followed, unhappily, was not fame but a footnote in medical textbooks duly noting "More's Paradoxical Sodium Radiation Syndrome," then twenty years of quiet decline: "My daughter, Samantha died; my wife ran off with a heathen Englishman . . . and I left off research, left off eating Christ in Communion, and took to sipping Early Times instead and seeking the company of the fair sex, as they used to say." The crucial phase of his discovery came twenty years later, in the mental hospital to which he had committed himself following a suicide attempt, while he lay recovering from "seizures of alternating terror and delight with intervening periods of immense longing." The idea struck him at the height of a great storm. He leapt out of bed and yelled at his fellow patients: "Don't be afraid, brothers! Don't cry! Don't tremble! I have made a discovery that will cure you! Believe me, brothers!" The response is worth quoting here: " 'We believe you, Doc!' the madmen cried in the crashing thunder, and they did. Madmen, like possessed souls in the Gospels, know when you are telling the truth. It was my fellow physicians who gave me trouble." Vintage Percy, the madcap tone as well as the view of medical wisdom. Tom's idea, "like all great scientific breakthroughs," was simple: to devise a wireless gadget that could measure the electrical activity of the separate centers of the brain, correlate the readings with "the manifold woes of the Western world, its terrors and rages and murderous impulses," and treat those woes by electrical massage of the corresponding centers. The lapsometer in fact is an ingenious invention and lends itself well to Percy's synthesis.

A "super-Negro" named Colley Wilkes helped Tom rig
up the first machine, though Wilkes did not share his view
of the soul. "Unfortunately," Tom says, "there still persists
in the medical profession the quaint superstition that only
that which is visible is real. Thus the soul is not real. Uncaused
terror cannot exist. Then, friend, how come you are shaking?"
Calling upon an old classmate who is now with Osaka Instruments and $150,000 from the sale of his wife's stock, Tom
has secured five hundred production models of More's
Qualitative Quantitative Ontological Lapsometer, otherwise
known as MOQUOL, and is ready for business.

Fortunately for him, Tom remarks, other people besides
himself have become unhappy of late: "Conservatives have
begun to fall victim to unseasonable rages, delusions of conspiracies, high blood pressure, and large-bowel complaints.
Liberals are more apt to contract sexual impotence, morning
terror, and a feeling of abstraction of the self from itself."
The syndromes described are those respectively of bestialism
and angelism. Tom himself suffers both at once, a condition
that is not at all uncommon. "A man, for example, can feel
at one and the same time extremely abstracted and inor-
dinately lustful toward lovely young women who may be perfect strangers." But some specifics are in order; and while
Tom watches for snipers, keeping an eye on the motel window
where his three sweethearts are embowered, he dictates into
a pocket recorder, for the sake of posterity and to claim
his due credit, a few cases in point.

His trial run with the lapsometer is P. T. Bledsoe. Heretofore Tom has tried the device only on himself, where he
uncovered "a regular museum of pathology, something like
passing a metal detector over the battlefield of Iwo Jima."
Now he turns it on Bledsoe, and we see Percy's synthesis
in the making as the lapsometer links medical and psychological conditions to political and social ones. Bledsoe is a
"generous Knothead" of sixty, a business executive and thirty-
third degree Mason who suffers from blinding sick headaches

and feels threatened by Negro, Communist, and Jewish conspiracies. His ambition is to move to Australia, where he spent a year of his youth. Tom suggests he do just that. "I'm not walking away from anything," Bledsoe replies stoutly, and Tom reflects that maybe he knows best. "It's just that in recent months I've found it an effective rule of therapy to accept as more self-evident every day a certain state of affairs, namely, that most people nowadays are possessed, harboring as they do all manner of demonic hatreds and terrors and lusts and envies, that principalities and powers are nearly everywhere victorious, and that therefore a doctor's first duty to his patient is to help him find breathing room and so keep him from going crazy." Tom brings out the first crude model of his invention and makes a pass over Bledsoe's skull, "feeling a bit like a phrenologist." On a hunch he focuses on the "red nucleus in the floor of the fourth ventricle" and asks Bledsoe about the nefarious Bildebergers. "To my astonishment and even as I watched, the needle swung from a moderate 2.6 mmv to a great whacking rage level of 9.4 mmv." Bledsoe is impressed that Tom knows his headache is returning and seems to feel better even though the lapsometer cannot yet cure it. Tom then notes a curious thing: "The very act of locating the site, touching the sore spot, so to speak, seemed to make him feel better." A bit of technological sorcery that recalls what Percy has said about naming.[17]

The second patient is Ted Tennis, an overarticulate graduate student who suffers from "massive free-floating terror, identity crisis, and sexual impotence." He is the embodiment of angelism, a disastrously abstracted type known to every psychiatrist: "the well-spoken slender young man who recites his symptoms with precision and objectivity—so objective that they seem to be somebody else's symptoms—and above all with that eagerness, don't you know, as if nothing

17. See for example Percy, "Naming and Being."

would please him more than that his symptom, his dream, should turn out to be interesting, a textbook case. *Allow me to have a proper disease, Doctor,* he all but tells me" (33). Ted is a classic example of the man who abdicates himself in deference to the experts. He speaks of feeling "considerable warmth and tenderness" toward his wife and cannot help wondering aloud about the "etiology" of the impotence. Tom talks the dialect to him: "I'd like to do a personality profile using a new tele-encephalographic technique." "Wow," is Ted's response, and like Bledsoe he seems better at the instant of being touched by this "scientific magic." "Who of us now," Tom muses, "is not so strangely alone that it is the cool clinical touch of the stranger that serves best to treat his loneliness?"

Over Brodmann 32, "the area of abstractive activity," Ted registers 7.6 mmv. Any reading over 6, Tom has learned, generally means that a person has "so abstracted himself from himself and from the world around him, seeing things as theories and himself as a shadow, that he cannot, so to speak, reenter the lovely ordinary world" but must orbit the earth and himself, "destined to haunt the human condition like the Flying Dutchman." Ted's anxiety registers a thunderous 8.7 mmv. Tom identifies with this condition himself: "We are two of a kind, winging it like Jupiter and spying comely maids below and having to take the forms of swans and bulls to approach them." In reporting his findings, Tom blurts out terms like "angelism" and "spiritual apogee." To him these are only technical terms, but that is no way to speak to a biologist who has cast off superstition.[18] "Look, Tom," Ted says. "All I want is a Bayonne-rayon training member." With the member he can help his wife "achieve an adequate response" even though good fortune may be denied to him. This prospective act is a grotesque parody of the calisthenics of alienation that Binx and Kate attempt

18. I may be wrong about this, but I cannot help suspecting Percy of choosing such terms to twit the legions of Ted Tennises who consider themselves liberated from tainted medievalism even while bending the knee superstitiously to what they conceive to be science.

on the way to Chicago. Tom has dozens of Bayonne-rayons in a drawer ("The untreatable maladies of any age, reader, may be ascertained from the free samples a doctor receives") but will grant Ted's request only on condition that he walk home the next day, six miles through the swamp, instead of taking the car pool. "At that time," Tom laments, the only treatment for angelism was "recovery of the self through ordeal." Ted agrees for the sake of Tanya, eager to do anything "to restore our relationship along the entire spectrum," and sets out hopefully. It turned out to be "every bit the ordeal I had hoped," Tom remarks. "So it came to pass that half-dead and stinking like a catfish, he fell into the arms of his good wife, Tanya, and made lusty love to her the rest of the night"—presumably with no talk of achieving adequate responses.

Ted's research as a graduate student centers on Monkey Island in the middle of the swamp, home of a colony of killer apes thought to be an unevolved descendant of one of man's ancestors: "No other ape kills for pleasure." The explanation chills, and here Percy addresses himself to the "monstrousness" loosed upon the world in this century as Tom, contemplating the question, digresses to sketch in his own version of the Fall. His lapsometer comes masterfully into play. "The question is: how to account for man's wickedness?" Biologists tend to look for a "wicked monkey in the family tree." Not so, says Tom; far more likely that something went wrong with man:

> If you measure the pineal activity of a monkey—or any other sub-human animal—with my lapsometer, you will invariably record identical readings at Layers I and II. Its self, that is to say, coincides with itself. Only in man do you find a discrepancy: Layer I, the outer social self, ticking over, say, at a sprightly 5.4 mmv, while Layer II just lies there, barely alive at 0.7 mmv, or even zero!—a nought, a gap, an aching wound. Only in man does the self miss itself, *fall* from itself (hence lapsometer!).

In such a passage we can see the true value of the lapsometer as a fictional invention. Human wickedness, it seems to confirm quantitatively, stems from a Fall no monkey knows, and consists of man's having fallen from *self*, from his own being, to become a shadow of himself.

Note that this Fall is more than the Cartesian mind-body split. "Mind" here is a socially conditioned self-consciousness looking back on one's "body," one's organism-self, especially upon the void that has come to occupy the juncture of mind and body from which man's being, *as man*, has vanished in the mind-body split. Instead of man, one becomes a monstrous angel / beast. The end of the world described in the novel's subtitle is really this end of the world in one's consciousness. If we raise the question again of why humanism leads to beastliness, the answer should now be more apparent. When one is emptied out in this fashion, a victim of the malaise, something moves in to fill the vacuum. "War is better than nothing," Percy remarks,[19] and all manner of ills—totalitarianism, murder, social rage—will serve equally well. What will not remain for long is emptiness; the void will be filled. Such a fact by itself could explain the monstrousness loosed upon our world.

In the twilight of the Eclipse such monstrousness can flourish. Dostoevski had a nightmare vision of it, as will be seen presently. The term *Eclipse* is mine, not Percy's, but it defines the fictional terrain of his novels. The Event described by Percy is the revelation of God's purpose manifested in time through the incarnation of the Word in Christ. The Eclipse is the "tempestuous restructuring of consciousness" of which Percy has spoken "which does not presently allow [man] to take account of the Good News."[20] Will Barrett exemplifies the condition, and all of Percy's novels take place on the far side of the Eclipse. Tom More has heard the Good News but learned not to listen. The novelist, Percy suggests, is "one of the few remaining witnesses to the doctrine of original sin, the ever-present imminence of disaster in paradise."[21]

---

19. Percy, "Hughes's Solipsism Malgré Lui," 492.
20. Percy, "Notes for a Novel," 12.
21. *Ibid.*, 9. Percy seldom presumes to speak on behalf of the novelist, preferring to speak only for himself, but here he was asked to do so.

The disaster in this paradise is that man has fallen from himself and lost access to his own inwardness, like Will Barrett, and is thus deaf to the Good News and a prey to whatever demons may be roaming the vicinity. That is the new Fall.

But suppose, Tom More thinks, he could "hit on the right dosage" with the lapsometer and "weld the broken self" whole! "What if man could reenter paradise, so to speak, and live there both as man and spirit, whole and intact man-spirit, as solid flesh as a speckled trout, a dappled thing, yet aware of itself as a self!" (36). In this superb trout image Percy gives us a glimpse of his earthly paradise.

Then, as if to make a final comment on the social conditions in which angelism thrives, he offers an aside before moving on to Tom's next patient. A sign at the vine-clad drive-in has advertised the same film for five years, something called *Homo Hijinks* that is billed as a "zany laff riot." In the last days of the "old Auto Age," it took a gimmick to get people out to the movies, in this case "an act of fellatio performed by two skydivers in a free fall on 3-D Ektachrome on a two-hundred-foot screen." A caricature of angelism as well as the film industry.

Tom's third patient is Charley Parker, the golf pro at the Paradise Country Club. A self-made man who from the condition of caddy has risen to become a prophet-activist of the game of golf, Charley is the kind of "sergeant-yeoman out of the hills" who always turns up to help out in emergencies, a "success" in life who is beginning to ask what it all adds up to. "What does it all mean, is the thing," he wonders aloud.[22] Charley is a blind devotee of progress whose success in eliminating labor costs on the golf course has put poor blacks out of work. His depression deepens when his son and namesake drops out of MIT and takes to the swamp, accusing Charley of hypocrisy and blaming him for starving the unemployed blacks. His "deep pineal reading," Tom

22. Golf is his religion, which gives this quandary dimension, especially if we recall Percy's apprentice novel *The Charterhouse*, where the golf course and country club had taken the place of the cathedral.

finds, is very low. Anger restores him momentarily; he absolutely feeds on the news. The best Tom can do for him at first is "historical therapy," a recalling of the good old days, "a recapture of the past and one's self." His son's accusations torment him. "The mystery of evil," Tom muses, "is the mystery of limited goodness." What has gone wrong with Charley is that he is a tinkerer, "a fellow who has to have one idea to worry with twenty-four hours a day"; his selfhood is all bound up with his enterprises. Later Tom is able to give him a "pineal massage" with the lapsometer, whereupon he returns to himself and begins spewing out projects, including the idea for a "golfarama," a "mystical idea of combining a week of golf on a Caribbean island with the Greatest Pro of Them All"—namely, Jesus—in a week of golf and revival meetings conducted by a member of the "old Billy Graham team."

Charley Parker is the portrait of a technological tinkerer. This "golfarama," which amounts to an extensive rotation trying to become a repetition, may not hold much promise; but lacking a pineal massage with Tom's lapsometer, it may be one of the best avenues open to the tinkerer in our society whose ego is too frozen into the patterns of his technological function to permit him a look at their underlying premises. As to the question raised by Charley's wife ("It wasn't his forty million dollars that filled in the swamp. He was just doing his job. Is it Charley's fault that Tifton 451 eliminates labor?"), ecologists and dropouts from technological society will undoubtedly answer yes. Like most of us, Charley is copping out. Whether or not his evil is limited goodness, the effects of his labors can be rapacious and blind.

What can happen when men just do their jobs is illustrated in the book Tom is reading when his fourth patient arrives. For weeks Tom has been reliving the Battle of Verdun in Stedmann's *History of World War I*. Half a million died there in a year-long struggle that left the battle lines unchanged. The horrors of Verdun are the horrors of abstraction: "white Christian Caucasian Europeans, sentimental music-loving

Germans and rational clear-minded Frenchmen slaughtering each other without passion." The effect here is even more ghastly than under the spirit of abstraction, where abstraction is fueled by resentment. Verdun involved a kind of world-historical absentmindedness, as Kierkegaard might have said, which forgets the value of human life: " 'The men in the trenches did not hate each other,' wrote Stedmann. 'As for the generals, they respected or contemned each other precisely as colleagues in the same profession' " (47). From this species of "professionalism," a form of abstraction in which function is divorced from value, man himself is a dropout.

The particular dropout from Charley's world who becomes patient number four is Charley's son Chuck. With his three years at MIT and the good looks of Phoebus Apollo, Chuck is a golden prototype of the counterculture. That he does not refuse the benefits of technology altogether is apparent when Tom goes with him and his wife at three in the morning to tend their ailing love child. Their chickee stands near an abandoned Confederate salt mine in the swamp, where they have set up to live "a perfect life of love and peace." Tom is invited to join them, and there is some good fun where Percy mocks their subcultural pretensions in the tones of Hemingway:

> "We're basically religious here, Doc."
> "Good."
> "We have God every minute."
> "Good."
> "Don't you see that I am God, you are God, that prothonotary warbler is God?"
> "No." (50)

Note that this tight-lipped hero is no Jake Barnes or Frederic Henry, but a befuddled Percyan hero who cannot say what is wrong with his life, denies he is a "liberated" Catholic, and is assailed by inexplicable longings.

Chuck, who smokes "rabbit" cannibis and has begun to "jump a bit, feet together, kangaroo style," is wild about the lapsometer, instantly aware of its possibilities: "Are you telling me that with that thing you can actually register the knotheadedness of the Knotheads, the nutty objectivity of the scientists, and the mad spasms of the liberals?" The danger of its setting off a Heavy-Sodium reaction in the swamp sets him off into a goat dance: "Doc, man you the wildest of all," he says ecstatically, falling into the dialect. "Doc, you got to stay here with us. Who's going to believe all that great wild stuff over there?" His glee at the prospect of them all doing each other in on the "glorious Fourth of July" betrays a countercultural resentment somewhat out of tune with ideals of peace and love. But Chuck believes, and enthusiastically parrots, what sounds like the official countercultural line: "You're a shaman. The scientists have blown it."[23] "Still and all, scientists are after the truth," Tom protests. But Chuck, with the limitations of his tribe, sees only the shaman in Tom and is no more ready to accept Tom's—and Percy's—esteem of science than is his wife Ethel, who resents Tom's diagnosis of "contradictory Judaism" in her, the belief that "the Jews are unique and that they are not." "I'm not listening to some bastard tell me I have a Jewish brain," she says, flinging the lapsometer at him; and as the salt on the bank spits and smokes, Percy foreshadows possible disaster in his familiar antic tone. "Brimstone, no doubt," Ethel says drily, and Tom replies, "As a matter of fact, it was."

It is Hester who believes Tom when he protests that scientists seek the truth. She is Tom's type, "post-Protestant, post-rebellion, post-ideology," reverted "clear back to pagan innocence like a shepherd girl piping a tune on a Greek vase." Hester is reading Erle Stanley Gardner, and her "lovely hollowed-out Holyoke vowels" capture him: "How stands it with a forty-five-year-old man who can fall in love on the spot with a twenty-year-old stranger, a clear-eyed vacant simple Massachusetts girl, and desire nothing more in this life than to move into her chickee?"

    23. On this subject see Theodore Roszak's *The Making of a Counter Culture* (New York, 1969), especially the final chapter.

The fact is that Tom's condition is more unstable than the Heavy Sodium. With his three girls in the motel, his fondness for gin fizzes and Early Times, and his named ambitions and nameless longings, he is a fine Percyan protagonist and guide for what lies ahead. And as Percy brings this first section to a close, there is a touch of the soap opera or Western movie that fits the burlesque rhythm he has chosen to give the novel. Will Tom make it to the pass with his lapsometer in time to head off the sweet beast of catastrophe? Tomorrow's episode will tell—but first our hero must return for a moment to the theme on which he opened.

"The U.S.A. didn't work!" Tom tells us on this Fourth of July. Maybe it never worked; maybe "the thing always had a flaw in it, a place where it would shear, and . . . all this time we were not really different from Ecuador and Bosnia-Herzegovina, just richer." Could it have been "the nigger business" all the time? And suddenly the joke goes sour:

> What a bad joke: God saying, here it is, the new Eden, and it is yours because you're the apple of my eye; because you the lordly Westerners, the fierce Caucasian-Gentile-Visigoths, believed in me and in the outlandish Jewish Event even though you were nowhere near it and had to hear the news of it from strangers. But you believed and so I gave it all to you, gave you Israel and Greece and science and art and the lordship of the earth, and finally even gave you the new world that I blessed for you. And all you had to do was pass one little test, which was surely child's play for you because you had already passed the big one. One little test: here's a helpless man in Africa, all you have to do is not violate him. That's all.
> One little test: you flunk! (57)

Here Percy touches the same wound Faulkner probes in his novels. The tone is as much Ike McCaslin's as Tom More's. But here we see a major departure from Faulkner. Yoknapatawpha County lies *behind* the Eclipse, in the ancestral regions obscured by time. The terrain of *Love in the Ruins* lies deep within the shadows of the Eclipse. And Percy makes no mention of the South. His vision encompasses the whole of the New Eden, the United States of America. The North has been examined by the same professor.

"The test was too much!" Tom protests. "What do you expect of man?" Even so, we almost passed. "You tested us because bad as we were there was no one else, and everybody knew it, even our enemies, and that is why they curse us." Nobody curses the Chinese. "Who ever imagined the Chinese were blessed by God and asked to save the world?" As for "Russia and the Russian Christ who was going to save Europe from itself: ha ha." Christendom has gone down the drain: "The dream over. Back to history and Bosnia-Herzegovina."

A trace of chauvinism seems to creep in here, along with a pinch of that pride brought to these shores aboard the Mayflower—the assurance that God is backing this enterprise. But before hastening to conclusions we might read what comes next: "I can save you, America! I know something! I know what is wrong! I hit on something, made a breakthrough, came on a discovery! I can save the terrible God-blessed Americans from themselves! With my invention! Listen to me. Don't give up. It is not too late." The final plea echoes the humor of Percy's remarks to the National Book Award press conference: "If my novel has any message, it is probably this: Don't give up, New York, California, Chicago, Philadelphia. Louisiana is with you. Georgia is on your side."[24]

Meanwhile, back at Paradise... And having sketched in the outlines of where we are on this peculiar Fourth of July, Percy leaves us with the sand trap smoking, the rattle of gunfire from up by NASA, and a lens-shaped yellow cloud hanging zeppelinlike over the horizon while he goes back to fill us in on just how we got here in the first place. Will Tom make it to the pass on time? Will his trusty lapsometer misfire, or, worse yet, fall into evil hands? Will the "terrible God-blessed Americans" pull the game out in the closing seconds?

Tune in tomorrow, same time, same station.

---

24. "The Authors That Bloom in the Spring," 24.

The Trial of Tom More

We return not to the thrilling days of yesteryear, but to a seemingly casual event three days earlier: "Someone took a shot at me at the breakfast table." This shot, quickly followed by two more, opens the novel as the first incident taking place in its present time. The three shots launch the action and also place us subliminally, touching the collective nerve of a nation traumatized by three shots in Dallas: the novel speaks not to an Auto Age, as Tom often refers to our own era, but to that Gothic era of assassinations identified with the name Kennedy. And Tom's response belongs equally to the same period: "As I was considering this at the top of my head, something at the heart of me knew better and I found myself diving for the corner even as I ruminated." He saves himself by "a reflex learned with the First Air Cav in the fifteen year war in Ecuador"—the conditioned response of an American of the 1960's.

The public nature of such conditioning is appropriate here, for now begins the public phase of Tom's ordeal. A later and more private one is to follow, but the first campaign of his war on two fronts takes place under the lights, so to speak, in the long middle sequence of the novel culminating in the comic shoot-out between Tom and Buddy Brown. Later the focus will turn inward; here it is on *them*, as the consensus anthropology is tested in the comic fires of The Pit.

As the contest opens the odds seem overwhelmingly against our shaky eccentric hero. On his forty-fifth birthday Tom lies on the floor of his enclosed patio, out of the line of fire, thinking of Doris, his lost wife. He is the perfect model of Kierkegaard's man whose house is without a beloved. Tom's prospects are not enhanced by what follows. At the moment of the first shot he is sipping Tang, drinking it warm because nothing works any more, not even his refrigerator. The USA went down the drain not because of polarization or pornography, he says; "what finally tore it was that things stopped working and nobody wanted to be a repairman."

He lies there looking up at Doris' books, swollen by rains to "fat wads of pulp": *Siddhartha, Atlas Shrugged, ESP and the New Spirituality.* Poor Doris had fallen victim to a weakness common to a certain type of Episcopal girl "just past youth"; she was ruined by "spiritual books" and "Gnostic pride."

The past comes into the story now as Tom lies ruminating about the last time he made love to her, here in the "enclosed patio," shortly before her departure with Alistair Fuchs-Forbes and his chum. "Here was where I had set a record: that of all cuckolds in history, I am the first American to be cuckolded by *two* English fruits." The scene recalled is good comic Percy. Tom presses what she insists upon calling his "conjugal rights" while Doris mouths one cliché after another from the new spirituality: "I'm going in search of myself"; "love should be a joyous encounter"; "spiritual growth is the law of life." She is en route to "making herself whole" at Alistair's handicraft retreat in Cozumel, the "last hope of the Western world," where "transcendental religion could rescue Western materialism." "We're so dead, Tom," she explains. Alistair is a "very tragic person. But he's a searcher like me, a pilgrim." The notions of people as dead and man as searcher or pilgrim are very nearly Percy's own. He satirizes her understanding of them, I think, because the worst enemy of truth often is not its opposite, error, but its next of kin, the cliché that encases and smothers it. "Pilgrim my ass," Tom says.

A serious note enters with mention of Samantha's death. Percy does not linger on it, merely introduces it; her death becomes important later, in the private phase of Tom's ordeal. Some eight years earlier Samantha had died a horrible death. Tom thinks Doris left because she never forgave him or God for it: " 'That's a loving God you have there,' she told me toward the end, when the neuroblastoma had pushed one eye out and around the nosebridge so that Samantha looked like a two-eyed Picasso profile" (72). He and Doris "chose not to forgive each other," he says later, and Alistair "happened to come along at the right time (273). Lacking forgiveness, Tom took to drink and Doris to the new spirituality, two familiar responses to great personal loss. Doris died and Tom's life moved into ever deepening shadows. So much for the remote past, which is prologue to his present state.

We get a glimpse of the more recent past through Dusty Rhoades, who gives Tom a lift to the Country Club in his bubble-top Toyota. Tom has evaded the sniper, at least for now. Dusty Rhoades is a fitting name for the conservative proctologist from Texas who has bought a plantation house called Tara and seeks to revive that faded apparition. Last Christmas Eve, Dusty had found his beautiful daughter, Lola, in Tom's arms in the deep grassy bunker of the eighteenth hole, a bit of "misbehavior in Paradise" for which he has not forgiven Tom. While they roll along listening to "Hills of Home," the Tara theme and Dusty's favorite tune, Dusty gives Tom to understand that the only honorable course open to him is to marry Lola and move into Tara: "You going to do right by Lola, or Doctor, I'm going to have your ass. Is that clear?"

In the meantime, as they clear Security at the sentry box and enter the "inner circle of Paradise," Tom has brought out his lapsometer and taken a reading on Dusty. He shows almost no coeliac anxiety, this "ex-fullback and hardworking surgeon, a man at home with himself and too busy to worry" about his pineal selfhood; "he may fear one thing or another but he's not afraid of no-thing, which is the worst of fears." But his love-sex ratio is reversed: "the reading from Brodmann Area 24, the locus of 'higher' or interpersonal relations, is a tiny 0.5 mmv while the hypothalamus, seat of organic sexual activity, registers a whacking stud-level 7.9 mmv," the wave of a "powerful, frequently satisfied, but indiscriminate sexual appetite." Dusty sees through Tom's evasions ("What you're saying is I'm messing around with my nurses") and demands to know if the lapsometer is "nonpartisan": "Does it also measure alcoholism, treachery, laziness, and white-trash morals?" An astute Knothead, fully polarized, as befits the proprietor of Tara in the new Southern Paradise, Dusty grasps the political implications of the lapsometer instantly. He is the exemplar of bestialism.

The empty pro shop reminds Tom of the affair with Lola, whom he had kissed there. "Women are mythical creatures," he remarks, thinking of the beautiful six-foot Lola with her gin fizz in hand. The memory prompts one of those ecstatic cries that recur as a motif throughout the novel: "Women! Music! Love! Life! Joy! Gin fizzes!" The theme is Percy's ode to joy, related to Kierkegaard's realm of the musical erotic; and like the retort to the waiting buzzards noted earlier it affirms life in the face of death, woe, and plain befuddlement. Tom, having only that day perfected his lapsometer and finished his article, is suffering from "simultaneous depression and exaltation." Why? Lola wants to know. "Well, I've won, you see. Won the big one. But it's Christmas Eve and I'm alone. My family is dead. There's nobody to tell." So he tells Lola, of course. "Her company stabilizes me. Abstracted still, my orbit becomes lower" (92). Note what happens. Tom remains abstracted—semi-angelized, we might say—but his orbit swings nearer the human—the condition of man as man. "Bending close to her, close to the upper reaches of her breast, is like skimming in silence, power off, over the snowy slopes of Kilimanjaro."[25]

Lola, who is united with herself in her love of music, "goes dreaming through the world safe and sure as Schubert's trout." A few "snapshots" of her with Tom's "Brownie," the lapsometer, reveal zero anxiety but an interpersonal wave "both powerful and truncated, lopped off at the peak like Popocatepetl." She has "a heart full of love and no one to give it to." It is inevitable that the muddled psychiatrist is soon "singing like a cello" between the knees of the lovely cellist. There seems to be no Puritanical note here, just as there is none in the musical-erotic realm described by Kierke-

25. The parallel with Hemingway's "The Snows of Kilimanjaro" would be interesting to explore, particularly Tom's angelism-bestialism and Harry's moral and physical decay. Hemingway's story has vultures to go with Percy's buzzards, and Percy's novel, like Hemingway's, shows the frozen carcasses of those aspiring to the heights.

gaard,[26] for which the cello is such an apt metaphor. The Percyan touch comes immediately thereafter when Tom becomes engorged with lymph and Lola saves his life at the cost of her reputation. "She could have gone, left me to die in the bunker, swell up and die and be found stiff as a poker in the foggy dew." But she fetched help, and Dusty, who found Tom without breath and "in some disarray," shot him full of epinephrine and brought him out of it. As his Christmas Eve then resumed its original plan, Tom watched Perry Como, now "seventy years young and snowy-thatched but hale as old Saint Nick himself," sitting on his stool singing "Silent Night" on the stereo-V.[27]

Evidently it was on Christmas morning, after listening to Perry Como, that Tom attempted suicide. Tom himself is not quite sure about it, but certainly watching Perry Como, "face orange, lips violet," do his youth act—that despairing travesty on a travesty of the Christmas spirit—would unsettle a man. Having been "assaulted at night by longings, succubi, and the hideous shellfire of Verdun," he awoke with his wrists cut and bleeding. "Seeing the blood, I came to myself, saw myself as itself and the world for what it is, and began to love life." Like any castaway of Percy's he took inventory: "After all, why not live? Bad as things are still when all is said and done, one can sit on a doorstep in the winter sunlight and watch sparrows kick leaves" (97). Brought out of orbit by Lola only to be swamped in the despair of Como's Christmas, Tom comes to himself through ordeal and is rescued by the small concrete favors of life, winter sunlight and sparrows kicking leaves.

His friend Max Gottlieb sutures his arteries without much ado. Tom recovers sufficiently to invite Ellen Oglethorpe, the nurse, to his bed, somewhat after the fashion of Frederic

26. In Søren Kierkegaard, in *Either / Or,* trans. David F. Swenson and Lillian Marvin Swenson (2 vols.; New York, 1959), I.

27. This is the only definite time clue I find in the book. Como coyly omits to give his age in *Who's Who.* In his letter to me of April 19, 1970, Percy said the novel took place some twenty years hence, which would place it in the early nineties, a little later than most reviewers have judged. The matter is trivial by the most generous standard.

Henry. But she declines, and his lust yielding to sorrow, he prays, "arms stretched out like a Mexican" and tears streaming down his face: "Dear God, I can see it now, why can't I see it at other times, that it is you I love in the beauty of the world and in all the lovely girls and dear good friends, and it is pilgrims we are, wayfarers on a journey, and not pigs, nor angels. Why can I not be merry and loving like my ancestor, a gentle pure-hearted knight for our Lady and blessed Lord and Savior? Pray for me, Sir Thomas More" (109). Percy follows deprecatingly with an "etcetera etcetera," but this passage without a trace of irony is a key to Tom's condition. He exists in a state of sin, which for Kierkegaard is the opposite not of virtue but of faith. Sin for Kierkegaard "does not consist in the fact that man has not understood what is right, but in the fact that he will not understand it, and in the fact that he will not do it."[28] Tom More is not Will Barrett; in his case "there is this little tiny transition from having understood to doing." The good "must be done at once," Kierkegaard says, but the "strength of the lower nature consists in dragging a thing out." The will has no objection, and "when the intelligence has become duly darkened" the two of them can "understand one another better" because the intelligence has surrendered to the will.[29] The everydayness duly darkening Tom's awareness is this understanding between his intelligence and his will. Ordeal rends it momentarily, and he recognizes himself to be the wayfarer he scorns in the fraudulent platitudes of Doris. It remains to be seen whether his condition will benefit by this fleeting insight.

The upshot of his suicide attempt was that he committed himself to the federal hospital, from which he went AWOL the following May, a couple of months before the novel's

28. Kierkegaard, *The Sickness unto Death*, 226.
29. *Ibid.*, 224–25. "And so there live perhaps a great multitude of men," Kierkegaard continues, "who labor off and on to obscure their ethical and religious understanding which would lead them out into decisions and consequences which the lower nature does not love, extending meanwhile their aesthetic and metaphysical understanding, which ethically is a distraction."

action begins. At present he is on his way back to the hospital to see Max.

Moving by stealth toward his objective, trying to outwit the sniper, Tom stumbles upon a conspiracy in the pagoda shelter on an island in the golf course. A three-man contingent of blacks is conversing beyond a partition while the Christian Kaydettes, a ridiculous marching group of baton twirlers, rehearse on the parade ground not far off. The plan of the blacks is to capture the Kaydettes on the Fourth of July and somehow to conscript the Ph.D.'s at Fedville as teachers for black children at the Honey Island school. A contrast emerges between Victor Charles, a local man who knows the whites and wants no one hurt, and Uru, a militant from the North untroubled by such misgivings. To the presumably sophisticated Uru, Victor is a hopeless Uncle Tom. Uru is an uprooted figure who belongs nowhere, with "a voice without antecedents, black yes, Midwestern perhaps, but mainly stereo-V, an announcer's voice, a Detroit disc jockey's voice." The three of them have shot a deer to feed the starving black children whose fathers have been put out of work as a result of Charley Parker's tinkering. "Well," says Willard Amadie, Tom's former caddy, "they going to eat today."

Tom moves on to the hospital and his old ward where his "old friends and fellow madmen" live: "They gaze at me, knowing me and knowing me not. I am like a dream they have dreamed before. A man standing at the window twitters his fingers, sending out radar beams to the vague, gauzy world, and cocks his ear, listening for returning blips. *Who are you out there?*" This is where he spent the best months of his life. "Here in the day room and in the ward we patients came to understand each other as only fellow prisoners and exiles can." The theme is familiar Percy: sanity in such times is not man's everyday condition, which is apt to be a pernicious despair, but a state of awareness to which one most likely comes through ordeal, perhaps through "madness" itself. True sanity resides in Being rather than in non-Being. The world outside the hospital, when Tom leaves the ward and goes AWOL, is almost too much, and Percy renders the moment phenomenologically in one sentence, as he often does in this novel: "Wham! there it was, the world, solid as a rock, dense as a doorknob" (107).

Tom's return to the ward produces a confrontation in which things are not at all what they seem. We see the sanity of "madness" and the insanity of "science" in the form of behaviorism as Percy's phenomenological treatment begins to yield dividends. The scene is crucial to his purpose because if the perspective of the novel is to be fully realized the reader must enter into it at this point.

Tom has a practical objective in coming to see Max: he wants Max to support his effort to secure funds for a crash program by which to develop his lapsometer and thus ward off disaster—a "mad" ambition, surely, though the reader can see the sanity of it. "Let's talk about this sense of impending disaster," Max says, therapist fashion, in the language by which demons are banished and a firm grip kept on the familiar world. He speaks common sense edified by science. But Tom detects "an oddity": "Max the unbeliever, a lapsed Jew, believes in the orderliness of creation, acts on it with energy and charity. I the believer, having swallowed the whole Thing, God Jews Christ Church, find the world a madhouse and a madhouse home. Max the atheist sees things like Saint Thomas Aquinas, ranged, orderly, connected up" (106). Tom, from his quirky private corner, sees the world's madness. Max, whose faith is in orderliness, cannot accommodate such a vision; his world is required to make sense. Prisoners or exiles like Dostoevski, Cervantes, and the two Thomas Mores have "seen visions, dreamed dreams," but "it is of no use in science unless you can measure it."

Earlier Max had "saved" Tom following his suicide attempt by naming his terror, "giving it habitation," knowing the worst of him and "naming it with ordinary words, English common nouns": Tom was having "troublesome mood swings," combined with "excellent insight." Now, as Tom speaks of "the soul of Western man," carelessly mentions the vines, and uses terms like angelism, Max the neobehaviorist is discomfited. "Belief. Truth values. These are relative things," goes the incantation by which he seeks to keep his world intact and banish the specter of the sniper and the conspiracy Tom has got wind of. On Tom's affair with Lola he says twice, "I am trying to see it as you see it," patronizing Tom's Catholicism. What worries Tom is that he feels no guilt, without which there can be no contrition or purpose of amendment and therefore no forgiveness of sin. Max wants to put Tom in a Skinner box[30] and "condition away the contradiction" so he will never feel guilt. "Then I'd really be up the creek," Tom says, and Max repeats, somewhat despairingly, "I'm trying to see it."

Max cannot see it, of course. His mind is imprisoned in its own assumptions. His behaviorism cannot negotiate with other faiths; it can only fall back into the new mumbo jumbo: "Belief. Truth values. These are relative things."[31] The reader who does not share Tom's Catholicism may be closer to Max's relativism, a sort of philosophical nowhere, but unless his imagination is too tightly bound he can share Tom's experience of events to come. And that imaginative element is important because the extent to which he participates will determine his response to the novel.

Much of the action now requires little explanation. Tom makes a visit to the Love Clinic, an elaborate sex research institute, and Percy's satire becomes rather broad as he gives us a multilayered scene with all sorts of absurdities taking place while the clinic's proudest exhibit, "Lonesome Lil," is dutifully masturbating beyond the viewing mirror. "Isn't it impolite not to watch her?" Tom wonders, his hand straying

30. Such a box in fact exists. B. F. Skinner once trained two pigeons to play Ping-Pong in such an enclosure.
31. In a review Percy once spoke of the "terrible despair of the assumption" underlying the argument "that in speaking of belief we have left truth behind" (Walker Percy, "Truth—or Pavlov's Dogs?" *America*, XCVII [1957], 307). For his views in depth on this subject see his essay "Culture: The Antinomy of the Scientific Method," *New Scholasticism*, XXXII (1958), 443–75.

along the vaginal computer to touch fingers with Moira, one of his true loves. Father Kev Kevin, a liberal schismatic who is now chaplain to the clinic, sits at the vaginal console reading *Commonweal,* a lay Catholic periodical for which Percy has often written.

Earlier in this chapter I spoke of the new Fall described in the novel. A sequence in this middle section of the novel shows the effects of this new Fall in a Southern context. Victor Charles appears to help when Tom passes out in a ditch near the animal shelter where Victor lives. Victor, whose loyalties are split between the black uprising and his ancient affection for Tom, warns Tom that he should move in with his mother. Something bad is going to happen. There is a scene illustrating the mutual concern and affection that often pervaded relations between white and black in the old days. Victor has returned from a remunerative job in Boston partly out of nostalgia for the old "shrimp jubilee," in which everybody—black and white—had spent the night on the beach catching shrimp by the light of gas lamps. Victor remembers Tom's family to one side of him and Leroy Ledbetter's to the other during one jubilee, a memory of olden days that is far more honest than the vision of Tara. Even now, Victor seems to have some feeling for Leroy, though Leroy now denies blacks entrance to his bar and helps keep them down. "It's so pitiful," Victor says. "You would think people with that much in common would want to save what they have."

A scene follows in which Percy describes a complicated breach of racial zoning that takes place in two seconds and brings the metallic taste of terror to Tom's throat. Tom recalls having tasted it after the Bantu uprising five years earlier when Leroy, then his partner in the Paradise Bowling Lanes, told him about the incident that triggered the uprising, Leroy's denial of an alley to a Bantu couple. Leroy is a seventh-generation Anglo-Saxon American like Tom, though "Protestant, countrified, sweet-natured," the sort who helps

out when you have a flat tire. Then where does Tom's terror
come from following the racial infraction?

> Not from the violence; violence gives release from terror. Not from
> Leroy's wrongness, for if he were altogether wrong, an evil man,
> the matter would be simple and no cause for terror. No, it came
> from Leroy's goodness, that he is a decent, sweet-natured man who
> would help you if you needed help, go out of his way and bind up
> a stranger's wounds. No, the terror comes from the goodness and
> what lies beneath, some fault in the soul's terrain so deep that all
> is well on top, evil grins like good, but something shears and tears
> deep down and the very ground stirs beneath one's feet. (152)

What is terrifying is not the evil men of Hollywood legend,
but the "good gone wrong and not knowing it," the "Southern
sweetness and cruelty." That is what shakes Tom.

We are in territory occupied by the spirit of abstraction,
that objectification of others, poisoned by resentment, that
sees only abstractions or symbols in place of living individual
humans. The "fault in the soul's terrain" is the rift in the
humanity of men that is the modern Black Death, that malady
no monkey knows, which has extended its sway even into
the intimate Southern domain of the shrimp jubilee. In a
remarkable passage that forms a centerpiece for Percy's comic
synthesis, Tom sees a vision of the new Christ in his own
reflection in the ancient pocked mirror behind the bar of
the Little Napoleon:

> In the dark mirror there is a dim hollow-eyed Spanish Christ. The
> pox is spreading on his face. Vacuoles are opening in his chest. It
> is the new Christ, the spotted Christ, the maculate Christ, the sinful
> Christ. The old Christ died for our sins and it didn't work, we were
> not reconciled. The new Christ shall reconcile man with his sins. The
> new Christ lies drunk in a ditch. Victor Charles and Leroy Ledbetter
> pass by and see him. "Victor, do you love me?" "Sho, Doc." "Leroy,
> do you love me?" "Cut it out, Tom, you know better than to ask
> that." "Then y'all help me." "O.K., Doc." They laugh and pick up
> the new Christ, making a fireman's carry, joining four hands. They
> love the new Christ and so they love each other. (153)

Undoubtedly some readers will see in this reflection the evidence that Tom More is the new Christ. I do not. The literary
landscape is overpopulated with Christ figures, it seems to

me, and it has become as difficult to circumvent as to create such symbols. Tom More is Tom More. What he sees in his own reflection is not himself as the new Christ but the *need* for a new Christ in a fantasy prompted by the racial predicament in which he finds himself.

In the limbo of chronic angelism-bestialism we find ourselves divided between our bestial impulses, which are fueled by hatred and violence, and our higher powers, which are stranded in abstract consciousness. One or the other normally predominates, but in either case our humanity, with its inwardness, is lost. So estranged do we become from each other—racially, socially, or personally—that we can relate to each other only through another we love. The old Christ is dead because we have become immune to the shining example; it cannot reconcile our angelic with our bestial selves. The new Christ lies drunk in a ditch. He needs us. He appeals to our love. Do you love me? Yes. "Then y'all help me." And in our love for him we unite our divided selves and join hands in the task.[32]

This is well and good, you may say, for the South or for some small town or rural community where a few strands remain of the social fabric, but what of the anonymous North or the poor old polarized USA, where as in New York "life is simple, every man's your enemy, and you walk with your eyes straight ahead?" What would it take to work a similar effect? Is there anyone we all love? Walter Cronkite, perhaps, who has been with us on many a sad or happy occasion? Red Skelton, who has made us laugh? When will the new Christ appear? Wait and watch, says Tom More; that is "the spirit of the new age" (387). In the meantime we know how it stands with us, and Percy is surely right about the way of the new Christ: you touch people where they live, not where they do not.

32. If I understand Kierkegaard, the same general relations obtain in the formula he sets down for the eradication of despair: "by relating itself to its own self and by willing to be itself the self is grounded transparently in the Power which posited it" (*The Sickness unto Death,* 147).

The hottest political issue going, Tom has told us, is euthanasia, and a call on old Mr. Ives prepares the way for the grand finale of this section, Tom's trial in The Pit. In the opening pages we learned that the nation's number one killer, by authority of the Surgeon General's report, is "Senior Citizens' anomie," locally known as the "St. Petersburg blues." It strikes even at "Gerry Rehab," where old folks in perfect physical condition inexplicably grow sad, "sit slack and empty-eyed at shuffle board and ceramic oven" despite the opportunity to develop their "creative and altruistic potential" (14). Mr. Ives, "a little bald-headed monkey of a man" from Tennessee whose eyes "fairly hop with—what? rage or risibility?" has been seen to "expose himself and defecate on Flirtation Walk." Worse yet, this overgarrulous man has gone mute. The diagnosis is "senile psychopathy and mutism," and unless Tom can save him, Mr. Ives is clearly slated for the "Happy Isles," meaning the "Permanent Separation Center" and the "Euphoric On-Switch" in a Georgia town appropriately called Jekyl.

The lapsometer reveals a furious redness in his red nucleus. Mr. Ives is "too damn mad to talk," Tom says; he trusts no one. A reading at Brodmann 28, the locus of concrete memory, shows a merry swing of the needle when Tom reminds him of their playing checkers together in his camper ten years ago on just such summer evenings. As yet Tom can only diagnose with the lapsometer, and he cannot prove anything even in diagnosis; but armed with his knowledge of Mr. Ives's condition he is better prepared for his trial-by-combat with Buddy Brown in The Pit, where the old man's fate is to be decided.

It is at this point that Percy's Mephistophilis appears in the person of Art Immelmann. He arrives, like Marlowe's figure, amid thunder, as Tom More sits in his office listening to Don Giovanni begin his descent into hell: "A bolt of lightning strikes a transformer with a great crack. Sparks fly. The ox-lot is filled with a rinsing blue-white light. Trees jump backward. The lights go out."[33] Unlike Marlowe's Mephistophilis, Immelmann is not invoked by Tom, the Dr. Faustus of this piece, but intrudes himself like an unwelcome drug salesman. In the lightning flames he "seems to come forward by jumps" with his big attaché case, shouting over the storm: "Funding is my game." Curiously old-fashioned with his flat-top haircut and white shirt, he looks like a "small-town businessman in the old Auto Age" but speaks the dialect of "one of those liaison fellows from Washington," as he presents himself, moving between the big foundations in the private sector and the National Institute of Mental Health. Immelmann has come to confer recognition on Tom's success in developing a technique that "maximizes and unites hardware and software capabilities," a "tool for dealing with the heretofore immeasurable and intangible stresses that are rending the national fabric." Percy gives the devil the best lines as Immelmann proceeds in the sophisticated lingo of the funding game to describe the lapsometer—the key to Percy's synthesis—as a tool "operative at behavioral, political, and philosophical levels." The people he represents are ready, as we might expect, to "fund an interdisciplinary task force and implement a crash program" to provide every physician and scientist in the country with a *MOQUOL* within a year's time.

A perfect tempter, offering just what the object of his designs wants and hopes for. He has even brought a contract transferring patent rights that he urges Tom to sign: standard procedure for any contract with the "private sector." Victory, Tom thinks, recalling his uncle's advice to "guard against the sadness of hubris." There is no doubt that Tom stands in peril, with his longings for the Nobel Prize, though he is not at this time in the market for voluptuousness; he already has Moira and Lola, not to speak of Ellen and Hester waiting in the wings. He is not trying to sell his soul but to donate

33. Immelmann's arrival makes an interesting comparison with the very similar entrance of Melville's salesman in "The Lightning-Rod Man," particularly in view of the anti-Catholic overtones of Melville's story.

his lapsometer. And who knows but that even Dr. Faustus, if Mephistophilis had spoken the language of "multilevel capacity" and "built-in logistical factors," might have sent him back to hell empty-handed? In any case Tom declines the offer to sign over his patent rights; and Art—it seems fitting that a contemporary Mephistophilis should be known by his first name—leaves by the back door, perhaps taking the short cut to the old Southern Hotel. But how would he know about the short cut? Tom wonders, and Percy ends the July First section on that mystifying note.

In the brief section of July Second, Property Rights Sunday is being celebrated in the Catholic Church. Monsignor Schleif-kopf, whose name means Knothead, preaches about those two fellow property owners, Joseph of Arimathea and Lazarus: "Dearly Beloved: we are reminded by the best commentators that Lazarus was not a poor man, that he lived comfortably in a home that he owned." Tom's Mother, Marva, a "realtor" who no doubt calls a house a "home," lives comfortably in her own physical habitation. "She sparkles with good health and is at one with herself." She is something of a prophetess, having predicted "four out of the last five assassinations,"[34] and is likewise immersed in astrology. She cautions Tom, who is a Cancer and therefore "deeply sensitive," to beware of Aries and Libra. (Ellen is evidently an Aries, and Moira, "that little Left snippet," a Libra.) The perfect match would be a Taurus—namely Lola—who by good fortune also stands to inherit Tara. Marva has a misty faith in the land: "Do you remember what Scarlett said about the land? Or was it in *The Good Earth*?" "Yes," says Dusty Rhoades, whose faith is a drier one. Marva's religion is a marshy compound of real estate and the occult, overlain by a shroud of Christianity. Wet or dry, Knothead faith is intimately bound to property.

---

34. A remarkable achievement, just the kind of achievement to be singled out for praise in a society such as the novel describes. Even more wonderful would be to find a way to do without the assassinations.

Far closer to the faith of Christ is the unlikely love couple from the swamp who chanced upon a Confederate Bible, "read it as if it had never been read before, the wildest unlikeliest doctrine imaginable, believed it, decided to be married and baptize their children" (188). As Sutter Vaught wrote in his casebook, "There is after all something worse than being God-forsaken. It is when God overstays his welcome and takes up with the wrong people."[35] Kierkegaard wondered how to introduce Christianity into Danish Christendom; how would Christ find entrance to Paradise Estates? By surprise, perhaps, through the naïvete of a love couple in the swamp, who take a fresh look at his story and catch at least a glimpse of what is there.

Finally the big day arrives, the day on which Tom is to meet Buddy Brown in The Pit. On his way to an appointment with the Director he runs into Buddy, who greets him with a pinch and a wink. "Son, this time I got you by the short hairs," says Buddy, a licentious man who keeps himself exceptionally clean. Now Buddy runs through the secular litany referred to earlier as Tom listens like Binx Bolling enduring his Aunt Emily:

> "It's the quality of life that counts."
> "Yes."
> "And the right of the individual to control his own body."
> "Well—"
> "And above all a man's sacred right to choose his own destiny and realize his own potential."
> "Well—"
> "Would you let your own mother suffer?"
> "Yes."
> "I don't believe you. I know you too well and know that you place a supreme value on human values."
> "Yes."
> "We believe in the same things, differing only in the best way to achieve them." (197–98)

The comedy of this scene arises from the incoherence of

35. Percy, *Last Gentleman*, 357. Note the similarity between the love couple here and the Tyree children of the earlier novel in their receptivity to the Good News.

the consensus anthropology, which suddenly becomes apparent. In the mouth of Buddy Brown, who has already made up his mind to ship Mr. Ives off to be executed, this talk of "a man's sacred right to choose his own destiny and realize his own potential" rings with mockery, but Buddy would be the last to detect it. The final line could be translated, "We're not really sure what we believe, so let's not quarrel, let's just do it my way." Buddy speaks a language of ideals drawn from the Judaeo-Christian tradition and operates on behaviorist assumptions. "It is the job of the satirist," Percy says, "to detect these slips and to exaggerate them so that they become known to everybody."[36]

The prelude to The Pit is Tom's visit to the Director. He enters as a patient, having forgotten that Monday is patients' day. Tom's hope is that the Director will help him secure funds to develop the lapsometer. Though the Director, as a behaviorist, is unlikely to smile on the notion of an ontological lapsometer, he is also dying of cancer. "A dying king, said Sir Thomas More, is apt to be wiser than a healthy king. A dying behaviorist may be a good behaviorist." But as it turns out, the Director patronizes Tom about the twenty-five million dollars he needs, reminding him of his "patient-staff status." The precarious balance of Tom's status is pivotal to the scene as he tips more and more in the direction of patient. The Director enjoins him to "hang in right where you are." Then, as the lapsometer lies on the desk between them "like a dog turd," he asks Tom: "Do you think you are well?" No, Tom says, seeing no particular connection between his answer and the merit of his proposal. But at the Director's "Well—?" his balance tilts: "My God, he's right. $25,000,000. An ontological lapsometer. I'm mad as a hatter." The Director inquires ironically about the lapse measured by the lapsometer: "A fall perhaps from a state of inno-

---

36. "The Authors That Bloom in the Spring," 23. See Percy's remark in footnote 10 on swamping the boat.

cence?"[37] whereupon Tom withdraws defeated, wanting to
practice medicine from his bed on the ward, "lie happy and
stiff on my bed, like a Hindoo on his bed of nails, and treat
sane folk and sane doctors from the sane world, which is
the maddest world of all" (207). He is now so addled that
he cannot speak coherently to his nemesis, Buddy Brown.
"I do not speak well. I've lost. I'm a patient."

It is in this condition that he signs away his patent rights
to Art Immelmann. The stage on which Percy's Faustus meets
his Mephistophilis is the men's room, where this emissary
from the dark regions of "funding" is in his element. A bit
earlier Art has identified himself as a coordinator, not the
man with the big ideas like Tom, just a "tinkerer." Now he
says obscenely, "Let me see your MOQUOL." He informs
Tom how he can turn the lapsometer from diagnosis to treatment, and he tells Tom what he wants to hear in Tom's
own private language. Like the diabolical figure who accompanies Hawthorne's young Goodman Brown through the forest, he has the gift of "discoursing so aptly that his arguments
[seem] rather to spring up in the bosom of his auditor than
to be suggested by himself." Tom wonders how a man who

37. If it strikes the reader that Percy is flailing away needlessly at a view of
man that is already discredited, I suggest a reading of Arthur Koestler's appendix
"On Not Flogging Dead Horses" *(The Ghost in the Machine* [New York, 1967],
349–53), in which Koestler denies that "the crudely mechanistic nineteenth century
conceptions" in biology, medicine, and psychology are really dead. Behaviorist
psychology, he says, still occupies a strategic key position" in all this. How is it,
he wonders, "that while Behaviourism is still floating like a dense smog over the
landscape, so many scientists of the younger generation, who are almost stifled
by it, keep pretending that the sky is blue, and Behaviourism a matter of the
past? Partly, I think, [because] though they have outgrown the sterile orthodoxy
of their elders, its terminology and jargon have got into their bloodstream, and
they cannot get away from thinking in terms of stimulus, response, conditioning,
reinforcement, operants, and so on.... Academics, brought up in [the reflex-
philosophy of Pavlov, Watson, and Skinner], may reject the more obvious absurdities
of Watson and Skinner, but nevertheless continue to employ their terminology
and methodology, and thus remain unconsciously tied to the axioms implied in
them."
Koestler too seems to be describing a kind of "consensus anthropology." Just
how "dead" these behaviorist assumptions are in Percy's novel is clear from the
power the Director wields in his summary dismissal of Tom's proposal as the figment
of a "patient-staff" subordinate.

looks like "the sort of fellow who used to service condom vendors in the old Auto Age" can know these things, but to his doubts Art replies, "Drink this drink and you'll never want a drink."

Tom drinks it, of course. Having himself been massaged by his own lapsometer, his terror now gone and his large bowel "slack as a string, clear as a bell," he signs the contract. His wishes are fulfilled. "Now you can use your talents for the good of mankind and the increase of knowledge," Art says, deftly touching the scientist's pride. "All you have to do is never look back and never be sorry as per agreement" (217). Tom seems to have closed a better deal than did Faustus, who promised never to think on God:

> Nor will Faustus henceforth. Pardon him for this,
> And Faustus vows never to look to heaven!
> Never to name God or to pray to Him,
> To burn His Scriptures, slay His ministers,
> And make my spirits pull His churches down.[38]

During this scene in the men's room Percy does something highly unusual. Art turns the lapsometer on Tom, and the effects are given phenomenologically. First Tom's anxiety level is raised until he feels "the Terror, but tolerable." He sees the wall urinals as "shaped like skulls." A "minus-seven Chloride dose" brings a dramatic effect: "Something in my diaphragm lets go. I realize I've been breathing at the top of my lungs for forty-five years." Then he notices his hand, a beautiful strong hand, but the hand of a stranger: "How can a man spend forty-five years as a stranger to himself? No other creature would do such a thing. No animal would, for he is pure organism. No angel would, for he is pure spirit." When a person is reconciled with himself and thus united as man-spirit, the author seems to be suggesting, he will experience his hand not as Roquentin does in Sartre's

---

38. Christopher Marlowe, *Doctor Faustus*, Act Two, Scene Two.

Nausea—as an alien fat-bellied crab lying on its back—but as a strangely beautiful manifestation of being.[39]

Percy then goes beyond this in the attempt to convey something extremely difficult to grasp. Art stimulates Brodmann 11, "the area of the musical-erotic." "Here the abstract is experienced concretely and the concrete abstractly." One loves a woman, for example, "both in herself and insofar as she is a woman," faithlessly and yet, as one loves music, truly. "A woman is the concrete experienced abstractly, as women." The love one experiences in this realm is that of the "scientist-lover," Art explains, and has its counterpart in scientific knowledge, which is "neutral morally, abstractive and godlike." Tom hears the "love music of man in particular for women in general" and the concept is translated into experiential terms as he begins murmuring to himself:

> Who am I?
> I am he who loves. I am in love. I love.
> Who do you love?
> You.
> Who is "you"?
> A girl.
> What girl?
> Any girl you please. You. (214).

Is this revelation that we find here, genuine insight, or the delusion of one who attempts, as Marlowe put it, to "practice more than heavenly power permits"?

The question is not easily resolved. One clue lies in the fact that the devil again has the best answers. Art insinuates himself into Tom's thoughts to get him to sign the contract:

39. A man regaining consciousness in a strange place and trying to recall what has happened, Percy says, catches sight of his hand: "It is as if he had never seen it before: he is astounded by its complexity, its functional beauty." What he experiences is a kind of "natural revelation" which can only be called "a revelation of being" ("Notes for a Novel," 10).

But the same hand, from a different conception of the world, might be viewed with disgust: "I see my hand spread out on the table. It lives—it is me. It opens, the fingers open and point. It is lying on its back. It show me its fat belly. It looks like an animal turned upside down. The fingers are the paws. I amuse myself by moving them very rapidly, like the claws of a crab which has fallen on its back" (Jean-Paul Sartre, *Nausea*, trans. Lloyd Alexander [New York, 1964], 98).

"Isn't it better to feel good rather than bad?" "Yes." "Isn't it better to be happy than unhappy?" "Yes." Who can dispute such arguments? The limitations of such reasoning are those of the musical-erotic, a term of Kierkegaard's that represents the highest achievement of the aesthetic sphere. Seen from the aesthetic sphere, the musical-erotic is the best of the good; seen from the ethical sphere, it is bad.[40] Don Juan is the personification of the musical-erotic, which in its immediacy can only be expressed in music, and it does not carry the connotations we attach to sensuality but is translated simply as "sensuousness—an amoral wild impulse following its purely natural urge."[41] That is its beauty and the upper boundary of its possibilities.

The public trial of Tom More culminates in the splendid comic uproar of The Pit. Sir Thomas More refused allegiance to the new order and was tried and beheaded for his crime.[42] Tom's trial is a little different. He too refuses allegiance to the new order, in this case a neobehaviorist order descended from B. F. Skinner,[43] but he is not beheaded. His trial consists of gladiatorial combat with one of Skinner's intellectual heirs for the life of poor old Mr. Ives—in The Pit, where Tom's assumptions and those of the behaviorists can be put to the empirical test. Is man simply an organism to be controlled and treated by proper conditioning, a mere piano key, or is he that testy and paradoxical being who emerged from Dostoevski's underground to proclaim his

40. At least that is how Percy told me he interprets Kierkegaard and what he attempts in this scene. Kierkegaard devotes almost a hundred pages to the musical-erotic in *Either / Or,* I.

41. Quoted from the notes to Kierkegaard, *Either / Or,* I, 447.

42. Sir Thomas More was Lord Chancellor of England under King Henry VIII. When the King divorced Queen Catherine to marry Anne Boleyn, More refused to swear fidelity to the new Act of Succession, unwilling as a matter of conscience to recognize any temporal lord as head of the church. He was indicted for high treason, convicted, and beheaded in 1535. His last words rang throughout Europe with his protest that he died "the King's good servant but God's first." See R. W. Chambers, *Thomas More* (London, 1935), the standard biography.

43. Since the publication of *Love in the Ruins,* B. F. Skinner has come out with a new book with a title Percy himself could not have improved upon: *Beyond Freedom and Dignity* (New York, 1971).

freedom and boast of his bad liver?[44] Can he find breathing
space in the new Crystal Palace of the behaviorists or will
he smash the windows in search of open sky?

Tom enters The Pit a decided underdog in the contest,
having been reduced to "patient" status, though after a
MOQUOL massage by Art Immelmann his heart is full of
love and his mind "like a meat grinder ready to receive the
raw stuff of experience and turn out neat pattycake principles." The steep slopes of the amphitheater are jammed with
students, who—like students in general, Tom thinks—are
a scurvy lot, half of them anti-euthanasics who revere Dr.
Spiro T. Agnew, the other half "qualitarians" following Hesse,
Skinner, and Justice William O. Douglas, who has presided
over a hundred million abortions in India and an equal
number of "painless 'terminations' of miserable and un-
productive old folk." As Buddy Brown and Tom square off
in this strange court a tacit behaviorist assumption emerges
that Mr. Ives is guilty of terminal failure to respond successfully to conditioning and that unless Tom, upon whom the
burden of proof rests, can somehow exonerate him, Mr. Ives
is necessarily to be shipped off to a painless termination.[45]

Buddy Brown leads off with his "differential diagnosis:

44. No excerpt can convey what Dostoevski's Underground Man has to say,
but for those unacquainted with him the following may help: "Then, you say,
science itself will teach man . . . that he does not really have either caprice or will
of his own and that he has never had it, and that he himself is something like
a piano key or an organ stop, and that, moreover, laws of nature exist in this
world, so that everything he does is not done by his will at all, but is done by
itself, according to the laws of nature. Consequently we have only to discover these
laws of nature, and man will no longer be responsible for his actions and life
will become exceedingly easy for him."

Then the Crystal Palace will be built, the Underground Man says sarcastically,
referring to the building erected in London for the Great Industrial Exhibition
of 1851, a symbol of the rising industrial-urban civilization. He denies that man
will ever pursue enlightened self-interest and proclaims that "man everywhere and
always, whoever he may be, has preferred to act as he wished and not in the
least as his reason and advantage dictated. . . . What man needs is simply independent
choice, whatever that independence may cost and wherever it may lead." Quoted
from Fyodor Dostoevski, *"Notes from Underground" and "The Grand Inquisitor,"* trans.
Ralph E. Matlaw (New York, 1960), Part VII, 22–23.

45. The intellectual arrogance of the assumption should be evident, but note that
if the assumption should be in error the cost is to be paid by Mr. Ives, who is
to be reduced in conformity with the reductivism of the behaviorist anthropology.

advanced atherosclerosis, senile psychosis, psychopathic and antisocial behavior, hemiplegia and aphasia following a cerebrovascular accident." Solid medical evidence from an expert, by the sound of it. Meanwhile Tom idles away his time admiring the beauty of his hand. Buddy omits to make a therapeutic recommendation; it scarcely seems necessary. "We are still waiting for your diagnosis, Dr. More," he says with the gentleness of victory. "I found no significant pathology," Tom replies, recommending that Mr. Ives be discharged. The conflict builds itself into the scene quoted at the beginning of this chapter, with Tom uttering the word *funeral* and the girls pulling their skirts down over their knees as the Director warns Tom to watch what he says. Mr. Ives's "bright monkey eyes" begin to snap. "I repeat," Tom says to the back rows. "If Mr. Ives is going to be referred to the Happy Isles of Georgia, which is nothing but a euthanasia facility, he has the right to know it and to prepare himself accordingly. And he has the right to know who his executioner is."

The Director threatens to send Tom back to the ward and Tom wonders if in fact that is where he belongs, but Buddy Brown saves him by forcibly giving him an alcohol test and pronouncing him "drunk as a lord!" Tom reacts by inhibiting Buddy's inhibitory centers with the lapsometer, confident that it will be enough just to "let Buddy be what he is." Buddy begins making lewd half-audible remarks and Tom moves on to Mr. Ives, further scandalizing the behaviorists with his metaphysics. "What is interesting [in Mr. Ives]," he says, "is the structure of his selfhood as it relates both to his fellow seniors in the Tampa settlement and to the scientists here." Let him speak if he is well, the students clamor. The lapsometer now comes to the rescue. Tom administers a "light Chloride dampening" to the red nucleus of Mr. Ives and a "moderate Sodium massage" to his speech area.[46] Mr. Ives begins to speak in a "deep drawling voice."

46. Sodium and chloride are united in common salt. Tom "cures" the patient by uniting his rage with his powers of speech, thus making the old man worth his salt.

The flavor of his remarks in the dramatic moments that follow emerges in his answer to the Director's query as to why he had behaved so outrageously to his fellow "retirees": "Doctor, how would you like it if during the most critical time of your experiments with the Skinner box that won you the Nobel Prize, you had been pestered without letup by a bunch of chickenshit Ohioans?" His explanation for not having walked or spoken for a month resounds with contempt: "There is only one kind of response to those who would control your responses by throwing you in a Skinner box," and that is to "refuse to respond at all." Tom recommends the old man be released and furnished with transportation back to Tennessee, where Mr. Ives's subsequent plans sound remarkably similar to sentiments expressed elsewhere by Tom: "Write a book, look at the hills, live till I die."

It is a superlatively funny scene and succeeds in discrediting behaviorist assumptions. The consensus anthropology is exposed as a fraud. Tom the underdog comes out on top and the whole circus disintegrates into farce as Art Immelmann, who has somehow got hold of Tom's box of lapsometers—"Now what the devil is he doing?" Tom wonders—proceeds to distribute them to one and all. Without a "pilot," he explains, they cannot hope to "go national": "That's boilerplate, Doc." Notwithstanding its dangers, the lapsometer proves a smashing success for Ted and Tanya, who are successfully interacting on the floor beneath the seats. "All we feared was fear itself," they chorus as he steps over them with a gentlemanly "Pardon." The libido of even the glacial Presbyterian Ellen threatens to break loose. "Did I say it aloud?" she asks Tom. And off they go, Tom between Max and Ellen, as the Director discovers how fair a fair youth can be, misquoting from the classics to a "handsome peach-faced lad" from an old-line Southern family.

The Temptation of Tom More

Sir Thomas More stood his ground good-humoredly and

was beheaded, later to be canonized a saint. It is difficult to foresee any such clear prospect for Tom at this hour of his triumph. Superficially he seems in little danger of hubris, with his manifold weaknesses and ailments and his three girls, heading into a Fourth of July on which his lapsometers are scattered over the landscape and he is being hunted by the same Bantus who aim to kidnap the Christian Kaydettes. On the other hand, as Tom himself might say, never have fame and power hovered so near. Students have applauded him, his girls are brimming with admiration, even the Director is now eager to get him under contract before MIT or Harvard latches onto him. And always, in the wings waiting, there is Art Immelmann, with his access to funds and high-powered committees. Tom has emerged victorious from his public trial; now he must face the deadlier temptations of hubris in the privacy of his mind.

The action in this second Fourth of July section centers on the hijinks of revolution and Tom's love tryst with his three girls in the broken-down Howard Johnson's, most of it good fun that breaks again and again into burlesque, at times threatening to become tiresome. But underlying all the funny business are the Faustus theme and a religious theme involving Samantha that is virtually unseen and yet emerges almost inexplicably from time to time. The death of Tom's daughter Samantha is the tragic face beneath the comic mask of Tom More. We have seen how well he can diagnose the ills of others. Now we have a chance to see how well he perceives his own, as within the panoramic public scene of the novel the private ordeal of its narrator now begins to put forth a subdued light that comes to suffuse and illumine the wider sphere.

It was the ghastly death of Samantha that put Tom on the skids some eight years earlier. She had been the cement holding his life together. Her death gave him an excuse to drink and go into decline. As his intelligence became more and more "duly darkened," he became mired deeper and deeper in the comic religious state in which he still lives, saying the right thing and doing the wrong.[47] The religious theme surfaces more and more as memories of Samantha and Doris are prompted by events.

As Tom leaves his house on this "hot still gold-green Fourth of July" the sight of P. T. Bledsoe's house burning cheerfully and unattended in the middle of Paradise Estates recalls to him how thirty years earlier, as a thirteen-year-old, he had "defiled himself" in the skeletal bathroom of the house, then under construction, amid the carpenter's litter of copper flashing and blocks of wood, "man's excellent geometries wrought from God's somewhat lumpish handiwork." A buzz on the Anser-Phone in his shirt pocket feels like a heart attack and produces "belated contrition": "God, don't let me die. I haven't lived, and there's the summer ahead and music and science and girls" (247).

While he waits for Moira to shower during their rendezvous at Howard Johnson's, Tom drinks a toddy and recalls his lost life with Doris in the old Auto Age before Samantha was born. Doris had never understood why he would leave her in the motel Sundays, during their travels, and find his way to mass in some nearby church. The passage is revealing:

> Now here was the strangest exercise of all! Leaving the coordinate of the motel at the intersection of the interstates, leaving the motel with standard doors and carpets and plumbing, leaving the interstates extending infinitely in all directions, abscissa and ordinate, descending through a moonscape countryside to a —town! Where people had been living all these years, and to some forlorn little mass, stepping up on the porch as if I had been doing it every Sunday for the past twenty years, and here comes the stove-up bemused priest with his cup (what am I doing out here? says his dazed expression) upon whose head hands had been laid and upon this other head other hands and so on, for here off I-51 I touched the thread in the labyrinth. . . . (254)

The labyrinth, it becomes clear in the context of the novel,

47. The phrase "duly darkened," quoted earlier, is from Kierkegaard's *The Sickness unto Death*, 225. Tom sinks into a condition Kierkegaard called continuation of sin: eternity has "only two rubrics, and 'everything which is not of faith is sin'; every unrepented sin is a new sin, and every moment it is unrepented is new sin" (236). For Kierkegaard on the comic religious, see footnote 14.

is the abstract "moonscape" terrain of modern urban society, this nowhere of which Binx Bolling has such a fear, with its interstates and standardized motels set down indiscriminately in the "green hills of Tennessee or out in haunted New Mexico." The thread in this labyrinth is the "forlorn" little church in a real town where people "had been living all these years," a concrete link with time and place, and the "stove-up bemused priest" upon whose head "hands had been placed."

Tom cannot say whether his exhilaration comes from "eating Christ" or from his "secret discovery of the singular thread" in this "geometry of Holiday Inns and improbable interstates," but the feeling seems to spring from the weird conjunction of terrain abstracted right out of time and a real place with ties going back, back, back. The experience is an existential repetition that enjoys the surprise of a rotation—suddenly out of the twilit labyrinth of the Eclipse, a thread leading all the way back to the Event.[48] Doris, being spiritual and seeing religion as spirit," could never understand "that it took religion to save me from the spirit world, from orbiting the earth like Lucifer and the angels, that it took nothing less than touching the thread off the misty interstates and eating Christ himself to make me mortal man again and let me inhabit my own flesh and love her in the morning." Now he has lost the thread and is himself lost in the labyrinth.

It was with Samantha that Tom used to go to mass on summer evenings, and now, as he carries on the tryst with Moira, the ghost of Samantha keeps coming back. It is her ghost that keeps a few embers alive in him. Moira is an empty-

---

48. Percy's essay on *A Canticle for Leibowitz* describes just such a conjunction in terms of an abscissa or time-line running left to right crossed by an ordinate consisting of "Something That Happened or Something That Will Happen on the time-line of such a nature that all points on the time-line are read with reference to the happening, as before or after, minus or plus" (575).

The existential repetition, Percy wrote in "The Man on the Train," is "the passionate quest in which the incident serves as a thread in the labyrinth to be followed at any cost" (490).

headed romantic caught in the common snares of inauthenticity. She asks naïvely, "Could we live in Paradise?" Tom carries her in his arms "like a child" and pats her "just as I used to pat Samantha when she had growing pains." Moira, while sharing in his fling, thus keeps fanning the embers of his memory. She plugs a quarter into the vibrating bed just as Samantha used to do. Her prodigality with her charms prompts an angry memory of the time Samantha was stood up by a boy from St. Aloysius: "Curse God, curse the nuns for arranging the dance, goddamn the little Celt-Catholic bastards, little Mediterranean lowbrow French-dago jerks. Anglo-Saxon Presbyterians would have better manners even if they didn't believe in God" (260). The memory calls up tears, bringing Tom closer to a recognition of his present state, and he feels guilt for accepting Moira's favors while she holds herself so cheap. "With her I feel like a man watching a child run around with a forty-carat diamond. Her casualness with herself makes me sweat."

The adventure with Moira is a rotation leading nowhere. Tom's dalliance in the bunker with Lola had been a rotation too, as he could not make his mother understand: "A perfect encounter, but it is not to be thought that we could repeat it" (176). But in promoting, with the aid of Dusty Rhoades, Tom's marriage to Lola, Marva is trying to propel him into the fake repetition of life at Tara. He is tempted by Lola's vision of him as "an agreeable H. G. Wells nineteenth-century scientist type, 'doing my researches' in the handsome outhouse of Tara" (338)—the same kind of researches, incidentally, that Aunt Emily had foreseen for Binx. "Come back to Tara," Lola begs him. "Come back and put down roots with Lola" (281). But even the music of this idyll, "happy old Haydn, whose music does not brook one single shadow of sadness," now seems to belong more to Vince Marsaglia, the gangster who had bought Tara from M-G-M, than to Tom More. When Tom says to Lola, "I've told you we can't go back to Tara" (316), he is doing more than echoing Thomas Wolfe. The mossy image of Tara is Percy's best lampoon of Southern sentimentality. The roads to Tara are dusty with the tramp of antebellum feet.

Tom's road to salvation takes another route, but first some other matters need attending to. He is taken captive by Uru and Victor, who drive him through Paradise in an armored golf cart[49] and imprison him in Monsignor Schleifkopf's office. Tom escapes through the air-conditioning vent, removing the screws from the grill with the "proper bronze sword" of the "somewhat prissy bronze archangel" Saint Michael—saved, this bad Catholic of the subtitle, by his knowledge of the sword, which he used "to fiddle with during the Holy Name meetings" (308). It was Saint Michael, we might recall, who led Adam and Eve out of Paradise after the Fall, while the "brandished sword of God before them blazed."[50] Tom leaves Paradise in a wild burlesque, setting off the carillon chimes, discarding Saint Michael's sword at the outside grill, kicking the grill loose during the major chord of "White Christmas," and coming out "feet-first, born again, ejected into the hot bright perilous world" of the Fourth of July, whereupon Lola rescues him on horseback and the two of them ride off on a mare called Yellow Rose while the carillon sounds "The First Noel" and Victor Charles exhorts Tom to "take care this little lady." "Isn't Victor wonderful!" Lola cries, catching a glimpse of old-time ways. "Tom, let's go to Tara!" But Tom, preferring moonscape to mold, directs her to Howard Johnson's instead.

Returning to the Love Clinic to retrieve Lola's cello, Tom learns he is being credited with a "breakthrough." At "Love" they have "implemented" his insight that "marital love often founders on boredom and the struggle to attain a theoretical orgasmic perfection" and with consummate imagination are

49. The idea for Percy's unpublished apprentice novel *The Charterhouse*, discussed in Chapter One, lends savor to this already piquant image of an armored golf cart touring Paradise.

50. John Milton, *Paradise Lost*, Book XII, line 633. Note the parallel too with the letter opener Aunt Emily toys with while lambasting Binx toward the end of *The Moviegoer*.

making a "fresh start" with "substitute partners." In this scene
Percy finally satirizes the misuse of the word *existential*: "Oh
dear!" Father Kev Kevin cries, watching Stryker lead Helga
into the Observer Stimulation Overflow Area. "If ever there
was an existential decision—!"

A conversation in this scene between Tom and Art
Immelmann suggests how one form of the monstrousness
of our century is born of the rift in man's nature that Percy
describes. Tom warns Art of the danger of applying the
lapsometer to the "prefrontal abstractive centers" of a man:
"It would render him totally abstracted from himself, totally
alienated from the concrete world, and in such a state of
angelism that he will fall prey to the first abstract notion
proposed to him and will kill anybody who gets in his way,
torture, execute, wipe out entire populations, all with the
best possible motives and the best possible intentions, in fact
in the name of peace and freedom, etcetera" (328). Art's
diabolic response to the horror of this vision is a delighted:
"Yeah, Doc! Your MOQUOL surpasses my most sanguine
expectations."

What Tom describes in his warning is not altogether new.
Consider the dream Raskolnikov has at the conclusion of
Crime and Punishment:

> While sick, he had dreamed the whole world was condemned to suffer
> a terrible, unprecedented, and unparalleled plague, which had spread
> to Europe from the depths of Asia. Except for a small handful of
> the chosen, all were doomed to perish. A new kind of trichinae had
> appeared, microscopic substances that lodged in men's bodies. Yet
> these were spiritual substances as well, endowed with mind and will.
> Those infected were seized immediately and went mad. Yet people
> never considered themselves so clever and so unhesitatingly right
> as these infected ones considered themselves. Never had they consid-
> ered their decrees, their scientific deductions, their moral convictions
> and their beliefs more firmly based. Whole settlements, whole cities
> and nations, were infected and went mad.[51]

51. This is quoted from the epilogue of Fyodor Dostoevski, *Crime and Punishment*,
trans. Sidney Monas (New York, 1968).

The affinity is apparent, though where Dostoevski is giving us a vision of future horrors Percy is trying to account for those already in evidence. With chronic angelism-bestialism man's essential humanity is divided between angelic and bestial elements, and he has little defense against the impulses that assail him. A vacuum will be filled. "War," as Percy said, "is better than nothing."[52] The effect may be worse when the motive force is an angelic dedication to abstract ideals than when it springs directly from the most bestial of hatreds. In either case the spirit of abstraction is at work and the price is paid by concrete human beings living in the world.

The only real immunization against such viruses is a truly human condition, man united with himself. How can the rift be healed? The novel, which was originally entitled *How to Make Love in the Ruins*, suggests possibilities. We learned from Kierkegaard that the "crowd" infected by these plagues is made up of individuals, and we have one such individual before us, Tom More. Now that we know the doctor's diagnosis of the others, we can return to how it is with him.

To Art's trumpeting that he has "already elicited positive interactions from both ends of the spectrum" with the lapsometer, Tom breaks in: "Goddamn, man, do you realize what you're saying?" Art winces at the mention of God, but to Tom's "Get out of my way" this satanic figure resorts to his old bag of tricks, mentioning Tom's prospect of winning the Nobel Prize, which leaves Tom with a "pleasant tingle" running across the sacrum. Later, Tom's allegation that "you and your goddamn foundations" are somehow responsible for what is happening, Art winces again and denies on principle that they "do" anything to anyone. "We only help people do what they want to do," he protests in a classic disclaimer of moral responsibility. "We facilitate social interaction in order to isolate factors." And here Percy has the devil himself quoting scripture in proclaiming that his people are "dedicated to the freedom of the individual to choose his

52. "Hughes's Solipsism Malgré Lui," 492.

own destiny and develop his own potential" (363). Hearing this pious claim from such a source, we should question it from anyone whose loyalties belong to other regions.

It is hardly surprising that Tom finally conquers his own hubris in the form of a plush post in Denmark in which to await his Nobel Prize. What is interesting is how he does it and why. It may be his invocation of Sir Thomas More that drives Immelmann hence, but what prompts him to resist in the first place? Neither a mechanical necessity of the plot, I think, nor the demands of any mythic or literary parallel outside the book, but the terms the author has set up within the novel: Tom's need to escape More's syndrome and to live as a human. Religion is instrumental, and in Tom's labyrinth the one remaining thread is his memory of Samantha.

The key scene is a flashback, triggered evidently by Uru's rejection of Tom's goodwill blessing[53] with a final: "You better go back, Doc, while you can." Tom does go back, in memory, to the day when he had stood by Samantha's bed. She asks, "Papa, have you lost your faith?" No, he says.

> "Then why don't you go to Mass any more?"
> "I don't know. Maybe because you don't go with me."
> "Papa, you're in greater danger than Mama."
> "How is that?"
> "Because she is protected by Invincible Ignorance."
> "That's true," I said, laughing.
> "She doesn't know any better."
> "She doesn't."
> "You do."
> "Yes."
> "Just promise me one thing, Papa."
> "What's that?"
> "Don't commit the one sin for which there is no forgiveness."
> "Which one is that?"
> "The sin against grace. If God gives you the grace to believe in him and love him and you refuse, the sin will not be forgiven you."
> (373–74)

---

53. Tom fumbles around like Will Barrett in trying to tell Uru what he knows Uru will not hear: "You got to get where we are and I'm not even sure you can do that" (373). Black militancy has progressed, but racial understanding seems to be about what it was back in the days of Will Barrett.

This sin against grace can no doubt be interpreted in strictly Catholic terms. But the novel goes beyond any sectarian confines to attempt a synthesis of religious and secular thought, and grace here has another dimension. What forms of grace are open to Tom More and to the rest of us who are exiled to the postmodern world?

Here again, I think, as in *The Last Gentleman,* grace is subjectivity or inwardness. The thread in Tom's labyrinth is the memory of Samantha, which has become the only link with his former faith. The sinful condition in which he lives is the opposite of faith. But the grace of inwardness can be viewed secularly as well. In the grip of the malaise we become lost in a limbo of objectivity. We have a clue to what grace might be in another memory of Samantha. Tom's heart was broken by her death. While she lived, "life still had its same peculiar tentativeness, people living as usual by fits and starts, aiming and missing, while present time went humming"; but even then he had foreknowledge that "the second she died, remorse would come and give time its bitter specious wholeness. If only—If only we hadn't been defeated by humdrum humming present time and missed it, missed ourselves, missed everything" (374). In the limbo of the malaise, present time defeats us. To catch it might be, as Chuck Parker says, to live "completely and in the moment the way the prothonotary warbler lives flashing holy fire" (368). Or better still, to reenter paradise and live there "both as man and spirit, whole and intact man-spirit, as solid flesh as a speckled trout, a dappled thing, yet aware of itself as a self!" (36).

The memory of Samantha pulls Tom out of his abstracted orbit and gives him access to his own inwardness, where he is whole and intact. In the illumination of his reviving faith his condition becomes apparent to him and he realizes he has been feasting on Samantha's death. When he had refused to take her to Lourdes, Doris, who though a dumbbell knew how to read his faults, saw that he refused in fear the girl might be cured. "What then? Suppose you ask God for a miracle and God says yes, very well. How do you live the rest of your life?" How indeed? Who can shoulder such a load? And with that recognition Tom leaves the realm of the comic religious, where he knows without doing, and resumes a life of doing as he knows.

The Samantha theme now recedes and Percy returns to Faustus. Recognizing what is working below the surface, we know that the actual spurning of Art's offer is a very minor victory. The scene itself is comical. "Our work here is finished," the novel's Mephistophilis remarks, gazing happily at the smoking bunker, in an echo of the concluding note of *The Tempest*. He manifests an evil influence over Tom, advancing lapsometer in hand. Tom cannot move from the spot. He peers through the smoke at his adversary, who declares: "The two of you will have to come." "If we both go, Chief," Ellen says in something like a farewell to the Garden, "maybe it will be all right." "We'll all be happy in Copenhagen," Art murmurs, breaking into song: *"Beautiful beautiful Copenhagen."* Then, echoing Helga of the Love Clinic with a "Let's go, kids," he touches Ellen, at which Tom closes his eyes and offers a good prayer, for a bad Catholic: *"Sir Thomas More, kinsman, saint, best dearest merriest of Englishmen, pray for us and drive this son of a bitch hence."* Opening his eyes, he finds Art "turning slowly away, wheeling in slow motion, a dazed hurt look through the eyes as if he had been struck across the face." Unlike Faustus, Tom had never sworn not to invoke the name of God or his representatives, and Art Immelmann is powerless against Tom's kinsman saint. The innocent Ellen feels sorry for Art as he vanishes into the smoke. The July action of the novel closes with Ellen smoothing Tom's eyebrows with her spit and urging that the two of them go home.

EAST OF THE NEW EDEN

The epilogue opens on a note of reconciliation. The mood is pastoral, and the change in Tom's life is nowhere better conveyed than in this passage worthy of Thoreau at his best: "Water is the mystical element! At dawn the black bayou breathes a white vapor. The oars knock, cypress against cypress, but the sound is muffled, wrapped in cotton. As the trotline is handed along, the bank quickly disappears and the skiff seems to lift and be suspended in a new element globy and white. Silence presses in and up from the vaporish depths come floating great green turtles, blue catfish, lordly gaspergous" (382). Our strivings now are ended, the tone seems to say. Life begins. The mood belongs to merry England, not the aspiring Elizabethan mood of Marlowe's *Doctor Faustus* but the quiet contentment he voices in "The Passionate Shepherd to His Love":

> Come live with me and be my love,
> And we will all the pleasures prove
> That valleys, groves, hills, and fields,
> Woods, or steepy mountain yields.

Five years have passed, enough for an age. "Now while you work, you also watch and listen and wait. In the last age we planned projects and cast ahead of ourselves." No more. Tom is reconciled at last, this time to himself.[54] "All any man needs," he says, "is time and desire and the sense of his own sovereignty."

The externals underlying this transformation are evident enough. He now occupies the slave quarters because the Bantus have won—not by force of arms but by oil money—and in a reversal of roles have taken over Paradise while Tom hoes collards in a more humble garden. Tom's showdown with Art Immelmann evidently failed to curb his ambition; he sank all his money into the lapsometer and it was insolvency, not broken pride, that brought out his humility. The aspiration symbolized by the lapsometer was one to "practice more than heavenly power permits," and we knew all along it would have to be duly chastened. The Bantus, on the other hand, are riding high, and a good share of the epilogue elaborates the old notion that the more it changes the more

54. The note struck here coincides with the union of body with soul that Whitman describes in Section 5 of "Song of Myself": "Swiftly arose and spread around me the peace and knowledge that pass all the argument of the earth...."

it stays the same. Colley Wilkes, the "super-Bantu" Tom had
diagnosed years before as "a self successfully playing at being
a self that is not itself" (112), counsels patience in the face
of the discrimination Tom encounters from the Bantu medical society. "These things take time," his wife explains. The
"Troubles" five years earlier, Colley remarks with equanimity,
were the usual thing: "People resorting to violence instead
of using democratic processes to resolve their differences."

If the lapsometer fails to effect a miracle cure in Tom's
life, as we knew it would, he has nevertheless stumbled upon
a simple and ancient remedy. His housing suggests its nature.
He no longer lives in the luxury of a mock-Paradise or visits
run-down motels with three beloveds, which is to say none;
instead he lives in the Slave Quarters with Ellen.[55] Back in
the old Howard Johnson's her virtue had been almost oppres-
sive, and throughout the novel she has been Tom's Girl
Friday, faithful to "Chief," joining in his triumphs and misfor-
tunes. Now it seems fitting that the "ripe Georgia persimmon
not a peach" should share his new quarters in a sort of modified intersubjective communion. I say *modified* because in
this novel perfection is not yet in evidence. There is a good
deal of plain old English-style muddling through. When Tom
goes to confession for the first time in eleven years the best
he can do is feel sorry he feels no sorrow for the sins he
confesses, though he willingly puts on the sackcloth as
penance. A tolerant fellow, he mixes easily with love couples
and Bantus as well as Presbyterians. Having escaped the false
paradise of the New Eden, he tends collards in a small plot
to the east while his less-innocent Eve stirs grits in the kitchen.

The outcome of Tom's private ordeal casts a light over
the public landscape of the novel, but Percy does not presume
to edify. Nor can the novel be construed as a defense of
a Christian life. "To defend anything is always to discredit

55. The Slave Quarters are "built like an English charterhouse," which recalls
the strict monastic order of the Carthusians, though Tom shares his apartment
and a king-sized bed with Ellen. From the charterhouse of Percy's apprentice novel
(see footnote 37 in Chapter One) to the Quarters is quite a distance.

it," Kierkegaard wrote.[56] The joyous tone of the epilogue speaks for itself. The consensus anthropology is revealed in The Pit as a fraud, but Percy does not insist the reader accept his own view of man. His comic synthesis will stand on either religious or secular premises. More's syndrome holds for both.

The novel offers another form of grace to its readers: the author's comic therapy. There is a connection, after all, between humor and wholeness. Whose ox has not been gored in this book? I doubt that anyone can read it without taking offense. But in the divided state of angelism-bestialism, humor can heal; it offers release from the grip of bestial aggressions even while restoring moral perspective. The comic is just what Emerson called it: "a pledge of sanity," the "balance-wheel" of the intellect.[57] With the spirit of abstraction rampant in our society, humor may be the only release from collective madness. It plays such a key role in *Love in the Ruins* that the novel's theme could be given in a paraphrase of the scientist's prayer: "Lord, grant that we be delivered from the Black Death and find ourselves in our love for You. Failing that, Lord, grant that we recover our humanity in loving and being true to one other. Failing that, Lord, grant us at least the power to stand back and see the humor of our predicament before it all collapses around our ears."

The novel ends hopefully, on Christmas Eve. "Barbecuing in my sackcloth," Tom says, opening the final section with a perfect tonal marriage of penance and celebration. He sneaks a few drinks of Early Times and goes in to carry Ellen, a "noble, surprisingly heavy, Presbyterian armful," to her new king-sized bed. Even the ivy imagery, which up until now has been identified with ruin, works for Tom as Percy ends the novel in a one-sentence summation of this tri-

56. Kierkegaard, *The Sickness unto Death*, 218.
57. See his essay "The Comic," in Ralph Waldo Emerson, *The Portable Emerson*, ed. Mark Van Doren (New York, 1946), 207. Percy's humor deserves a chapter to itself.

umphant comedy: "To bed we go for a long winter's nap, twined about each other as the ivy twineth, not under a bush or in a car or on the floor or any such humbug as marked the past peculiar years of Christendom, but at home in bed where all good folks belong."

The epilogue is a triumph, the kind of gold we rarely find these days in fiction, and it is earned. It is difficult to think of any novel that ends on a note of such authentic affirmation. My own feeling about the novel can best be compared to the moment following the midnight mass where the children of some love couples and young Thomas More shoot off firecrackers. "Hurrah for Jesus Christ!" they cry, in another echo of Dostoevski.[58] "Hurrah for the United States!"

Hurrah for Walker Percy! Hurrah for what is left of the USA! Maybe the New Eden did not work. On the other hand, given the peculiarity of the age, maybe there is yet time for every man to be a king, if only of a poor collard patch in the garden of being.

58. See the last footnote in Chapter Three.

6

Toward a Rediscovery of Being

In the joy of naming, one lives authentically. No matter whether I give a name to, or hear the name of, a strange bird; no matter whether I write or read a line of great poetry or understand a scientific hypothesis, I thereby exist authentically as a namer or a hearer, as an I or a Thou—and in either case as a co-celebrant of what is.[1]

Being can not be indicated, it cannot be *shown;* it can only be alluded to, a little as some third person now disappeared is alluded to amongst friends who knew him formerly and keep his memory green.[2]

The novelist, Percy says, is "less like a prophet than he is like the canary coal miners used to take down into the shaft to test the air. When the canary gets unhappy, utters plaintive cries and collapses, it may be time for the miners to surface and think things over."[3] Percy himself has a fine nose for atmosphere, and the canary in him has certainly been uttering plaintive cries, particularly in *Love in the Ruins*. But he does more than warn of noxious atmosphere, and to complete this study of his novels we should consider them against the background of his theory of art as a reversal of alienation. In the novels we have often seen the character who is trapped in the cul-de-sac of his private consciousness.

1. Percy, "Naming and Being," 153.
2. Gabriel Marcel, *Metaphysical Journal*, trans. Bernard Wall (Chicago, 1952), viii.
3. Percy, "Notes for a Novel," 7.

Most of us can recognize in ourselves a degree of the same condition; at times we may feel like the poor lonesome ghosts of *Love in the Ruins,* locked in our own machinery. It is a matter of hope then that art can be a form of liberation.

"There is no such thing, strictly speaking," Percy says, "as a literature of alienation." The modern literature of alienation is in reality "the triumphant reversal of alienation through its re-presenting," an "aesthetic victory of comradeliness, a recognition of plight in common." When Kafka "read his work aloud to his friends, they would all roar with laughter until tears came to their eyes." The alienated commuter riding a train "exists in true alienation which is unspeakable," but the commuter reading a book about an alienated commuter riding a train "rejoices in the speakability of his alienation and in the new triple alliance of himself, the alienated character, and the author. His mood is affirmatory and glad; Yes! that is how it is!"[4] And that is the responsibility of the novelist: to speak it, to tell how it is, and thus to deliver us from our private prisons into a common world.

For an example of this phenomenon in Percy's fiction we might take Jamie Vaught, the boy who must die in *The Last Gentleman.* As the novel opens he is thoroughly abstracted from himself, reading Wittgenstein and pursuing the vertical search, imprisoned in abstraction without knowing it. Then Will Barrett appears to become his companion, and the games they play are the key opening the way for him on his final journey. "This was the game they played: the sentient tutor knowing quite well how to strike the dread unsounded chords of adolescence, the youth registering, his mouth parted slightly, fingernails brushing backward across his face. *Yes, and that was the wonder of it, that what was private and unspeakable before is speakable now because you speak it*" (155). The italics are Percy's, and it is not only with adolescents that we find "dread unsounded chords." Anyone with small children can

4. Percy, "The Man on the Train," 478.

witness how we all enter the human community as our fears and hopes find a home through the joy of naming.

A novel can produce the same effect. Unhappily it often fails to turn out that way because of inauthentic naming. One of the main obstacles in fiction is the proliferating cliché artist. Percy has spoken of the "compulsive liberal novelist" who accepts the "strict condition that no Negro or Jew may be admitted to fiction unless he has been previously canonized."[5] Is it any wonder that in such a novel the realities go unnamed, leaving us more stranded in alienation than ever? In *The Moviegoer* we have the novelist Sam Yerger, one of whose novels, written in Chiapas, deals with "the problem of evil and the essential loneliness of man" (168), which Percy calls "the most frequently used blurb on the dust jackets of the last ten thousand American novels."[6] An earlier novel of Sam's, described as "an impassioned plea for tolerance and understanding," had not been well received in Feliciana, but a nostalgic new book called *Happy Land* was commended in the reviews as a "nice blend of a moderate attitude toward the race question and a conservative affection for the values of the agrarian South" (170). Mort Prince, in *The Last Gentleman,* has a book called *The Farther Journey* in which a Connecticut writer dallies with a neighborhood housewife he is not even attracted to as "the exercise of that last and inalienable possession of the individual in a sick society, freedom" (133). And readers of *Love in the Ruins* may not be cheered to learn that in the 1990's "old favorites endure, like venerable Harold Robbins and Jacqueline Susann, who continue to write the dirty clean books so beloved by the American housewife" (19). Read enough of these blurbs and you understand why Sutter Vaught in *The Last Gentleman* could respect John F. Kennedy: "With all the hogwash, no one has said what he was. The reason he was a great man was that his derisiveness kept pace with his brilliance and his beauty and his love

5. *Ibid.,* 492.
6. Percy, "Notes for a Novel," 8.

of country. He is the only public man I have ever believed" (342).

Before he published a novel of his own, Percy had turned his existential lights on American fiction. Mark Twain "hit upon an admirable rotation" in Huck Finn's trip downriver, he wrote in 1956, but Tom Sawyer's drifting over the Sahara in his balloon is a "standard comic-book rotation." Hemingway practices the "literature of rotation, escape within escape." In *A Farewell to Arms* he achieves rotation "to the fourth power": first, the American in Bohemia, escaping the everydayness of life in America; second, the *tenente* who has "gotten clean away from the everydayness of Bohemia"; third, the same Frederic Henry "escaping the everydayness of the Italian army"; and fourth, in a "concealed reversal" that is "offered as an undesired turn of events," Henry getting "clean away" from Catherine and the baby and thus escaping the everydayness of having "settled down and raised a family." Thomas Wolfe, on the other hand, lying in his berth while the train makes its passage in the night through lonely Midwestern towns, is well placed to encounter repetition or the Return. "He may be lost and by the wind grieved but he is withal triumphant." Marquand "hit the motherlode" in *Point of No Return* by applying "the device of the Return to the promising vein of exurbanite alienation." Charles Gray is the "suburban counterpart of Joseph K.," a "gentle wayfarer who is true to himself in the search for himself." Marquand's formula can be summed up as "suburban alienation recognized, plus the way out of the Return, plus a gentle disillusionment stoically borne."[7]

Writers like Sam Yerger and Mort Prince create a major problem for the novelist who wants to explore the same terrain seriously. These cliché artists are the goody-goodies who are the thieves of art, in the sense in which Rita Vaught is discussed in Chapter Four. They flood the market with false coin and debase the currency. In the terms of the epi-

7. All the judgments in this paragraph are from Percy, "The Man on the Train."

graph from Rilke that heads this study, they claim to show the face of the god. For the novelist who writes from a Christian position the problem is acute: "The old words of grace are worn smooth as poker chips and a certain devaluation has occurred, like a poker chip after it is cashed in."[8]

Confronted by all these difficulties, the novelist falls back upon his resources. He may proceed like Kierkegaard, not "*directly* with the matter one wants to communicate" but by "accepting the other man's illusion as good money."[9] Percy often does likewise; he does not attempt to show the face of the god, to approach from the space that lies before it. The novelist, he says, uses "every ounce of cunning, craft and guile he can muster from the nether regions of his soul." The tools of his trade have come to be, necessarily, "violence, shock, insult, the bizarre": "How can one possibly write of baptism as an event of immense significance, when baptism is accepted but accepted by and large as a minor tribal rite somewhat secondary in importance to taking the kids to see Santa at the department store." Flannery O'Connor explained, Percy says, that she created bizarre characters because "for the near-blind you have to draw very large simple caricatures."[10] The challenge is to take those who are as "dumb" as Val's Tyree children in *The Last Gentleman* and make them hear: "When they do suddenly break into the world of language, it is something to see. They are like Adam on the First Day" (289).

When this endeavor succeeds, important things happen. The novelist recovers the miracle, repeating the primal act of symbolization. "Naming is unique in natural history," Percy

8. Percy, "Notes for a Novel," 13.
9. Søren Kierkegaard, *The Point of View for My Work as an Author: A Report to History and Related Writings,* ed. Benjamin Nelson, trans. Walter Lowrie (New York, 1962), 40. Lewis A. Lawson stresses Percy's indirect approach in his essay "Walker Percy's Indirect Communications," though I think when he says Percy succeeds in "filtering through Binx's consciousness a considerable amount of existentialist (usually Kierkegaardian) statement" (874), he risks misleading the reader who sees in "statement" a form of edification.
10. Percy, "Notes for a Novel," 13–14.

writes, "because for the first time a being in the universe stands apart from the universe and affirms some other being to be what it is. In this act, for the first time in the history of the universe, 'is' is spoken."[11] We can see in this statement the fruits of Percy's apprenticeship in the philosophy of language, and the excitement he found in the discovery of symbolization, which stimulated a burst of writing in the fifties as he constructed a bridge between his love of science and his existentialism. "In the joy of naming," he says, "one lives authentically." Man's ailment in part is an exhaustion of his symbols. To rediscover being, he must renew them or find new ones. Only then will he "exist authentically as a namer or hearer, as an I or a Thou—and in either case as a co-celebrant of what is."[12]

Percy has demonstrated the power to name the previously unnamable. The judges for the National Book Award in 1962 commended *The Moviegoer* as "a truthful novel with shocks of recognition and spasms of nostalgia for every—or nearly every—American." These recognitions are difficult to achieve because what Percy sets out to name are just those things which lie beneath the threshold of awareness—that which we do not know we know. And as Marcel says, Being cannot be indicated or shown; it can only be alluded to. It is this consideration, I believe, that dictates Percy's oblique approach. A Percy novel is a kind of "hollow form, a negative mold," as Rilke said of *The Notebooks of Malte Laurids Brigge*. The positive casting one could make from it, if it were a bronze, might be "happiness, assent—most perfect and most certain bliss."[13] But with the general exhaustion of symbols, and with the cliché-mongers claiming to unveil the face of

---

11. Walker Percy, "The Act of Naming," University of Houston *Forum*, I (1957), 7.

12. Percy, "Naming and Being," 153.

13. See the epigraph from Rainer Maria Rilke at the head of this book, which is taken from a letter written by Rilke in 1915. The full text has been reprinted in Richard Ellmann and Charles Feidelson, Jr. (eds.), *The Modern Tradition: Backgrounds of Modern Literature* (New York, 1965), 707–708.

the gods, Percy chooses to approach by a dialectic. He can only allude to what is there.

The novel remains a promising instrument in such an endeavor. "In some ways," Percy told an interviewer, "we are (as novelists) at a point in history like the revolution in physics which occurred around 1900."[14] What he has in mind is the deliberate phenomenology of the modern French novel in particular—the novel undertaken as exploration, which he takes to be as far removed from Dickens and Tolstoi as Planck and Einstein are from Newton.[15] In his latest article Percy proposes the "novelistic" approach to the psychiatric patient as the "sole remaining alternative" to the "analytic-psychical" approach of Freud and the "organismic-behavioristic" approach of Skinner. The worlds Freud and Skinner describe, he says, are "demonstrably right and useful in their way, but how do you get from one to the other?" For "novelistic" we might substitute "phenomenological," for "the novelist must first and last be a good phenomenologist."[16] In view of the limitations of the scientific method discussed in the opening chapter, Percy believes, the novel—or for that matter the cinema—may prove to be the instrument best suited for exploring what it is to be a man living in the world, though to date neither the modern French novel nor any other seems to have grasped the possibilities.[17]

The new novelist, Percy says, tends to move in on territory once held by the theologian. "It is the new novelist who, despite his well-advertised penchant for violence, his fetish of freedom, his sexual adventurism, pronounces anathemas upon the most permissive of societies which in fact permits him everything."[18] This view echoes what he said in 1958

14. Brown, "An Interview," 6.
15. Percy to Luschei, April 19, 1970.
16. Walker Percy, "Toward a Triadic Theory of Meaning," *Psychiatry: A Journal for the Study of Interpersonal Processes*, XXXV (1972), 17.
17. Percy to Luschei, April 19, 1970.
18. Percy, "Notes for a Novel," 11. The reader should be aware that Percy ordinarily claims to speak only for himself. Here he was asked to speak for "the novelist."

in objecting to moral relativism in anthropology: "It is not enough to study a culture element with only the objective of discovering its immanent role in a culture. It is also necessary to judge it accordingly as it does or does not contribute to the development of the potentialities of human nature."[19] The new theologians, such as Harvey Cox, may not judge the world except as it fails to measure up to such ideals as participatory democracy, but novelists like Norman Mailer, Philip Roth, Wilfrid Sheed, and John Updike make sweeping moral judgments on American society, as prophets or avenging angels or as Swiftean satirists.[20]

Percy himself certainly pronounces anathemas upon the consensus anthropology in *Love in the Ruins,* but he never launches indiscriminate attacks on science as such. The novel contains hints of a counterreaction under way that Walter M. Miller, Jr., calls the "Simplification," a response to destructive technology that entails the blind destruction of science and technology and spawns "bookleggers" who rescue books from the bonfires.[21] The Simplification itself would be anathema to Percy. "It's all very well for some young people and a few aging gurus to attack science and technology and go live in the ruins in love and peace," he told the NBA press conference. "On the other hand, it is not a small thing either to turn your back on 2,000 years of science and art and progress and tradition."[22]

The question we must face, he believes, is what it is "to be a man in a world transformed by science." He criticizes the existentialists for their "contempt of science."[23] The question of living in such a world is one that science itself cannot deal with. The novelist exploring our predicament, Percy says, finds in himself and in others "a new breed of person in whom the potential for catastrophe—and hope—has sud-

19. Percy, "Culture: The Antimony of the Scientific Method," 473.
20. Percy to Luschei, April 19, 1970.
21. Percy, *"A Canticle for Leibowitz,"* 576.
22. "The Authors That Bloom in the Spring," 23–24.
23. Brown, "An Interview," 6.

denly escalated . . . . The psychical forces presently released in the postmodern consciousness open unlimited possibilities for both destruction and liberation, for an absolute loneliness or a rediscovery of community and reconciliation." What has happened is a "tempestuous restructuring" of consciousness resulting from "the absorption by the layman not of the scientific method but rather the magical aura of science whose credentials he accepts for all sectors of reality."[24]

The scientific method neither deserves nor makes such a claim. The layman needs to acquaint himself with its limitations. And other instruments of knowledge are required. If the question is how to release man from his absolute loneliness in a rediscovery of community, certainly the novel, with its power of naming, is one such instrument. Percy's novels diagnose a condition he has named the malaise. Something Kierkegaard said of the physician's remarks beside a sickbed applies to his diagnosis: "although it can be fully understood only by one who is versed in medicine, yet it must never be forgotten that it is pronounced beside the sickbed."[25] The patient has a sickness and thus a vital interest in the diagnosis, though he may need assistance in reading some of the names. The terms of it are primarily existentialist; in fact Percy says his three novels to date complete a group and could be read as a gloss on Kierkegaard.[26]

At the time of this writing he has an idea for a novel with an island theme, something perhaps related to his essay "The Message in the Bottle," though in a strict sense he is not yet "working" on a new book. Recently his interests seem to have returned to the philosophy of language, the subject of his first major essay. His latest essay advances a triadic theory of meaning, built upon the foundations laid by Charles Sanders Peirce, the neglected genius of American

24. Percy, "Notes for a Novel," 11–12.
25. Søren Kierkegaard, *Fear and Trembling* and *The Sickness unto Death*, trans. Walter Lowrie (New York, 1954), 142.
26. He told me this and said he would never write another like them.

philosophy, whose time Percy thinks may have come.[27] Percy
attaches great importance to this other undertaking—more,
if anything, than to his novels. A preliminary reading shows
him to be elaborating an idea he took up in his first essay
almost two decades earlier.[28] "A signal is received by an organism in an *environment*," he writes, making a primal distinction.
"A sentence is received and uttered in a *world*."[29]

What other novelist or physician could make such an affirmation? To raise the question is to recognize something about
Walker Percy. Only a man versed in philosophy could wisely
risk such an assertion. Not even a man with Percy's gifts
could write Percy's novels, unless he were grounded in
philosophy and medicine. The emphasis of this book is on
the novels, where his great achievement may prove to have
been translating Kierkegaard into concrete American terms.
Such a task cannot be accomplished by intellect alone. Certainly in Percy an existentialist sensibility has taken root in
America, a fact that could signal a turning point in American
fiction. He has staked out a claim on behalf of the novel
that brings to mind Henry James—a large claim, for a
medium so often pronounced dead, and one that would serve
equally for film. No medium could hope to satisfy such a
claim without heeding James's reminder that no good novel
will ever proceed from a superficial mind.[30]

Wait and watch, says Percy's most recent protagonist. The
author himself waits hopefully. He does not see many signs
of the new era he hopes for, and he feels more derisive
than most writers about the Age of Aquarius and the new
religiousness in some of its forms.[31] But as he wrote a few
years ago, "the notion of man graduating from the religious
stage to the political is after all an unexamined assumption.

27. Percy, "Toward a Triadic Theory of Meaning." See footnote 16.
28. The question is treated briefly in Chapters 1 and 2. Percy works from what
Marcel calls the "metaphysic of *we are*" in going beyond Suzanne Langer's treatment
of symbolization.
29. Percy, "Toward a Triadic Theory of Meaning," 9.
30. See James's famous essay "The Art of Fiction."
31. Percy to Luschei, April 19, 1970.

It might in fact turn out that the modern era which is perhaps two hundred years old and has already ended will be known as the Secular Era which came to an end with the catastrophes of the Twentieth Century."[32]

Conceivably he might become absorbed in his writings on language and never complete another novel, though that possibility seems unlikely in view of the forces that led him to fiction in the first place. If he should never write another novel, the loss would be felt beyond the boundaries of the literary world, for the malaise has moved in for the duration, by all the evidence, and we have few writers whose vision can penetrate it. Percy learned his way of seeing mostly through the existentialists, but we cannot categorize a man of such varied talents in a phrase. We have to grant him his uniqueness. No one can predict with any assurance where his inclinations may lead him, though his views have shown a durable consistency. His pilgrimage bears watching, for who else do we have in America who writes superlative novels out of a considered philosophical position and a professional knowledge of medicine? And what contemporary who *is* our contemporary speaks to our predicament from a sense of his own sovereignty as this man does? It looks as if we too will have to wait and watch and listen.

32. Percy, "Notes for a Novel," 12.

Bibliography

I. Works by Walker Percy

Novels

The Moviegoer. New York: Noonday Press, 1967. Originally published by Alfred A. Knopf, 1961.
The Last Gentleman. New York: Farrar, Straus and Giroux, 1966.
Love in the Ruins. New York: Farrar, Straus and Giroux, 1971.

Excerpts from the Novels

"Carnival in Gentilly," University of Houston *Forum*, III (Summer, 1960), 4–18.
"*The Last Gentleman:* Two Excerpts from the Forthcoming Novel," *Harper's Magazine*, CCXXXII (May, 1966), 54–61.
"Excerpt from *The Last Gentleman*," *The World of Black Humor*, ed. Douglas M. Davis (New York: E. P. Dutton & Co., 1967), 229–45.

Philosophical Essays

"Symbol as Need," *Thought*, XXIX (Autumn, 1954), 381–90.
"Symbol as Hermeneutic in Existentialism: A Possible Bridge from Empiricism," *Philosophy and Phenomenological Research*, XVI (June, 1956), 522–30.
"The Man on the Train: Three Existential Modes," *Partisan Review*, XXIII (Fall, 1956), 478–94.
"The Coming Crisis in Psychiatry," two parts, *America*, XCVI (January 5 and 12, 1957), 391–93, 415–18.
"Semiotic and a Theory of Knowledge," *Modern Schoolman*, XXXIV (May, 1957), 225–46.

"The Act of Naming," University of Houston *Forum,* I (Summer, 1957), 4–9.

"Metaphor as Mistake," *Sewanee Review,* LXVI (Winter, 1958), 79–99.

"Symbol, Consciousness, and Intersubjectivity," *Journal of Philosophy,* LV (July 17, 1958), 631–41.

"The Loss of the Creature," University of Houston *Forum,* II (Fall, 1958), 6–14.

"Culture: The Antinomy of the Scientific Method," *New Scholasticism,* XXXII (October, 1958), 443–75.

"The Message in the Bottle," *Thought,* XXXIV (Autumn, 1959), 405–33.

"Naming and Being," *Personalist,* XLI (Spring, 1960), 148–57.

"The Symbolic Structure of Interpersonal Process," *Psychiatry: A Journal for the Study of Interpersonal Processes,* XXIV (February, 1961), 39–52.

"Toward a Triadic Theory of Meaning," *Psychiatry: A Journal for the Study of Interpersonal Processes,* XXXV (February, 1972), 1–19.

Other Essays

"The Willard Huntington Wright Murder Case," *Carolina Magazine,* XLIV (November, 1934), 4–6.

"The Movie Magazine: A Low 'Slick,' " *Carolina Magazine,* XLIV (March, 1935), 4–9.

"Stoicism in the South," *Commonweal,* LXIV (July 6, 1956), 342–44.

"The American War," *Commonweal,* LXV (March 29, 1957), 655–57.

"A Southern View," *America,* XCVII (July 20, 1957), 428–29.

"The Southern Moderate," *Commonweal,* LXVII (December 13, 1957), 279–82.

"Decline of the Western," *Commonweal,* LXVIII (May 16, 1958), 181–83.

"The Culture Critics," *Commonweal,* LXX (June 5, 1959), 247–50.

"Seven Laymen Discuss Morality," *America,* CIII (August 27, 1960), 12–13.

"Red, White, and Blue-Gray," *Commonweal,* LXXV (December 22, 1961), 337–39.

"How to Succeed in Business Without Thinking about Money," *Commonweal,* LXXVII (February 22, 1963), 557–59.

"Hughes's Solipsism Malgré Lui," *Sewanee Review,* LXXII (July–September, 1964), 489–95. An essay-review on Richard Hughes's *The Fox in the Attic.*

"Mississippi: The Fallen Paradise," *Harper's Magazine,* CCXXX (April, 1965), 166–72.

"The Failure and the Hope," *Katallagete* (Journal of the Committee of Southern Churchmen, Nashville) (Winter, 1965–66), 16–21.

"From Facts to Fiction," *Writer,* LXXX (October, 1967), 27–28, 46. Reprinted from *Book Week.*

"Notes for a Novel about the End of the World," *Katallagete* (Journal of the Committee of Southern Churchmen, Nashville) (Winter, 1967–68), 7–14.

"New Orleans Mon Amour," *Harper's Magazine*, CCXXXVII (September, 1968) 80–82, 86, 88, 90.

"Walter M. Miller, Jr.'s *A Canticle for Leibowitz*," in David Madden (ed.), *Rediscoveries* (New York: Crown Publishers, 1971), 262–69. Reprinted in *Southern Review*, n.s. VII (April, 1971), 572–78.

Reviews

"Truth—or Pavlov's Dogs?" *America*, XCVII (June 1, 1957), 306–307. A review of William Sargant's *Battle for the Mind*.

"Modern Man on the Threshold," *America*, CV (August 12, 1961), 612. A review of Ivar Lissner's *Man, God, and Magic*.

"Virtues and Vices in the Southern Literary Renascence," *Commonweal*, LXXVI (May 11, 1962), 181–82. A review of Norris Lloyd's *A Dream of Mansions*, Marion Montgomery's *The Wandering of Desire*, and Thomas Chastain's *Judgment Day*.

Letter

Letter to the author, April 19, 1970.

II. Works on Walker Percy

Critical

Atkins, Anselm. "Walker Percy and Post-Christian Search," *Centennial Review*, XII (Winter, 1968), 73–95.

Blouin, Michel T. "The Novels of Walker Percy: An Attempt at Synthesis," *Xavier University Studies*, VI (1968), 29–42.

Bradbury, John M. "Absurd Insurrection: The Barth-Percy Affair," *South Atlantic Quarterly*, LXVIII (Summer, 1969), 319–29.

Byrd, Scott. "The Dreams of Walker Percy," *Red Clay Reader*, (1966), 70–73.

Bryant, Jerry H. *The Open Decision: The Contemporary American Novel and Its Intellectual Background* (New York: Free Press, 1970), 273–77.

Cheney, Brainard. "Secular Society as Deadly Farce," *Sewanee Review*, LXXV (Spring, 1967), 345–50.

———. "To Restore a Fragmented Image," *Sewanee Review*, LXIX (Autumn, 1961), 691–700.

Douglas, Ellen. *Walker Percy's "The Last Gentleman": Introduction and Commentary* (New York: Seabury Press, 1969). A pamphlet, 28 pp.

Henisey, Sarah. "Intersubjectivity in Symbolization," *Renascence*, XX (Summer, 1968), 208–14.

Hoffman, Frederick J. *The Art of Southern Fiction: A Study of Some Modern*

Novelists (Carbondale, Ill.: Southern Illinois University Press, 1967), 129 –37.

Hoggard, James. "Death of the Vicarious," *Southwest Review*, XLIX (Autumn, 1964), 366–74.

Hyman, Stanley Edgar. "Moviegoing and Other Intimacies," *Standards: A Chronicle of Books for Our Time* (New York: Horizon Press, 1966), 63–67.

Kazin, Alfred. "The Pilgrimage of Walker Percy," *Harper's Magazine*, CCXLIII (June, 1971), 81–86.

Lawson, Lewis A. "Walker Percy's Indirect Communications," *Texas Studies in Language and Literature*, XI (Spring, 1969), 867–900.

———. "Walker Percy's Southern Stoic," *Southern Literary Journal*, III (Fall, 1970), 5–31.

Lehan, Richard. "The Way Back: Redemption in the Novels of Walker Percy," *Southern Review*, n.s. IV (April, 1968), 306–19.

Luschei, Martin. "The Sovereign Wayfarer: Walker Percy's Diagnosis of the Malaise." Ph.D. dissertation, University of New Mexico, 1970. *(Dissertation Abstracts International*, XXXI, No. 10, 1971.)

Maxwell, Robert. "Walker Percy's Fancy," *Minnesota Review*, VII (1967), 231–37.

Tanner, Tony. *City of Words: American Fiction, 1950–1970* (New York: Harper & Row, 1971), 260–62.

———. *The Reign of Wonder: Naivety and Reality in American Literature* (New York: Perennial Library, 1967), 349–56, 358. Originally published by Cambridge University Press, 1965.

Thale, Jerome. "Alienation on the American Plan," University of Houston *Forum*, VI (1968), 36–40.

Thale, Mary. "The Moviegoer of the 1950's," *Twentieth Century Literature*, XIV (July, 1968), 84–89.

Van Cleave, Jim. "Versions of Percy," *Southern Review*, n.s. VI (October, 1970), 990–1010.

Interviews and Sketches

Brown, Ashley. "An Interview with Walker Percy," *Shenandoah*, XVIII (Spring, 1967), 3–10.

Carr, John (ed.). "Rotation and Repetition," in *Kite-Flying and Other Irrational Acts: Conversations with Twelve Southern Writers* (Baton Rouge, 1972), 34–58.

———. "An Interview with Walker Percy," *Georgia Review*, XXV (Fall, 1971), 317–32.

Cremeens, Carlton. "Walker Percy, the Man and the Novelist: An Interview," *Southern Review*, n.s. IV (April, 1968), 271–90.

Serebnick, Judith. "First Novelists—Spring, 1961," *Library Journal*, LXXXVI (February 1, 1961), 597.

"The Authors That Bloom in the Spring," *Publishers' Weekly,* CXCIX (March 22, 1971), 22–24.

"The Sustaining Stream," *Time,* LXXXI (February 1, 1963), 82.

Index

Abdication, 27–28, 150, 162, 185–86
Abraham, 35, 61–62, 165
Abstraction: as labryinth, 14; crowd as, 25; explained, 30–34; defined, 31; existentialist revolt against, 32; and resentment, 33; spirit of, 33–34, 37, 173, 191, 205, 224, 225, 231; and institutions, 54n; vs. individual existence, 59, 91–92; failure of, 88; and sex, 97; from self, 113, 150, 162, 165, 184, 185, 233–34; and Verdun, 190–91; mentioned, 21, 29n, 63, 75, 90, 97, 104, 198, 227. *See also* Philosophy, modern; Angelism
Absurd, the, 50, 61
Adam, 153, 223
Ahasuerus, 77, 99, 103
Alabama, 131, 163
Albuquerque, N.M., 147, 162
Alienation: and literature, 13, 56, 234, 236; and scientific method, 19 and n; and ordeal, 41; rotation as deliverance from, 47; in American cities, 116; and sex, 98, 102; and vision, 99; art as reversal of, 233–34
Alltäglichkeit. See Everydayness
America, United States of: crisis mood of, 17; philosophical temper of, 19, 33; and existentialism, 19–20, 103; compared with nineteenth-century Denmark, 22; present condition of, reflected in Percy's novels, 70, 112, 169, 175, 176, 181, 238; God and, 80, 175, 193–94; prosperity of, 115;

Americans lost in, 116; as pluralistic society, 139–40; and history, 175, 193–94; downfall of, 193, 195; prospects of, 232
Amnesia: in movies, 72; and Will Barrett, 112, 113, 115n, 118, 129, 132, 140, 150, 152, 153, 155; as perfect device for rotation, 142
Anderson, Sherwood, 10n
Angelism: symptoms of, 185–87; treatment of, 187; and religion, 221; and mass murder, 224, 225; mentioned, 184, 189, 198, 203
Angelism-bestialism: symptoms of, 173, 184, 206; and loss of being, 188; and evil, 205; and war, 225; both religious and secular, 231
Anomie, 20, 207. *See also* Malaise
Anonymity, 21, 22, 47
Anthropology, 7–8, 54, 240
Anthropology, the consensus: *Love in the Ruins* built upon, 170; described, 172–73; challenged by Tom More, 174; tested, 195; revealed as fraud, 218, 231; mentioned, 210–11, 212n, 240
Anxiety: and everydayness, 21; and being, 43; and bad art, 47; illustrated in *The Moviegoer*, 81, 91, 106
Aquinas, Saint Thomas, 12, 34, 174, 202
Aristophanes, 108n
Art: and intersubjectivity, 53, 56; and everydayness, 88; as reversal of alienation, 233–34
Astrology, 209

Atheism, 202
Atlas Shrugged, 196
Auden, W. H., 75
Authenticity: and the crowd, 25; and intersubjectivity, 29–30, 233; and death, 43–44, 109; and rotation, 47; and naming, 233

Bad faith: defined, 26; and death, 26–27, 43, 93, 161, 171; and bustling activity, 82–83; Kierkegaard on, 200n
Behaviorism: as flat-earth view of mind, 37; limitations of, 203; Koestler on, 212n; as new order, 215; assumptions discredited, 218; mentioned, 172, 177, 202, 211, 216
Being: Heidegger on, 23, 43; Marcel on, 40, 233; and anxiety, 43–44; Percy on, 48, 214n; road to, 63; in Percy's novels, 70n, 74; and inwardness, 114; loss of, in angelism-bestialism, 188; recovery of, 232; and exhaustion of symbols, 238; and naming, 238
Bellevue Hospital, New York City, 5
Bestialism, 184, 197–98
Birmingham, Ala., 3
Black Death, modern. *See* Angelism-bestialism
Blacks. *See* Race relations; South
Boredom, 23, 24
Boston, 204
Breisach, Ernst, 23, 42
Brothers Karamazov, The, 109n
Browning, Robert, 87
Buber, Martin, 54n
Bucks County, Pa., 138
Buddhism, 120
Burlesque, 219, 223
Butler, Rhett, 98

Camus, 6, 8, 15, 103
Canaan, the New, 175
Canticle for Leibowitz, A, 221n
Carolina Magazine, 10
Castaway: man as, 39–40; and Jews, 88; Will Barrett as, 152; Tom More as, 175; mentioned, 14, 80, 199. *See also* Wayfarer
Cather, Willa, 160n
Catholicism: Percy and Catholic writers, ix; Percy's conversion to, 12; Church split into factions in *Love in the Ruins,* 178; family tradition of Tom More; on the sin against grace, 226–27; men-

tioned, 69, 95, 146n, 153, 164, 191, 203, 208n, 228
Cervantes, 142, 202
Cheney, Brainard, 76n, 135n
Chicago, 90, 95, 96, 99–100, 101, 116
Chinese, the, 194
Choice, the: in Kierkegaard, 59, 63; necessity of, 87, 150; inability to choose, 120, 149. *See also* Leap of faith
Christ, the new, 205–206
Christ figures, 205–206
Christianity: William Alexander Percy on beautiful dead language of, 4; and Western culture, 36, 175; and a modern incapacity, 36, 188–89; Percy on uniqueness of, 40, 120; the good news of, 40, 153, 161, 166, 167, 188, 210n; rites of, 107n, 164–65, 181, 183; and resurrection, 109; and lostness of the American in America, 116; Guardini on post-Christian era, 118; eliminated by Will Barrett, 120, 166–67; in new South, 144; in the consensus anthropology, 172; as outlandish, 193, 210; and property worship, 209; *Love in the Ruins* not a defense of, 230; and the novelist, 237; mentioned, 13n, 94, 98, 150, 163, 178–79, 190, 211
Chomsky, Noam, 13n
Cinema, 239
Cohn, David, 10
Columbia University College of Physicians and Surgeons, 5, 11
Comedy, 231, 232
Commonweal, 204
Communists, 185
Confederacy, the, 140, 146, 151, 191
Conformity, 25
Confucius, 139
Consciousness, postmodern, 240–41
Conservatives, 176, 184, 192
Contingency, 42, 80, 99
Copenhagen, 228
Counterculture, 176, 191, 192
Covington, La., 11, 12, 17
Cowardice, 25, 27
Cox, Harvey, 240
Crime and Punishment, 224
Crowd, the, 25
Crusoe, Robinson, 15, 88
Curtailed I, the, 22, 26, 27, 58, 63

Dachau, 108
Dallas, 195

Dante Alighieri, 3, 169
Dasein, 23
Death: in life, 21, 22, 64, 76, 89, 104, 112; masked by modern society, 26–27; I and my death, 26–27, 42, 111–12; and bad faith, 26–27, 93, 161, 171; in abstract vs. concrete terms, 33; and nothingness, 42; of loved ones, 42, 227; Rilke on, 44; physicality of, 71, 108, 196; management of, 93, 109, 110, 161, 164; as astonishment, 113; of Will Barrett's father, 136–37; imminent, as searching existentialist light, 146; and women, 164; of Jamie Vaught, 164–66; and Western world, 175; mentioned, 69, 72, 95, 111, 173, 196, 219
Death Comes for the Archbishop, 160n
Democrats, 181
Denmark, 22, 210
Descartes, 188
Despair: and inauthenticity, 24; and bad faith, 41, 43; and bad art, 47; Kierkegaard on his personal, 57; as prelude to the choice, 59, 104; that is unaware of being despair, 76, 83, 89, 177, 201; Ahasuerus as type of, 77; vs. the search, 79; and sex, 98, 102; recognition of, 99–100; and religious awareness, 105; of behaviorist assumptions, 203; Kierkegaard on eradication of, 206n; mentioned, 65, 82, 103
De trop, 157n
Dickens, Charles, 239
Dignity of the individual, 173n
Disease as dis-order, 5n
Divine Comedy, The, 169
Dr. Faustus, The Tragical History of, 229
Don Giovanni, 207
Don Juan, 49, 77, 93, 103, 215
Dostoevski, Fyodor: value to Percy, 6, 8; humanity of characters created by, 7; the Underground Man in Percy's novels, 76, 79, 177; on hyperconsciousness, 122; on the Underground Man, 122n; nightmare vision of future, 188, 224–25; and the behaviorists, 215–16; the Underground Man quoted, 216n; on dangers of science, 224; mentioned, 109n, 118, 160n, 202, 232
Dru, Alexander, 58, 59

Eden, the New, 193, 228, 230, 232
Education, 27, 147
Egocentrism, 54–55, 162, 166
Einstein, Albert, 239
Eiseley, Loren, 39 and n, 170
Emerson, Ralph Waldo, 11n, 16, 22, 59n, 231
Empiricism, 30n, 33
English, the, 68, 229
ESP and the New Spirituality, 196
Euripides, 86
Euthanasia, 170–71, 181, 207, 217
Eve, 223, 230
Everydayness: defined, 21; explained, 21–24; Marcel on, 22, 23; and ordeal, 41, 72, 78; and rotation, 45, 82; and the bomb, 64; and visibility, 78, 124; as despair, 79, 80; and the scientist or artist, 88; and love, 148–49; as sin, 200; in Hemingway, 236; mentioned, 63, 85, 93
Evil, 24, 169–70, 173, 187–89, 190, 204–205
Existence: and recognition of death, 26; overlooked by modern philosophy, 32; vs. thought or abstraction, 58, 88, 91–92, 114; and faith, 59; vs. probability, 78; vs. possibility, 104n; vs. order, 147n; vs. romanticism, 157n
Existentialism: and the malaise, x; existential vs. logical correction of vision, x; and Percy's philosophical quest, x, 12, 13, 20, 30n; need for understanding of, to Percy's novels, x, 18, 19; defined, 8, 34n; Percy as existentialist, 8, 242; foreign to American philosophical temper, 19–20; existentialist sources of Percy's novels, 19–63; individual against crowd in, 25; categories of, distinguished from logical, 29; and empiricism, in Percy, 30n; as revolt against abstraction, 32; and transcendence, 38; theistic vs. atheistic, 38; and Hegel, 65n; as perspective in *The Moviegoer*, 101; criticized by Percy for contempt of science, 240; taking root in America, 242

Faith, 59. *See also* Kierkegaard; Leap of faith
Fall, the, 174, 223
Fall, the new, 174–75, 187–89, 204–206
Fallout, The, 115n

Farber, Leslie H., 7
Farce, 218
Farewell to Arms, A, 236
Faulkner: Sartre on, ix; Percy's escape
    from influence of, 9; and Percy's boy-
    hood, 9, 10; and Percy's style, 10, 16,
    143; and Percy's novels, 67, 102, 123,
    198; and Kierkegaard, 101*n*
Faust, 77, 103
Faustus, Dr., 174, 179, 208, 209, 212,
    213, 219, 228
Finitude, 26–27, 42
Fitzgerald, F. Scott, 128
Foote, Shelby, 10 and *n*
French, the, 191, 239
Freud, Sigmund, 12, 43, 99*n,* 121, 239
Future. *See* Time
Future consciousness, 129

Gatsby, The Great, 128
Gaylord Farms Sanatorium, Conn., 11
Gentleman. *See* South
Germans, 190–91
Geworfenheit, 39
Ghost in the Machine, The, 212*n*
Gone with the Wind, 98, 209
Good Earth, The, 209
Good news, the. *See* Christianity
Gordon, Caroline, 14
Grace: absence of, 112; and abdication,
    162; as inwardness, 167, 227; divine,
    174; after the new Fall, 175; the sin
    against, 226–27; humor as, 231
Graham, Billy, 190
Greece, 193
Greenville, Miss., 9, 10, 12
Griffin, John Howard, 138
Ground Zero, 116*n*
Guardini, Romano, 118, 129, 167
Guilt, 203

Harris, Joel Chandler, 115*n*
Harvard, 121, 123, 182
Hawthorne, Nathaniel, 11*n,* 212
Hegel, Georg Wilhelm Friedrich, 6, 32,
    65*n*
Heidegger, Martin: value to Percy, 8;
    and everydayness, 21, 23; on death,
    26–27, 42; and Percy's castaway, 39;
    on anxiety, 43
Hemingway, Ernest: Percy's agreement
    with, on influence of Mark Twain, 9;
    and Percy's fiction, 96, 191, 199–200;

    achieves rotation to fourth power,
        236; mentioned, 140, 198*n*
Homo viator. See Wayfarer
Hope, 148, 168, 240
How to Make Love in the Ruins, 225
Hubris, 208, 219, 226
Huckleberry Finn, The Adventures of, 9,
    142, 153, 159
Hughes, Langston, 10
Humanism: Percy on scientific, 36, 64;
    humanists vs. seekers, 104; and beast-
    liness, 170, 188; view of man of, 172
Humor: levity as mask in Percy's novels,
    82; Kierkegaard on passion of, 95*n;*
    of Sir Thomas More, 179; the comic
    religious as last stage before faith, 179
    and *n;* and wholeness, 231. *See also*
    Burlesque; Comedy; Farce; Satire
Hyperconsciousness. *See* Self-conscious-
    ness
Hysteria, 155*n*

Identity, 134. *See also* Repetition; Search
Idiot, The, 118
Immanence, 49, 61, 141, 162, 166
Impersonation. *See* Role-playing
Inauthenticity: antithesis of meaningful
    life for existentialists, 24; explained,
    24–30; defined, 25; and tyranny of the
    majority, 25; and death, 43, 109; in
    art, 47; and rotation, 48; in the
    movies, 73, 79; and role-playing, in
    Percy's novels, 73, 84, 104; of movie
    magazine fans, 82*n;* and abdication,
    in Percy's novels, 91, 136; and living
    through others, 99; and sex, 99*n;* of
    television laugh shows, 157; in nam-
    ing, 235; mentioned, 63, 115. *See also*
    Abdication; Bad Faith; Role-playing
Individual, the: limitations of scientific
    method for, 6; lost in scientific writing,
    7; truth resides in, 25; vs. the crowd,
    25; and danger of absorption into
    function, 32; and statist philosophies,
    33; and spirit of abstraction, 34; and
    faith, 63; lost in the illusion of possibil-
    ity, 117
Infinite passion: explained, 57–63; vs.
    postulate outside of oneself, 58; ap-
    pearance of phrase in Kierkegaard,
    58*n;* vs. Little Way in *The Moviegoer,*
    77; not shared by Kate Cutrer, 108;

vs. objective remove of Will Barrett, 114

Intersubjectivity: and sovereignty, 28–30; and objectification of others, 29; and symbolization, 29; and rotation, 48; explained, 52–57; Marcel's definition of, 53; vs. self-consciousness, 53, 84, 85; shared secret the mainspring of, 54, 95; egocentrism a barrier to, 54–55, 162; and consciousness, 55; Percy's definition of, 55; and art, 56; the leap into, 63; as communion, 107n, 230; as transcendence, 162; in naming, 233, 238; and the literature of alienation, 234

Inwardness: in Kierkegaard, 58–59; as grace, 114, 167, 189, 227; and religion, 120; humor as, 179; humanity bound to, 206

Irony: Kierkegaard on, 95n; Percy's use of dramatic, 117; of Will Barrett's family, 122; Percy's reliance upon, 122; Will Barrett's lack of, 135, 163; concentrated in Sutter Vaught, 149; in ending of *The Last Gentleman*, 167; mentioned, 119, 120

Isaac, 62

Israel, 193

James, Henry, 143n, 242

James, William, 12

Jaspers, Karl, 8, 39

Jean Christophe, 86

Jesus, 147, 152n, 190, 205–206, 232

Jews: and despair in Kierkegaard, 77n; and the search, 88–89; Binx Bolling as the Wandering Jew, 99; the recognition of Kate as Rachel, 99–100, 101; Kate's failure to perceive own Jewishness, 108; anti-Semitism, 146, 185; contradictory Judaism, 192; mentioned, 182, 202

Job, 43, 50, 165

John the Baptist, 175, 178

Jung, Carl Gustav, 7

Kafka, Franz, 104n, 234

Kaufmann, Stanley, 16

Kazin, Alfred, 12, 16

Keats, John, 10

Kennedy, John F., 235–36

Kennedy era, 195

Kierkegaard, Søren: value to Percy, 6,

8, 19; and Emerson, 21–22, 59n; on everydayness, 22; on his own era, 22; on the curtailed I, 22; on boredom, 24; on the crowd, 25, 33; on seduction, 29; on Hegelian idealism, 32; on the original sin of modern philosophy, 32, 58; on anxiety, 43; on rotation, 45–46, 47; on repetition, 49–50; aesthetic stage of, 49, 59–60, 77–78, 77n, 93, 98, 101, 104 and n, 124n, 137, 163n, 215; ethical stage of, 49, 59–60, 98, 106, 108, 137, 163n; religious stage of, 49–50, 106, 108, 163n, 165–66; three stages of, 49–50, 57, 65n; youth of, 57–58; on the infinite passion, 57–63; on house metaphor for condition of life, 58, 76; on knight of infinite resignation, 59, 60–61; on knight of faith, 59, 60–63, 165; on despair, 76, 77; and Ahasuerus, 77; and Don Juan, 77; and Faust, 77; and house metaphors in Percy's fiction, 77, 108, 110, 195, 230; knight of faith in Percy's novels, 95 and n, 101, 105, 106; knight of infinite resignation in Percy's novels, 95n, 106; on humor, 95n, 179; and Faulkner, 101n; on keeping silent, 108n; and grace, 114; on truth, 114n; on possibility, 117; on forgetting, 120n; on self-recovery, 155; comic religious mode of, 179, 219–20, 228; and the musical-erotic, 198, 199, 215; on sin as the opposite of faith, 200; on the eradication of despair, 206n; and Christianity in Christendom, 210; on continuation of sin, 220n; on defending anything, 230–31; indirect approach of, 237; on the physician's diagnosis, 241; translated by Percy into American terms, 242; mentioned, 26, 27, 36, 88, 107–108, 112, 120, 122, 123, 191, 225

Knight of faith. *See* Kierkegaard

Knight of infinite resignation. *See* Kierkegaard

Knopf, Alfred A., Inc., 16

Koestler, Arthur, 37, 212n

Ku Klux Klan, 122

Langer, Suzanne K., 12, 242n

Lanterns on the Levee, 13

Lapsometer: key to Percy's comic synthesis, 174–75, 208; role of, in *Love in*

the Ruins, 178, 183–84, 187; links medical, scientific, and political conditions,
184; powers of, 191–92, 207, 212;
effects of, illustrated, 213, 214, 217,
218, 224

Last Gentleman, The: runner-up, National
Book Award, 16; and abstraction, 30;
and ordeal, 41; intersubjectivity in, 52,
234; discussed, 111–168; as pilgrimage of incapacitated pilgrim, 112, 113,
114; Ground Zero as starting point
for postmodern pilgrimage, 116, 127;
Will Barrett's pilgrimage, 130, 145,
149, 150, 152, 163; pilgrim vs. gentleman, 158; pilgrim misses import of
pilgrimage, 166; mentioned, 173, 210,
227, 234, 235, 237

Lawson, Lewis A., 67n, 77n, 106n, 155n,
156n, 158, 237n

Lazarus, 209

Leap of faith: and attaining the religious
stage, 49; possible only after the
choice, 59; compared to dancer's leap,
62; into the intersubjective communion, 63; of Binx Bolling, 105, 106;
of Jamie Vaught, 165–66; and Will
Barrett, 167; mentioned, 20, 66, 87,
101

Leaves of Grass, 16

Lee, Robert E., 146

Levittown, Pennsylvania, 139, 140

Liberals, 139–40, 176, 184, 192, 204

Liberty, 9

Literature, 51, 56. *See also* Percy, Walker

Louisiana, 182

Love in the Ruins: on lying, 29; as comic
synthesis of modern thought, 169; discussed, 169–232; peculiar comic quality of, 170–71; Tom More in comic
religious mode of Kierkegaard, 179;
time period of, 199n; as synthesis of
religious and secular thought, 227,
231; as comic therapy, 231; mentioned, 16, 20, 25, 34, 98n, 113n, 126n,
206, 225, 233, 234, 235, 240

Madness, 201, 202

Magic Mountain, The, 14–15

Mailer, Norman, 139n, 240

Malaise, the: and scientific method, x;
Percy's encounter with, 17; partly the
result of effort to understand it, 19;
opaque without existentialist modes of

perception, 20; and inauthenticity,
24; and bad faith, 26; and modern
industrial society, 34; and view of
man, 37; summary of, 63; as fallout,
64, 105, 115–16, 118; *The Moviegoer*
a diagnosis of, 70; as fog or gas, 81;
and moviegoing, 81–82; transported
to Appalachians, 84; and sex, 98, 135–
36; in South, 144; *Love in the Ruins*
Percy's most comprehensive diagnosis
of, 169; as vacuum, 188; and present
time, 227; Kierkegaard and Percy's
diagnosis of, 241; as enduring feature
of American life, 243; mentioned, 46,
82, 90n, 111. *See also* Alienation

Man, view of, 12, 15. *See also* Anthropology; Wayfarer

Marcel, Gabriel: value to Percy, 6, 8; on
metaphysic of *we are*, 13n, 242n; aim
of, in writing plays, 14; on mysteries
vs. problems, 18; on everydayness, 22,
23; Percy includes philosophical
method of, 30; on identity, 31; on
modern society, 31; on abstraction in
friendship, 32; on functional view of
man, 32; on spirit of abstraction, 33–
34; on concrete mode of thinking, 34;
on man as wayfarer, 37–38; on disquiet, 38; on spatial analogues, 40; on
being, 40, 233, 238; on contingency,
42; on the death of loved ones, 44;
on intersubjectivity, 52–55, 56–57; on
the shared secret, 53, 54; definition
of philosophy of, 56; on transcendence, 105; on preconceived ideas,
115n; mentioned, 27n, 36, 84, 162,
174

Marcus Aurelius Antonius, 67

Mark Twain, 9, 122, 142, 154, 236

Marlowe, Christopher, 207, 208, 214,
229

Marquand, John P., 236

Mauvaise foi, 26. *See also* Bad faith

Mayflower, 194

Mead, George Herbert, 55n

Mechanism of disease, 5

Melville, Herman, 86, 208n

Mencius, 139n

Mephistophilis, 179, 207, 208, 209, 212,
228

"Metamorphosis, The," 104n

Milton, John, 223n

Mind-body split, 188

Mississippi, 4*n*, 9, 11, 131
Mississippi River, 142, 159
Modern period. *See* Time
More, Sir Thomas: conception of man, 174; relation to Tom More, 174; humor of, 179; invoked as saint, 200, 226, 228; on dying kings, 211; biography of, 215*n;* demise of, 218–19; mentioned, 182, 202
More's syndrome. *See* Angelism-bestialism
Moviegoer, The: Binx Bolling left over from own search, 3; outline of Percy's pilgrimage, 4; sermonizing of W. A. Percy in, 5*n;* Percy's breakthrough with, 15; wins National Book Award for 1962, 16; writing of, 16; everydayness omnipresent in, 21; and inauthenticity, 24; and role-playing, 26; and God's existence, 35; and repetition, 48–49; discussed, 64–110; insufficient latitude of, 111–12; comments of National Book Award judges on, 238; mentioned, 11, 116, 123, 128, 132, 134*n*, 135, 141, 163, 173, 186–87, 222, 223*n*, 235
Moviegoing, 93, 94
Movies: Percy on movie magazine fans, 11, 82*n;* specific references, in Percy's novels, 72, 75, 87, 92, 98, 100, 104, 189; and the search, 79; peculiar reality of stars, 81
Musical-erotic, 198, 199, 214, 215
Mystery: Marcel's definition of, 18; and Percy, 18, 20; Heidegger on, 42; Pascal on, 43, 80; of death, 71; confronted by self-assurance, 82

Naming: and being, 23, 233; and Adam on the First Day, 153; and the lapsometer, 185; of fears, 202, 234–35; inauthentic, in fiction, 235; as unique in natural history, 237; and authenticity, 238. *See also* Symbolization
National Book Award, 16, 173*n*, 194, 238, 240
Nausea, 6, 7, 83, 147*n*, 157*n*, 214
Negroes. *See* Race relations; South
New Canaan, 175
New Eden, 193, 228, 230, 232
New Mexico, 28, 148, 160*n*, 221
New Mexico, University of, 151
New Orleans, 17, 64–111 *passim*, 176

New York City, 111, 114, 116, 123, 129, 206
News from beyond the seas, 14, 80, 120, 153, 165. *See also* Christianity
Newton, Sir Isaac, 239
Nietzsche, Friedrich, 38–39
North: Percy on intellectual establishment of, 25*n;* cities of, 99; as homeless, 116; Southern view of, 121–22; unhappiness of, 144–45, Percy's message to, 194; and new Christ, 206
North Carolina, University of, 5, 10, 82*n*
Northerners, 81, 159*n*, 177
Notebooks of Malte Laurids Brigge, The, 2, 44, 238
Notes from Underground, 6, 216*n*
Nothingness, 42
Novel, the. *See* Percy, Walker

Objectification: of others, 29, 31, 32, 34, 87*n;* of self, 31, 88, 91. *See also* Abstraction
Objectivity: Percy on, 19*n*, 162; Kierkegaard on objective thought, 22; as way of viewing oneself, 28; as sole measure of human worth, 32; and the castaway, 39; Marcel on, 40; vs. inwardness in Kierkegaard, 58; as absence of grace, 114; and religion, 120; and vision, 120; as limbo, 120, 227; Will Barrett as objective witness, 166; in psychiatry, 185
O'Connor, Flannery, 237
O'Hara, Scarlett, 209
O'Neill, Eugene, 11 and *n*
Ordeal: explained, 41–44; encounter with nothingness as ultimate form of, 42; shock and recovery of vision, 42, 78, 124, 199; defined, 44; the great catastrophe, 64, 113, 118, 130, 175, 178, 179; and everydayness, 72, 78, 80, 200; as deliverance, 91; shock in Percy's novels, 93, 113, 150, 164, 171; war as fun, 94 and *n;* eschatological-thrill anecdotes, 96; bad news as good, 133, 193; and angelism, 187; and sanity, 201; of Tom More, 219, 230; mentioned, 63, 71. *See also* Death

Paradise: Percy's mock, 174, 175–223 *passim;* earthly, 189, 227
Paradise Lost, 223*n*
Pascal, Blaise, 43, 80

Past, the. *See* Time
Pavlov, Ivan Petrovich, 212*n*
Peirce, Charles Sanders, 241–42
Percy, LeRoy (father of Walker), 4
Percy, Walker: intellectual odyssey of, ix,
    3–18, 20–21; philosophical and per-
    sonal crisis of, 3–9; personal circum-
    stances, 4 and *n*, 5, 9; ordeal by tuber-
    culosis, 4, 5–6, 9, 11, 124*n;* formal
    education, 5, 10, 11; conversion from
    physician to novelist, 5*n*, 12;
    encounter with the existentialists, 6;
    personal characteristics of, 8*n*, 16–17,
    90*n;* literary apprenticeship, 9–11,
    14–16; marriage, 11; conversion to
    Catholicism, 12; literary break-
    through, 15–16; critical success, 16;
    three years of psychoanalysis, 16; as
    diagnostician, 20; and readership,
    101*n*
—Philosophical views: influences on, x,
    6; philosophical essays, 12–14; dis-
    cussed, 19–63; symbolization as
    bridge from empiricism to existential-
    ism, 30*n;* view of man closest to Mar-
    cel, 35; on ethical secularism, 36; on
    scientific humanism, 36; on *news* vs.
    knowledge, 39; on naming, 56; sum-
    mary of, 63; satire of popular use of
    existential, 224; discovery of symboliza-
    tion, 238; criticism of existentialists
    for contempt of science, 240; the
    novels as a gloss on Kierkegaard, 241;
    an existentialist sensibility in America,
    242; on the modern era, 243
—Literary views: the novel and the limi-
    tations of scientific method, 7–8, 14,
    239; the novel as phenomenological
    exploration, 7–8, 74 and *n*, 239; on
    the Southern oral tradition, 11; novel-
    ist compared to scientist at dead end
    of traditional hypothesis, 15; on the
    satirist's aim, 181; on role of the novel-
    ist, 188, 233, 234; on art as a reversal
    of alienation, 233–34; on the compul-
    sive liberal novelist, 235; on American
    novelists, 236; the novelist and the
    cliché artist, 236–37; on the novelist
    writing from a Christian position, 237;
    on the revolution in modern French
    novel, 239
—Style: European influences on, 6;
    influence of Mark Twain on, 9; and
    Faulkner, 9, 10; stylistic debt to
    Camus, 15, 103; discovery of own
    voice and tone, 15–16, 64, 70, 71, 111;
    humor, 65, 89, 210–11; phenomeno-
    logical method, 74, 112, 129, 140, 202;
    use of house metaphors, 77, 108, 110,
    195, 230; influence of Sartre's *Nausea*,
    83*n;* satire, 89–90, 120, 137, 138, 139,
    140*n*, 173*n*, 181, 222–23; elliptical and
    understated, 110; rhythm, 111, 137,
    193; use of omniscient viewpoint,
    116–17; use of sex, 135; use of time,
    140; rhetoric, 143; protagonists, 193;
    oblique approach, 237, 238–39;
    novels as negative molds, 238. *See also*
    Irony
—Works: the two streams, 8; philosophi-
    cal essays, 8, 12–14; apprentice writ-
    ings, 9–11, 14–15; most intensive diag-
    nosis of the malaise, 64; a postmodern
    pilgrimage, 111; a comic synthesis of
    modern thought, 169, 174–75, 205,
    227; literary achievement, 242, 243.
    See also *Last Gentleman, The; Love in
    the Ruins; Moviegoer, The*
Percy, William Alexander (cousin):
    raised Walker and brothers, 4; ser-
    monizing of, 4*n;* death of, 5; and Wal-
    ker's going to medical school, 5*n;* and
    Faulkner, 9; influence of, on Walker,
    10; on religious questioning of Percy
    boys, 13; on soldiering, 71*n;* on World
    War I, 94*n*
Phenomenology: as method in Percy's
    novels, 74; Percy's definition of, 74*n;*
    as method in *The Last Gentleman*, 112,
    129; of modern French novel, 239.
    See also Percy, Walker
Philip the evangelist, 84*n*, 161, 166, 167
Philosophy: and literature, 8; Kier-
    kegaard's criticism of modern, 32, 58;
    modern, moves wholly within imma-
    nence, 49; Marcel's definition of, 56.
    See also Percy, Walker
Pica, Greenville High School, 10
Pilgrimage, See *Last Gentleman, The*
Planck, Max, 239
Plot, 177
Point of No Return, 236
Possibility: Kierkegaard on the individu-
    al as, 22; and rotation, 45; Will Barrett
    and pure, 113, 160, 163, 164; Kier-
    kegaard on illusion of, 117; Percy on,
    142
Postmodern era. *See* Time

Postulate, life as, 58, 167
Predicament, man in, 8
Present, the. *See* Time
Price, George, 50
Princeton, 123, 134, 137, 151
Problem, Marcel's definition of, 18
Progress, 177, 189, 216n
Prophet, The, 89
Psychiatry: reductive view of man of, 7;
Percy's three years of analysis, 12;
Percy on coming crisis in, 13; and writing as therapy, 16; dispossession of
layman in, 28; pride of patient in self-
objectification, 31, 150, 185–86;
American, silence of, on existentialist
themes, 36; intersubjectivity in, 54n;
being told vs. discovering in, 91–92;
as chic cureall, 96; role-playing in
analysis, 117, 121; psychoanalysis as
sweet mother, 119, 124; psychoanalysis as barren, 125; jargon of, 133–34,
202; psychiatrist as narrator of *Love
in the Ruins,* 175; Percy on novelistic
approach to patient, 239
Puritans, 175
Puritanism, 198

Race relations: whites on blacks, 102,
107, 185; in North, 120, 201, 139; sexual mores of blacks, 136–37; sexual
mores of whites, 136–37; the castaway's view of, 151n; downfall of
U.S.A., 193; militant blacks vs. Uncle
Toms, 201; and the new Christ, 206;
toward end of century, 226n, 230. *See
also* South
Recollection, 51
Reductivism, 7, 216n
Relativism, 203, 240
Religion, 13, 53. *See also* Infinite passion;
Repetition; Wayfarer
Repetition: explained, 48–52; as conversion of rotation, 50; aesthetic vs. existential, 51; definition of, 51; in literature, 51; as used up, 93; existential,
in Percy's novels, 99, 100, 142, 155,
221; as future experience, 128–29; as
the Return, in *The Last Gentleman,* 141,
142, 155; and death of Jamie Vaught,
165; as historical therapy, 190; Tara
as fake, 222; and Thomas Wolfe, 236
Republicans, 144, 181
Resentment, 33, 34, 188

Return, the, 50–51, 130. *See also* Repetition
Richmond, 140
Rilke, Rainer Maria, 2, 40, 44, 76, 237,
238
Robbins, Harold, 235
R. E. Lee, 146
Role-playing: and inauthenticity, 24;
definition of, 26; playing native, 28;
and ordeal, 42; in place of the choice,
58, 83, 97; soldiering, 67; fraternity
alumni, 69; the model citizen, 74–75;
borrowed from the movies, 87, 98,
104; social, 89, 99, 108; in psychiatry,
91, 92; sexual, 98, 135–36, 143–44;
stoic gestures, 105; Will Barrett's
mutability, 117, 120, 132n; among
Southerners, 132; Kitty Vaught as
rehearsal, 135; of fictional self, 230.
See also Inauthenticity
Romanticism, 68, 87, 88, 94, 157
Rotation: explained, 44–48; vs. repetition, 50–51; limitations of, as lifestyle,
77–78, 104, 105; aesthetic, 79; and
everydayness, 82; existential, 92, 95;
as used up, 93; amnesia the perfect
device for, 142; to the second power,
159n; as bonus for repetition, 221;
Hemingway's use of, 236; mentioned,
63, 73, 190
Roth, Philip, 240
Royce, Josiah, 53n
Rubin, Louis D., Jr., 9
Russia, 194

St. Michael, 181, 223
Salvation, 154, 164–65, 166n
Sanborn, Patricia, 38
Sandburg, Carl, 10
Sanity, 201–202, 212, 231
Santa Fe, N.M., 154, 160, 161
Saranac Lake, N.Y., 14
Sartre, Jean-Paul: on Faulkner, ix; value
to Percy, 6, 8; *Nausea* as phenomenological exploration, 7; concept of bad
faith, 26; Percy's disagreement with,
29, 55n; and transcendence, 38; and
the stare, 53n; Marcel's criticism of,
55; influence of, on Percy, 83n, 147n;
metioned, 44, 157n, 213–14
Satire: Kierkegaard on, 108n; Percy on
satirist's job, 173n; Percy on aim of,
181; *Love in the Ruins* as futuristic, 169
See also Percy, Walker

Science: self as vacuum in worldview of, 6; and existence, 28; veneration of, 28, 113, 129, 162, 178, 180, 186, 241; and self-objectification, 31, 97, 162, 165; as pose, 69, 75, 87, 91, 222; and romanticism, 87; as the other side, 124–25; as secret club, 132; vanity of scientists, 179, 213; and superstition, 180; the scientist's prayer, 180; as God-given, 193; as faith, 202; and the musical-erotic, 214; Dostoevski's fears of, 224; and naming, 233; and existentialism in Percy, 238; Percy's defense of, 240; and postmodern consciousness, 241; mentioned, 68, 119, 176, 192

Scientific humanism, 36, 64, 97, 172

Scientific method: shortcomings of, x, 6, 241; Percy's admiration for, 5; gaps left in our knowledge by, 17; as agent of alienation, 19; and layman, 162; limitations of, and the novel, 239

Search, the: existential, 34–41, 48–52, 57–63, 68, 74, 78, 79, 90, 93; aesthetic, 45–48, 50–52; of Binx Bolling, 64–110 *passim;* existential, as unifying thread of *The Moviegoer,* 73; and the movies, 79; definition of, 79, 80; and God, 79–80; and Southern aristocratic tradition, 86, 103; horizontal vs. vertical, 88; vertical, definition of, 88; horizontal, 90; occurs to Binx Bolling, 99; vertical, 234

Self-consciousness, 84, 85, 97, 110, 122

Self-deception, 26. *See also* Bad faith

Sex: post-Christian, 96; research, 97, 203, 223–24; and the malaise, 98 and *n,* 99*n;* Percy's treatment of, 99*n;* symbolism, 102; and psychoanalysis, 121; instinct of Will Barrett, 126; and therapy-group jargon, 133; role-playing in, 135–36, 137, 143–44; mores, 136–37; as religion, 138–39; as escape from abstraction, 162; and technical aids, 186

Shakespeare, William, 10, 86, 107

Shared secret, 53, 54, 95

Sheed, Wilfrid, 240

Shock. *See* Ordeal

Siddartha, 196

Sin: original, 188; continuation of, 200, 220*n;* as opposite of faith, in Kierkegaard, 200, 220*n,* 227; forgiveness of, 203; and Christ, 205; against grace, 226–27; penance for, 230

Skinner, B. F., 13*n,* 177, 203*n,* 215, 239

Skinner box, 170, 203, 218

Smith, Hallett, 174

"Snows of Kilimanjaro, The," 198*n*

Socrates, 114

Sound and the Fury, The, 10, 121, 123

South: Percy and literary tradition of, ix, 9, 11; aristocratic tradition of, 66–70, 72, 73, 77, 83, 100–103, 105, 107; Southerners in North, 99, 116, 120, 131, 132; clash of generations in, 100–103, 123; the Southern gentleman, 122, 133–34, 136, 137, 139, 150, 151, 158; the Southern past, 122, 123, 140, 159; young men of, 123, 125; Will Barrett's return to, 130, 141, 144–45; the Southern community, 131, 142; chauvinism of, 132*n;* blacks in, 132*n,* 158 and *n,* 185, 201; women of, 137, 144; race relations in, 138, 146, 163, 176–177, 204; as immanent, 141; sex roles in, 144; happiness of, 144–45; the new, 144–45, 153; racial strife in, 151, 154, 156; present racial impasse in, 158–59; predicament of white moderate, 158–159, 226*n;* sweetness and cruelty of, 205; and the new Christ, 206; antebellum nostalgia of, 222–23

Southwest, 111, 116, 148, 152

Sovereign wayfarer, 48, 63, 166

Sovereignty: and inauthenticity, 25; Percy on, 27; loss of, by abdication, 27; and intersubjectivity, 28–30; definition of, 48; illustrated in *The Moviegoer,* 81; living vs. engineering a life, 125; and Will Barrett, 150; at death, 166; the sense of, 229, 243

Speculative philosophy. *See* Abstraction

Stoicism, 66–67, 102*n,* 105, 156 and *n,* 158, 159

Strange, The, 16*n,* 103

Subjectivity. See Inwardness

Suicide: of Percy's father, 4; in Percy family, 4*n;* as means to life, 97; of Will Barrett's father, 136–37, 155–58, 159; Tom More's attempt, 183, 199, 200

Sullivan, Harry Stack, 43

Susann, Jacqueline, 235

Swift, Jonathan, 240

Symbolization: as basically human need,

12; symbol distinguished from sign, 12; and loss of visibility, 23; and inter-subjectivity, 29, 55; as possible bridge between existentialism and empiricism, 30n; Marcel on, 55; as basis of consciousness, 55; and the novelist, 237–38; exhaustion of symbols part of man's ailment, 238. *See also* Naming

Tara, 197, 204, 209, 222, 223
Tate, Allen, 14
Technology, 190, 191, 240
Tempest, The, 228
Texas, 197
Theory. *See* Abstraction
Therapy, group, 120, 134
Thoreau, Henry David, 84, 85, 228
Thought. *See* Abstraction; Existentialism; Infinite passion; Philosophy
Thrown-ness, 23, 39
Tillich, Paul, 57
Time: existential vs. historical, 128; Will Barrett's amnesia and post-Christian shakiness about, 129; cyclical vs. historical, 129n; present, and the malaise, 227
Time, periods of:
—Premodern: Will Barrett's return to the Southern past, 140, 141
—Modern: society of, 26–27, 31, 100–101, 102, 221; Guardini on end of, 119n, 167; seen from postmodern, 129; Confederate fantasy of, 140–41; monstrousness of, 169–70, 173; Percy on modern era, 243
—Postmodern: and a new incapacity, 112; Guardini on nature of, 118–19 and n, 167; and Christianity, 120, 166; phenomenological rendition of, 128 –29; *The Last Gentleman* as pilgrimage through, 130; left behind by Will Barrett, 140–41; grace in, 227; Percy on restructuring of consciousness in, 241
Tolstoi, Leo, 239
Townsend, Mary, 11
Transcendence: recognized by all existentialists, 38; Marcel's definition of, 38, 115–16; Kierkegaard on, of ethical stage, 49–50, 61; of everyday condi-
tion, 63; as aspiration toward purer mode of experience, 115–16; as abstraction, 120, 162; the American Southwest as transcendent, 148, 160; definition of, 162; incomprehensible from immanence, 165–66
Trial, 43n, 50 and n, 165
Truth, 25, 57, 114n, 196, 203
Twain, Mark, 9, 122, 142, 154, 236
Tyranny of the majority, 25

Underground Man. *See* Dostoevski
United States of America. *See* America, United States of
Updike, John, 240

Van Cleave, Jim, 67n
Van Dine, S. S., 10–11
Verdun, Battle of, 190–91, 199
Voegelin, Eric, 129n

Wandering Jew, 77, 99, 103
Walden Pond, 84
War: World War II, 5, 17, 94; World War I, 33, 68, 71n, 94n, 190–91; Civil War, 68; Korean War, 69, 78, 85, 87, 99, 100, 104; war in Ecuador, 181, 195; as better than nothing, 188, 225
Watson, John Broadus, 212n
Wayfarer: explained, 34–41; defined, 37; and horizontal search, 88; precariousness of man's position, 174; in Tom More's prayer, 200; mentioned, 63, 80, 103, 105, 110, 177
Whitehead, Alfred North, 28, 33
Whites. *See* Race relations; South
Whitman, Walt, 16, 229n
Williamsburg, Va., 141
Wittgenstein, Ludwig, 234
Wolfe, Thomas, 16, 222, 236
Women: as movie magazine readers, 82n; as love objects, 87; American college, 89; in *The Last Gentleman,* 134n; as hearty, 155; and death, 164; musical-erotic view of, 198, 214
Wright, Willard Huntington, 10–11

Yankees, 116, 122, 133, 140
Yeats, William Butler, 181